# 750
# RACER

As part of our ongoing market research, we are always pleased to receive comments about our books, suggestions for new titles, or requests for catalogues. Please write to The Editorial Director, Patrick Stephens Limited, Sparkford, Nr Yeovil, Somerset BA22 7JJ.

# 750 RACER

### EVERYTHING YOU NEED TO KNOW ABOUT BUILDING AND RACING A LOW-COST SPORTS-RACING CAR

## PETER HERBERT
in association with
## DICK HARVEY

Patrick Stephens Limited

© Peter Herbert 1996

First published in 1996

British Library Cataloguing-in-Publication Data:
A catalogue record for this book is
available from the British Library

ISBN 1 85260 447 6

Library of Congress catalog card number 96 075172

Patrick Stephens Limited is an imprint of
Haynes Publishing, Sparkford, Nr. Yeovil, Somerset BA22 7JJ.

Designed & typeset by G&M, Raunds, Northamptonshire
Printed in Great Britain by
Butler & Tanner Limited, London and Frome

# CONTENTS

# ACKNOWLEDGEMENTS

I wish to thank amateur racing drivers everywhere, and members of the 750 Motor Club in particular, for their inspiration and assistance in the preparation of this book.

Special gratitude must also be extended to Allan Staniforth who, in his inimitable way, and abetted by Dick Harvey, talked me into, and guided me through, the awesome task of writing this, my first book.

Finally, I am indebted to Gail Slater who, with remarkable patience, turned my scribble into a semblance of prose; and to my wife Philippa for supporting with good humour a terminal motorhead.

# Chapter 1

# HEAVEN CAN WAIT

**O**n the morning of Sunday 16 October 1988, while at Mallory Park, Richard George Harvey, racing driver, car constructor, raconteur and pillar of 750 Motor Club society, died. To be precise, he died five times.

At Silverstone the previous day, Dick had failed narrowly to retain his 750 Formula Championship, close friend and rival Mick Harris having snatched the crown. But at least a Darvi had again secured the coveted Goodacre Trophy, and Harvey was magnanimous in defeat.

Easing his own red and blue Darvi 86.9 out of the paddock and onto the picturesque Leicestershire circuit that autumnal sabbath morn, Dick began practice in relaxed mood. Championship pressures were lifted, yet as a racer he still wanted to win. After a couple of gentle laps to warm up the tyres and reacquaint himself with the track, he accelerated hard downhill through Devil's Elbow and hit the Kirkby Straight with foot nailed to the floor to begin a hot lap.

Firmly in top gear, with the tachometer needle brushing 8,000, Dick moved to the right as he approached the pit-lined start–finish area to pass a pair of novice drivers running in tandem. Disastrously, the second of the two chose that moment to pull out of the other's slipstream. By involuntary reflex the Darvi swerved to the right to avoid contact, and ran headlong into the end of the pit lane barrier. Car and driver stopped dead from more than 100 mph in the space of 2 ft.

There is a theoretical limit to how much deceleration the human heart can withstand, and this had been exceeded by some margin. Dick Harvey's personal fuel pump stopped. Medically he was dead.

Had this happened on the M25 Dick would have stayed dead. However, for all its dangers motor racing takes safety very seriously. Sitting close by the track behind a fully loaded cornet the size of a Klansman's hat was Doctor Vlatchsis, indulging his passion for ice-cream. The Medical Officer acted quickly. Tossing his snack to one side he sprinted to the trapped driver's aid and, using whatever skill and violence were necessary, cajoled the Harvey heart back into action, allowing the injured driver to be carefully released from the remains of his car. During the high-speed ambulance ride to Leicester General Infirmary life tried to slip away again no less than four times, but on each occasion it was brought back. There is a widely held theory amongst the 750 racing fraternity that on each arrival at Heaven's Gate the bar was closed, hence Dick's prompt returns to earth.

A scary tale? Certainly. Yet not one without optimism. An amateur racing driver at the wheel of a home-built car survived an horrific accident by virtue of the structural integrity of his own design and workmanship, together with prompt and dedicated medical attention. Furthermore, this driver's enthusiasm for his chosen brand of motor sport survives undiminished.

This is the story of contemporary 750 Formula racing viewed through the eyes of that one man.

## Chapter 2

# IN THE BEGINNING WAS THE WORD 'SEVEN FIFTY'

**A**dolf Hitler, reputedly not a competition licence holder and most certainly less than a fun person, made many people's lives miserable between 1939 and 1945, including those with a passion for motor racing. When Adolf's six-year European tour was brought to an enforced end, enthusiasts throughout the Continent were eager to resume their sport, and less than four months after Germany's unconditional surrender the Grand Prix de la Libération was held in Paris over the roads of the Bois de Boulogne. The race was won by the Bugatti of French resistance hero Jean-Pierre Wimille, which was entirely fitting.

British motor racing devotees were equally anxious to race again. However, without access to closed public roads, or to a ready supply of raceable machinery, things took a little longer on the British side of the Channel.

Prior to the Second World War, Austin Sevens had enjoyed a distinguished racing career. Conceived surreptitiously by Sir Herbert Austin so as not to alert fellow directors to expenditure of which they were unlikely to

approve, and designed in secret by the 18-year-old Stanley Edge at Sir Herbert's Lickey Grange home, the Seven was launched in 1922 at the Longbridge factory's Whit Monday carnival. For a company already in receivership this was a pretty ballsy move. Yet the accompanying claim that here was a car which would provide 'motoring for the millions' turned out to be no idle pretension.

The Seven's compact original form – 9 ft long, less than 4 ft wide, with a weight of 7 cwt – belied its sophistication. A 747 cc side-valve water-cooled engine produced a modest 10.5 hp at 2,400 rpm, giving the little Austin a top speed on the unexciting side of 40 mph. However the motor proved eminently tunable. Consequently the Seven was to provide the basis for the most popular inexpensive sports cars of the '20s and '30s. Indeed, no self-respecting wag-about-town of modest means would be seen dead without his wide cap, cravat, Oxford bags and Nippy, Ulster or, better still, Gordon England modified Brooklands Super Sports ver-

sion of the car. How else could a chap whisk Cynthia, Sybille or Dorothea up to the West End for a show and a spot of dinner, or to Henley for a picnic by the river, yet still remain competitive at the odd Shelsley hillclimb?

There was a tradition of competitive motoring at Austin, the guv'nor himself having raced in the early days when one sat on one's machine rather than in it. So it was only to be expected that Sir Herbert would commission a number of lightweight, fabric-bodied racing specials even before the standard car was in production.

A class win in the 1923 Italian Grand Prix at Monza and a second in class to a Maserati in the 1931 running of the world's greatest road race, the Mille Miglia, were barely believable international achievements. On home ground a works supercharged Seven Ulster won the 1930 Brooklands 500 at the incredible average speed of 83.4 mph. Although the victory was on handicap, the velocity alone clearly demonstrated the little Austin's potential, particularly as it was sustained for more than six hours around the bumpy, banked track. The drivers were S.C.H Davis, 'Sammy' to his friends, and the Earl of March, 'Your Lordship' to his friends. (Actually, this is not true – he was known as 'Freddie'.)

These were the days when without contacts or wealth you did not race – 'the right crowd and no crowding' was the contemporary attitude. Davis was a talented driver and motoring writer whose words appeared in *The Autocar* under the pseudonym 'Casque'. The Earl of March was a gentleman sportsman who later, as the Duke of Richmond and Gordon, established the Goodwood racing circuit on the Second World War Westhampnett airfield within his Sussex estate. In recognition of their Brooklands success Sir Herbert sent them an appreciative letter and a cheque for £50. Even in 1930, fifty quid split two ways was unlikely to change an Earl's lifestyle for the better, but it would certainly have kept

Sammy's familiar pipe topped up for a few weeks.

At club level Sevens swept all before them in races, rallies, sprints, hillclimbs, reliability trials and consumption tests.

Talented engineer Murray Jamieson steadily developed first the side-valve, particularly in single-seater 'Dutch Clog' form (so named because of their likeness to the wooden footwear from Holland), then twin overhead-camshaft versions of the engine which enabled the diminutive 750 Austins to remain highly competitive right up to the outbreak of the Second World War. Indeed there were some, perhaps blessed with terminal optimism rather than clear vision, who saw Longbridge as Britain's only potential source of serious opposition to the all-conquering Silver Arrows of Auto Union and Mercedes Benz.

Tragically, Jamieson lost his life while spectating at Brooklands in 1938, when J. Paul's

Delage left the track following a collison with another car during the International Trophy race, and ploughed into the crowd.

Drivers of the calibre of Pat Driscoll, Charlie Dodson and Charles Goodacre were the mainstays of the factory team under the management of Austin's Australian son-in-law Arthur Waite, himself a successful driver. Driscoll, the equipe's number one, was a former motor cycle racer who attributed his considerable speed on four wheels to the comparative safety he felt after risking his neck for so many years astride a powerful Norton around Brooklands' bankings. Dodson was also an ex-rider and TT

*'Works' twin cam: C.D. Buckley enters Pardon hairpin at Prescott in 1939. Note the twin rear wheels on the Austin which were popular at the time for speed hillclimbing, giving increased adhesion at the startline and out of tight uphill bends. (Austin Motor Company)*

winner, while Goodacre was an engineer in the Longbridge Experimental Department.

Others who enjoyed 'works' drives were stars of the day Kay Petre and Prince Bira. Canadian-born Mrs Petre was an unassuming lady of awesome ability behind the wheel. Her exploits included lapping Brooklands at an average of more than 134 mph in an even then venerable 10.5-litre Delage. Hardly a 'girlie' thing to do. Later she became motoring correspondent of the *Daily Mail*.

Prince Birabongse of Siam, Bira to his chums, came to England with cousin Chula for an education and became captivated by European motor racing. Small but perfectly formed, the stylish prince made his name in MGs and ERAs run by the family White Mouse Equipe.

However, perhaps the quickest Austin racer of them all was Bert Hadley. The manner in which he became a racing driver, and a 'works' driver at that, is real *Boys Own* stuff. Hadley was Pat Driscoll's mechanic: 'A very good boy but lazy' was how he was described by the team leader. One day whilst testing at Donington Bert asked Austin's brilliant race designer Murray Jamieson if he could have a go in one of the two twin-cam single-seaters on hand. This was a request that had been made on several occasions before, but so far warming the cars up in the paddock and driving them onto the starting grid had been the limit of the chubby little fellow's racing experience. But on this sunny day the studious Jamieson relented and, dressed in his mechanic's overalls and borrowed goggles, Hadley was allowed out for five careful laps. As he left the pits and dis-

appeared from view, the wily Jamieson sent Driscoll out in the other car to catch, but not pass, the mechanic to observe how he drove.

Lap after lap Hadley would come past, to be followed some time later by Driscoll, the gap never closing. Eventually Pat pulled into the pits to enquire where Bert had gone and whether he was off the road somewhere. Apparently Driscoll had been driving flat out. Had the name of the team ace been Ayrton, the speedy 'arriviste' would probably have been rewarded by a smack in the mouth and a new clause in his contract, but we speak of simpler days when raw talent was rewarded. Hadley became a factory driver, and very successful he was too, giving the Austin team its final victory and the Imperial Trophy at Crystal

Palace. Indeed, such was Bert Hadley's talent that both Auto Union and Mercedes expressed interest in his services. But sadly Germany's quest for world domination extended far beyond motor racing, and in 1939 a full 'works' Austin Seven racer was switched off for the last time, never to be restarted.

Shortly before the enforced close of this motor sporting era, a letter appeared in the January 1939 edition of the magazine *Motor Sport* at the instigation of its widely respected editor Bill Boddy. Headed 'A 750 Club if

*'Holly': the founder of 750 Formula racing, Holland Birkett, waving the chequered flag at the finish of the 1954 Relay Race at Silverstone. This annual end-of-season event is now held at Snetterton, and carries Birkett's name. (Courtesy of Mike Peck)*

wanted', the proposition was that a club be formed for the impecunious Austin Seven enthusiast, and its first meeting was held at Virginia Water on 13 April 1939. The response was promising, and thus the '750 Club' was launched, the membership being amused that the name would be mistaken for a nightclub by the uninitiated.

During the war years petrol rationing and little inconveniences such as the loss of all membership records following the bombing of club headquarters restricted 750 Club activities. But members met where possible, and otherwise kept in touch with one another via the *750 Bulletin*. One of the mainstays of this band of enthusiasts during this dark period was

*'U2 can afford to go motor racing': Arthur Mallock at Silverstone in 1950 giving his famous Mallock Austin, WJ 1515, a thorough workout. Built for racing and trials, this car was the forerunner of Mallock's very successful series of racing cars which began with the U2 Mk 1 in 1958. (Guy Griffiths)*

Holland Birkett, a veterinary surgeon from Fleet in Hampshire. Affectionately known as Holly to one and all, and usually accompanied by a large Alsatian dog on his motoring adventures aboard one of a number of Austin Seven specials or a delectable Bugatti Type 40, Birkett emerged into peace time as Club Captain, and when motor racing resumed in Britain in 1949 it was he who devised a new motor racing formula to cater

for any impecunious, would-be Austin Seven-based racing car constructor and driver. This formula was not only to allow thousands of enthusiasts to drive competitively, and many to go on to much greater things, it was also to lay the foundation for Britain's current key position within world motor racing.

Sadly, Holland Birkett's life was ended prematurely in 1963 when his Auster light aircraft crashed on the French coast at Stella Plage near Le Touquet-Paris-Plage. However, his name lives on in the 750 Motor Club's Birkett Relay Race, held for many years at Silverstone but now run at Snetterton each autumn.

His suggestion of a 750 Formula first appeared in the September 1949 edition of *Motor Sport*, with the invitation for

*Pit stop for Arthur: a sportily clad Mallock patiently waits as his mechanics attend to his car's needs. Note imaginative use of what appears to be a length of scaffold pole as trialing fiddle brake, pre-Nomex pullover, and minimalist spectator protection. (Howard Venning)*

those interested to write to Birkett. By December 56 letters of support had hit Holly's desk together with many verbal assurances. And so 750 racing was born.

The basis for the fledgling formula was the side-valve, conventionally aspirated Austin Seven engine block, crankcase, gearbox, rear axle and chassis frame. The bore and stroke was not to exceed 2.26 in x 3 in, so allowing for nominal rebores. Bodywork was to comply with RAC regulations of the time. Front suspension and fuel were unrestricted.

In common with many other small motor clubs of the period, the 750 Club could not yet afford to run a motor race on its

*They're off! Seven Fifty race start at the September 1952 Silverstone SUNBAC meeting. Future publisher Patrick Stephens is in pole position in the Stoneham and went on to win. Car 110 (back right) is already applying opposite lock! (Patrick Stephens Collection)*

own, so once again Birkett inspiration was brought to bear. The Seven devotees got together with a number of similarly impoverished clubs to form the Eight Clubs, and it was they who organized the first 750 Formula race on 3 June 1950 at Silverstone. There were 16 starters, and the winner was Charles Bulmer, later to become editor of *Motor*, at the wheel of Tom Lush's Ulster. Another notable competitor that day was Colin Chapman, making his racing debut in a 1172 cc Ford-engined Lotus Mark II, and he won a 16-lap scratch race following a terrific scrap with Gahagan's Type 37 Bugatti.

The following year Chapman dominated the 750 Formula in his Lotus Mark III. Technically advanced, with skilfully braced spaceframe chassis, soft but well-damped suspension, hydraulic brakes and desiamezed inlet ports, only the car's temperamental nature denied it the 750 Cham-

pionship. Indeed, the Lotus exhibited the characteristics that were to typify much of its creator's later work, leading to the unkind suggestion that 'Lotus' stood for 'Lots Of Trouble Usually Serious'. Chapman's enterprising interpretation of 750 Formula rules was to hold him in good stead when later coming to grips with Formula One regulations. The promptly banned twin-chassis Lotus 88 of 1981 was a typical Chapman *cause célèbre*, where his innovative attempt to capitalize upon a peerless grasp of 'ground effects' (the use of aerodynamic suction to create a low-pressure area beneath a chassis to force tyres onto the track surface) brought him into conflict with the sport's authorities. However, six Formula One World Championships for Lotus are an irrefutable testimony to the engineer's imagination and ability.

Holland Birkett was concerned about the sophistication of the Lotus, fearing that it

*'The Omen'. Star of this and other films such as* No Love For Johnnie *and* Charlie Bubbles, *actress Billie Whitelaw presents the winner's garland to future Marcos founder Jem Marsh at Brands Hatch in 1959. The young Marsh is at the wheel of his Speedex, and was at the time involved with Frank Costin in the building of the prototype Marcos. Billie Whitelaw is step-sister to former 750 racer J.B. 'Johnnie' Moore. (Jon Cowley)*

might deter newcomers from entering what was supposed to be a simple and affordable form of motor racing. Fortunately the formula's saviour was not long in coming.

Aptly named Simplicity, Jack French's car was built in just six weeks in 1953, and promptly outpaced the Lotus Mark III on occasion, albeit no longer in Chapman's hands. This remarkable car represented all that 750

*Speedex lives on: second owner Richard Eade seen cornering at Debden. (Courtesy of Mike Peck)*

racing stood for by being uncomplicated, inexpensive and competitive; and although never to take outright championship honours, it inspired a generation of impecunious enthusiasts.

Many were the cars that followed: Mallock Austins, built by the man who was to become the backbone of Clubmans racing with the famous U2, Arthur Mallock; the Broadley Special, produced by cousins Graham and Eric Broadley, who later founded

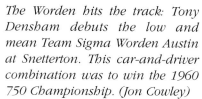

*The Worden hits the track: Tony Densham debuts the low and mean Team Sigma Worden Austin at Snetterton. This car-and-driver combination was to win the 1960 750 Championship. (Jon Cowley)*

Lola Cars, prolific producers of virtually every kind of racing car known to man; the Stoneham 750 Special of Patrick Stephens, the construction of which was narrated by the future publisher in his book *Building and Racing My 750*, which further popularized the 750 movement; the Speedex of Marcos founder Jem Marsh; the low and mean-looking, Tony Densham-devised Worden of Team Sigma, which broke away from the traditional Seven Special shape to set new 750 racing performance standards; and the amazing Forrest Saloon, which remained so true to its

*Mike Forrest towers over his amazing creation: the Forrest Saloon at rest in the Brands Hatch paddock in 1961. (Courtesy Mike Peck)*

*Complexity: Jim Yardley at Oulton Park. (Courtesy Mike Peck)*

Austin Seven origins that the box-like body was retained but with more than 9 in sliced off its roofline. Weight was offset by aerodynamics when compared with conventional open-top approaches to the formula. Assisted further by equally original engine lubrication and tuning, Mike Forrest's machine was a cost-effective and competitive visual delight, rather like dropping an American drag racing 'Funny Car' onto a grid of Formula Fords. Complexity, with dry-sumped, almost horizontal motor, and, possibly the ultimate, the Cowley, concluded the 750 Formula's Austin-powered period. Bill Cowley's creation, which sported twin Weber carburettors and de-siamezed ports, extracted a worthwhile power increase

*The Forrest in action: entering Druids at Brands Hatch in the company of David Boorer's DEB. (John D. Farlid)*

from the ageing side-valve motor by the use of a twin-plug head. Two separately driven distributors allowed each set of four plugs to spark in turn, so ensuring complete combustion.

The clear link between 750 racing of the 1950s and '60s, and Britain's current pivotal position in world single-seater and sports car racing, can be seen if you take a look at the personalities common to both eras. Consider Chevron founder Derek Bennett, Lola's Eric Broadley, Lotus creator Colin

*What the hell was that? Reg Nice in his Austin Seven Ulster appears to be taken by surprise at Silverstone by a low-flying Nigel Cowley in the car his father created. (Harold Barker)*

Chapman, Cosworth co-founder Mike Costin and future Grand Prix driver John Miles, Formula One design engineers Gordon Murray, Maurice Phillippe, Tony Southgate, Len Terry and Derrick White, and prolific Clubmans car producer Arthur Mallock – all cut their teeth and honed their skills (to overdose heavily on the metaphors) as racing car designers in the 750 Formula, and have progressed to designing successful racing cars at the very highest level, including Formula One World Championship winners.

By the mid-'60s the face of British club racing had changed

*The Cowley: Nigel Cowley gives what is probably the ultimate Austin-engined 750 Formula car its head at Snetterton. (Fred Scatley)*

considerably since the heady days of 750 racing's post-war beginnings. With a wide range of both production-based and purpose-built racing cars available, competitors no longer looked automatically towards 750s for affordable motor sport. Similarly, with the advent of Clubmans, Formula Ford and Formula 3, the choice of a foothold on the ladder up to Formula One was much greater.

The 750 Club had by this time revealed itself to a less than startled public to be indeed a motor club rather than a nightspot by becoming the 750 Motor Club. Now organizing racing for a wide range of cars, it still remained true to its credo 'Leaders In Low Cost Motor Sport'.

But the passage of time produced the first major crisis in the club's history. The faithful Austin Seven power unit that had formed the basis of the 750 Formula for its first 15 years was long out of production. Elderly crankshafts were breaking like raw carrots. There were also some Seven *aficionados* who considered the engine worthy of preservation as an historic treasure, viewing the propulsion of wayward conrods through the sides of such gems, while sitting flat in top down Silverstone's Club Straight, as bordering on the sacrilegious.

Lengthy and passionate debate took place on the subject of the 747 side-valve Austin's replacement. On the face of it, the engine from beneath the bonnet of a plastic three-wheeler was an unlikely choice, but using the means of propulsion from Reliant's flying tripod made sense. Available in 750 cc side-valve or 600 cc

overhead-valve form, the larger of the two was actually based upon the Austin engine it was to replace. Indeed, before the war the Austin motor itself had powered Reliant's diminutive three-wheeler delivery vans. Later, in order to keep pace with contemporary traffic, Reliant had uprated these engines. However, the introduction by the government of a maximum weight requirement for motorcycle taxation eligibility necessitated an all-new unit. Reliant produced an all-aluminium, three-bearing, wet-lined 600 cc little beauty which was to prove eminently tunable, this eight-port headed number just begging to have its standard 23 bhp doubled. Long-term production stability, ready availability at an affordable price, and the makers' enthusiastic support were further points in its favour.

Reliant-powered cars were permitted from 1966, and a further generation of inventive constructors and adventurous drivers was spawned. The larger 850 cc ohv engine, a development of the 600, was

*Silverstone at Snetterton: current 750 Motor Club Chairman Michael Fetherstonhaugh in his Team Sigma Austin Seven-based car in 1959. The fully enveloping body was designed and made by Michael with the help of Harry Worrall, and replicas of the body were later marketed by Jem Marsh as the Speedex Silverstone. (Jon Cowley)*

admitted to the formula in 1987 following an interim 750, and continues to this day, still capable of setting new lap records with every new season.

A gentleman by the name of Bryan Clayton was one of the first to convert to Reliant motivation, having tired of his elderly Austin engine regularly becoming unglued. Fittingly named 'Vitesse', Clayton's car and driving dominated the '66 season and pointed the way for serious 750 Formula combatants. Yet it is a reflection of the imagination and technical ability of many 750 Motor Club members that a side-valve-powered car won the 750 Championship as recently as 1973. That car was the Warren, so named for no better reason than that it was the name of the road in which Jerry Evershed lived. He and driver Robin Smythe demonstrated that it was possible to build a rear-engined 750 racer within rules stipulating the use of a solid rear axle. This was cunningly achieved by turning the engine through 180° to point the gearbox towards the front of the car, then chain driving, by means of a jackshaft, a short propshaft to the differential. The reversed rotation of the engine in this position was counteracted by the axle being turned upside down, so ensuring that, unlike in Italian tanks, there were not four reverse gears and one forward. In addition to such a radical layout, the motor was supercharged by a Godfrey blower, although forced induction was later to be banned.

Tragically, both Evershed and Smythe were to succumb to the ravages of cancer within two years of their success, robbing the sport of two its more talented enthusiasts.

Other notable constructors and racers of the formula's Reliant period have included Dave Newman, whose DNC Mk 5 was of semi-monocoque construction which utilized 2 in aluminium-skinned side panels with foam filling built up on the regulation spaceframe. Powered by a dry-sumped motor set so low that the flywheel emerged through the floor, the DNC sat on 10 in diameter Mini racing wheels and slicks. Dick Hartle used rubber bands in tension to suspend his Tristesse. Ray Wilson set up the Omag 2 with minimal ground clearance by utilizing rubber bushes in compression as sus-

pension. Dick Harvey and Mick Harris, of whom probably more than you can bear later, were the creators of the mid-engined Darvi 877 with Group C style all-enveloping body. And most recently there has been John Morris, who with ex-Broadspeed engine-builder Mike Kenny and former Lucas engineer Tom Hewlitt devised the all-conquering Marrow, which won the 750 Championship in 1990 and '91 in Phil Myatt's hands, and in 1992 and '93 with Andy Jones at the wheel. Of conventional front-engined layout, the power unit is set well back and angled towards the centre to facilitate lowline all-enveloping bodywork finished in white striped green, hence the car's vegetarian-friendly name.

The rules governing 750 racing have evolved by necessity over the years, but in essence they remain true to their modest Austin Seven origins. Reliants have replaced Austins in the engine bay, any production four-speed gearboxes and live rear axles are now acceptable, and the incorporation of two 2 in x 2 in steel chassis members has supplanted the obligatory use of an Austin Seven chassis. Originally such tubing took the form of a three-sided 'top hat' section with a fourth side welded across the bottom. Now a 2 in square single piece of steel is allowed. Aerofoils, slick tyres and, of course, extensive safety equipment are also now in, but changes have been so gradual and minimal that it is still possible to be competitive with a 20-year-old car. In what other formula, apart from historic racing, can that be said? Indeed, 750 racing is most probably the

longest running motor racing formula in the world.

The attractions of 750 racing are enormous. Run by 100-octane motorheads for those with a similar affliction, this is real motor racing at Reliant Robin prices. The excitement and glamour are there in abundance, but the participants are generally down-to-earth people who work hard for a crust during the week in commonplace jobs in order to go racing at weekends.

For the most part, professional racing drivers are anonymous young men. They have interchangeable physiques, personalities, skills, pace and aspirations. Life in 750 racing is different. There are fat drivers and thin drivers, young drivers and old drivers, fast drivers and slow drivers, and their wide variety of characters, strengths and flaws are there for all to see. This is what makes being part of it all so enjoyable.

Without sponsorship or hefty prize funds, 750 racers race for the love of it, and money is kept firmly in perspective. There is a healthy irreverence towards big spenders, and although the odd motorhome may show up, it had better be a beat-up Transit rather than a Winnebago. Indeed, should someone have a new flysheet on their tent, questions are likely to be asked as to where the cash came from. Into this world stepped Dick Harvey, and through his experience and ideas you will see how you too can design, build and race a 750 Formula car for sensible money, and become part of a most enjoyable form of motor racing with a fine tradition.

# Chapter 3

# ENTER DICK HARVEY PADDOCK LEFT

George Jeffrey started it all. George was a guy with more patter than Moses' flip-flops, allegedly changing addresses as often as his ladies. Jeffrey Racing Cars produced a 750 racing car kit, a review of which on the pages of *Cars and Car Conversions* caught the eye and imagination of an impressionable young High Wycombe industrial chemist.

Prior to this apocalyptic moment, Dick Harvey's motoring adventures had been limited to the Queen's highway, albeit at speeds of which Her Majesty would have disapproved. His first car was a side-valve Ford Anglia 100E. This was followed by an Anglia 105E, the first unsuspecting recipient of Dick's tuning attentions. With the benefit of advice from Alan Kitchen, an experienced mechanic at Norman Reeves, the local Ford dealership, the 1200 cc engine was modified to such effect that, sitting on its lowered and stiffened suspension and 5J wide wheels, the Harvey Anglia regularly saw off 1650 cc Angleboxes, the boy racer icon of the sixties.

*Last and lapped: Dick Harvey gingerly negotiates Becketts at Silverstone in the Jeffrey Mk III. Inadequate engine lubrication plagued Dick's 1972 debut season. Note home-made fully enveloping bodywork. (Dick Harvey collection)*

An introduction to kit car construction followed in the form of a Mini Marcos. Jem Marsh's aesthetically challenged plastic rat was initially powered by an 850 cc motor, a subsequent 1000 cc unit never seeming as sweet.

These early wheels took Dick, brother Jon, and their pals to Silverstone, and they became hooked on motor racing. Dick in particular considered himself something of a wheelman, and well capable of mixing it with the best of them on the wide expanses of the Northamptonshire circuit. But as many budding racers learn, being the rat's pyjamas on the A43 in an Anglia is far removed from going through Woodcote in an open racer, wheel to wheel with a bunch of like-minded nutters.

The 'Triple C' article changed the course of Dick Harvey's life and, following a couple of telephone calls, he and his brother set out in Jon's Thames van for deepest Oxfordshire. There, in a war-surplus Nissen hut on the edge of an old airfield near Minster Lovell, to the west of Witney, lurked Jeffrey Racing Cars, and in exchange for a wad of used fivers, Dick received a basic chassis and a set of drawings. These were duly loaded into the van and brought home, to be installed in the family garage next to Chez Harvey.

This garage was something of a character. In the antique trade it would have been considered 'distressed'. Built of asbestos and timber, the structure had an alarming habit of going all lozenge-shaped whenever the doors were opened. Accordingly all entries and exits were executed in double-quick time. Some years

later it was demolished by the simple measure of leaving a door open.

Within this death-trap Dick built his first 750 racer in 1971. A fully enveloping, two-seater sports glassfibre body was designed and fitted onto alloy pods astride the Jeffrey chassis, to which were added a 642 cc Reliant motor (600 plus 80 thou), Reliant gearbox and Morris Minor back axle.

First race was at Aintree in 1972, an event notable for a hole at Beechers Bend that could have swallowed Shergar and probably did, the circuit owners presenting the 750MC with a ludicrous repair bill for £800 following the savaging of a fence by an E-type, and the Jeffrey's oil light glowing ominously throughout the practice. Paddock 'experts' prescribed a liberal dose of a notable additive, and knowing no better, Dick obliged. This was a bad move. The additive formed a nasty big glob in the sump, blocking the oil ways and blowing the engine after just one lap.

Three more races followed during that first season, as did two more blow-ups. In the final race of the year, at Silverstone, the car chugged round to finish last and lapped. Not quite the triumphant debut hoped for, but in the true spirit of 750 racing young Harvey remained undeterred.

The problem was poor engine lubrication. The standard Reliant system relied upon a Mini oil pump positioned within the sump, this being driven off the side of the camshaft by a long shaft. Unfortunately, when subjected to the sort of revs unknown to a three-wheeler being gingerly conducted down to Tescos by its

God-fearing owner, the 'skew gears' that drove the oil pump and distributor would strip, leaving the hapless racer with a power unit on the point of going ballistic.

Dick believed he could improve upon the Jeffrey, and who wouldn't have? Yet despite his stormy baptism in the ways of 750 racing, Dick owed his introduction to race driving to George Jeffrey, and indeed many were the drivers who were able to enter the sport inexpensively with one of George's cars, including successful club racers Mike Chittenden, Rod Hill and Richard Stephens.

During the winter preceding the 1973 season a new car was built. The racer was constructed in ten weeks, the brothers attending evening classes in welding to develop their brazing skills. This car made use of the running gear from the Jeffrey mounted onto a new chassis covered with a Clubmans-style body featuring a functional two-seater cockpit with separate front mudguards. The oil circulation system was revised by dry-sumping, and Dick raced this car with encouraging results for three years. The inspirational name Darvi was the work of brother Jon, and as this was Dick's second attempt at building a racer it was designated the Mk 2.

At about this time Mick Harris arrived on the scene. An apprentice mechanic at Norman Reeves, Mick was sent to Dick by Alan Kitchen to be dissuaded from wasting his money and energy on modifying his Anglia. This Dick did to such good effect that Mick was recruited as unpaid race meeting help to the Darvi equipe. And so the happy triumvirate of

*Beginning of the Darvi dynasty: the 'Clubmans'-bodied Mk 2 seen at Lydden's Devil's Elbow in 1975 pursued by Ray Wilson's Omag. Wilson was later to create the ultra-low Omag 2 which used rubber bushes in compression as suspension. (Chris Todd)*

Dick, Mick and Jon would pile into the latter's old Viva van and tow the Darvi Mk 2 up and down the country to racing circuits far and wide.

*Early aerodynamic experiments: the Mk 2 with more angular 'evolution' bodywork powering through Russell at Snetterton in the days when it was a proper bend. Note grooved slicks, perpetrators of the infamous 'three bite shuffle'. After being sold to Peter Thompson, then becoming the Banana Special, this car disappeared without trace for 17 years before being discovered recently in a barn at Thame, not 20 miles from its High Wycombe birthplace. (Fred Scatley)*

Like Mick, Jon was a mechanic. A brief stay at Norman Reeves preceded a spell at March and involvement with the Formula 2 test team in the days of Jean-Pierre Jarier and Jacques Coulon. Later, based in the South of France at Circuit Paul Ricard, he helped run the Antar-sponsored March F3 effort in the French Championship for rally drivers Jean Ragnotti and Philippe Albiera. Subsequently Jon was to become Adrian Reynard's first employee.

On one occasion the van's

head gasket blew on the M1 whilst travelling home from Mallory Park. That morning a character by the name of Len Large had driven his family up to Leicestershire to watch the racing, and being a car salesman had liberated a 10-mile-old Marina 1300 demonstrator. On his return trip Len spotted the stranded team and offered to tow them off the motorway. So away they went, Mr Large, wife and kids in the Marina pulling Dick, Mick and Jon in the van, which in turn was pulling the Darvi and trailer. Quite a sight, and not one to amuse the local constabulary. By the end of the M1 things were going so well that Len insisted on towing them all the way home. The Marina was well run-in by the time they reached High Wycombe.

*The adjuster car: the lower and leaner Darvi Mk 3 appeared in 1976 and was designed to run on 10 in diameter wheels. Note rear trim flap, aerofoils not being permitted at the time. (I. Booth and A. Pattison)*

Soon Mick Harris became as absorbed in 750 racing as Dick, and they began sharing the Darvi. At that time entries were often so large that two races would be held, with selection for which one being according to practice times. Dick would drive the 'fast' races, Mick the 'slow' – an arrangement that reduced costs considerably.

The Darvi Mk 3 saw the light of day in 1976. The intention had been to complete it during the previous year, but the death of Dick's father on St Patrick's Day 1975 relegated motor racing to its proper place in the grand scheme of things, and the car lay in the garage for several months unfinished. Designed to run on 10 in diameter Mini wheels which offered lower gearing and ride height, together with less rolling resistance and smaller frontal area, the Mk 3 was an 'adjuster car'. Most key settings were adjustable, with such items as multi-choice suspension pick-up points and radius arm mountings via a range of holes in the chassis. The Mk 2 was

sold to Peter Thompson and disappeared into the West Country; when last seen it was painted yellow and going under the name of the Banana Special.

Dick and Mick continued their sharing arrangement with the Mk 3 and steadily, by judicious experimentation with the car's vast variety of settings, they began to get the Darvi to work in a very satisfactory manner. The problem with having access to such a range of variables was that it was always tempting to fiddle with something, and frequently the car would be changed between practice and races. It was never accepted at this stage that perhaps the driver was being beaten rather than the car.

The Darvi Mk 3 allowed Mick Harris's natural talent as a driver to flourish, and he won several 'slow' races. At one Mallory Park meeting the car had three drivers. Due to a 70-strong entry, three races were held. As usual Dick and Mick did the 'fast' and 'slow' races, then the car was lent to Colin

*Dick on the limit: actually he was way over, and promptly spun! Note single-piece GRP top and rear aerofoil which have been added to a developing Mk 3. (Dick Harvey collection)*

'Buzby' Robinson. 'Buzby' (so named because he was always on the telephone) was down to drive the Panda with master metal-worker John McPharland, but inconveniently both drivers qualified for the third race. Jokingly, McPharland suggested to the Darvi drivers that Robinson race the Mk 3, and to everybody's surprise Dick agreed. When race time came so did the rain, and the Foster Wheeler engineer was a little reluctant to take up his Darvi drive, but Dick and Mick put it to him that if they were prepared to hang about and get wet so should he be, so into the cockpit he strapped himself. Not having practised the car, Robinson was made to start ten seconds after the rest. However, it is a measure of both his driving and the car's capabilities that he still won the race, his one and only victory.

A postscript to this heart-warming story is that shortly afterwards the delighted guest driver sent Dick a bottle of malt whisky as a mark of gratitude. This gesture was to instigate a life-long devotion to malts by the Harvey palate.

For 1977, following the sale of the Mk 3 to air traffic controller Steve Quinton (it is now owned by Northerner Ian Blackwood), Dick produced the Darvi Mk 4. Basically this was a tidied up Mk 3, with better aerodynamics and 13 in wheels in order to capitalize upon supplies of second-hand slicks that were becoming available.

Prior to this time, treaded racing tyres were *de rigueur*, hard old Dunlop CR81s being the popular choice. But with Formula 3 now running on untreaded soft compound rubber, partly used stock soon found its way into the sticky hands of the impecunious 750 men. Dick cultivated a source of such tyres in the form of Eddie Jordan, then wheeling and dealing his way up through the lower single-seater formulae to his current position in the lime-light of Formula One. The Darvi constructor would buy the soft fronts, ideal for a light 750 Formula car, a hot-rod driver

would buy the harder rears, and Dick would drive up to Jordan's Silverstone base where the fast-talking Irishman, often on two phones at once, would point him towards a pile of discarded rubber. The price was cheap, but everything had to be taken. So the basket cases went to the tip on the way home, the good stuff was sorted into sets, and any surplus was sold to fellow 750 men for £60 per set, the price of one new tyre. As this ever cost-conscious formula only allowed one set of tyres to be used per meeting, it was common practice to cut three grooves in them to allow some displacement of water in the unlikely event of it raining in England. Dick accordingly performed the necessary surgery upon his bargain basement Goodyear G50s.

Complete with larger 748 cc

*The Darvi Mk 4: back on 13 in diameter wheels, and complete with March F3 nose-cone and exposed side-draught FZD Dellorto carburettor, Dick Harvey and Mick Harris became regular front runners in this car during 1977. (Richard Towndrow)*

engine, smoother one-piece body top, and a modified ex-March F3 nose-cone courtesy of 'the bruvver', Dick's learning curve as both a builder and driver of racing cars took a steep

upward turn, and during the 1977 season he took a couple of second places in the 'fast' races, while Mick became a regular winner of the 'slow' events. However, these simplistic race descriptions should not be taken too literally, for often the two drivers' practice times were very similar, yet clearly it was impossible for them both to drive the car in the same race. Inevitably Mick's presence in the 'slow' races led to dark mutterings and grumblings

amongst the great paddock unwashed, and so it was decided in the interests of peace and harmony that Mick would take over the Mk 4 and Dick would build a Mk 5.

The Darvi Mk 5 was a refined Mk 4, and hit the track in time for the 1978 season. This car was to serve its owner well for a remarkable five seasons. In conceiving this, his fifth racer, Dick took to heart Arthur Mallock's thinkings on static weight distribution. Basically, any asymmetrical layout such as that adopted by a Clubmans-style 750 Formula car is bound to have a problem of weight distribution as the driver sits off-centre. With all this weight on the right-hand side of the car, and a light-alloy engine on the left doing little to offset it, Dick looked at ways of redress-

*Darvi domination: Dick in the Darvi Mk 5 (car 3) and Mick (Darvi Mk 4/5) share the front row of the grid at Snetterton with musician Gary Randal's Hague, just out of shot. (Fred Scatley)*

ing the balance. He laid out the bare chassis on his garage floor, weighed various components on the bathroom scales, and distributed them in such a way as to optimize static weight distribution. And lo and behold, by putting the battery, fuel tank and one or two other minor items on the left side of the car, the balance was almost perfect without doing anything too radical. That was to come later.

Meanwhile, Mick Harris had been building his new car up on the Darvi Mk 4 chassis, and when it appeared in 1979 it was designated Mk 4/5. Mick and Dick were well matched in their essentially similar cre-

ations, and during one season took 17 pole positions between them. As Dick was three stone heavier than Mick, this suggests that weight distribution is as important as overall weight.

Harris won his first 750 Championship race in 1979 at Lydden. Harvey had to wait until 1980 for his maiden victory at Silverstone, eight long years after the Aintree débâcle. Hardly overnight success, but in a form of racing where car performance is similar, and where many protagonists are vastly experienced due to having made the formula their home, this is not unusual. Wins and good placings for the Darvi

*Now that's what's called a motor race: Mick Harris goes on to beat Dick Harvey to the flag, Dick's Mk 5 displaying a little kerb rash around the nose. (Fred Scatley)*

duo continued during the years that followed, culminating in Mick Harris winning the 1982 and '83 Championships.

An informed independent

*DNC sandwich: Dick in the Mk 5 and Mick in his Mk 4/5 give Iain Sclanders, in a DNC, something to think about through Russell at Snetterton. Note that sidepods have crept into Darvi thinking, in contrast to the more exposed wheels of the DNC. (Fred Scatley)*

assessment of a 750F racing car builder's work is usually difficult to obtain, but late in 1979 Dick received such an appraisal from one of the best. Former Lotus Formula One driver John Miles, now a development engineer for Lotus, track-tested several 750 Formula cars at Silverstone for *Autocar*, and the Darvi Mk 5 was amongst them. Miles was very impressed with the Darvi, observing that it was 'beautifully sorted'. He went on to say that 'turning-in stability was incredible', that the steering had 'superb feel', and of the braking, that 'a giant hand simply clawed the speed back'.

Dick was similarly impressed by John Miles. A gentle, unassuming man who was the absolute antithesis of the popular concept of the modern, hard-nosed F1 pilote, the son of the late actor and Mermaid Theatre impresario Sir Bernard Miles clearly had talent to burn. At the time, a good 750 lap

*Birkett Relay Race 1983: Dick Harvey's Darvi Mk 6 is overshadowed by a Caterham Seven and Aston Martin DB4 at Silverstone. (Harold Barker)*

around Silverstone's club circuit, using all the track and lots of revs, was in the region of 1 min 10 sec. Never having sat in the car before, and sticking to a self-imposed 7000 rpm rev limit, Miles was circulating the Darvi in 1 min 10 sec within five laps. Unfortunately, the intervention of the lunch break followed by the onset of rain prevented him 'going for a time'.

In July 1982 Dick received an unwelcome birthday present: he was made redundant. Aeropreen, for whom he had worked as a foam development chemist, had been bought by Dunlopillo and a spot of 'rationalization' took place. With no income now the racing had to stop.

But 750 racing was by now firmly in the blood. Life without it was unthinkable. So Dick continued to turn up at races to watch or do a little mechanicking. Former 750 Champion Bob Simpson suggested that Dick Harvey Racing Services be established, for Dick had been in 750 racing for 11 years by now and had earned considerable credibility as a driver–con-

structor. Who better to provide for the odd and varied needs of the 750 racer?

The one-man business was set up in the small prefabricated garage next to his home, financed by the sale of the Mk 5 to Lancashire quarry owner Bill Brown. This transaction involved an expedition to Blackburn, a part of England where Southerners believe the M6 becomes cobbled. On Dick's arrival there, crisp greenies exchanged hands, the construction of the trans-Pennine M62 having been good to the quarry trade.

Subsequently the car passed first to the late Gary Dobbin, a most popular and enthusiastic 750MC member with a talent for utilizing otherwise useless pieces of equipment for motor racing purposes. An example of this gift was the Prince Charles and Lady Di tea tray which, when applied with magnetic numbers, made a fine pitboard. You won't find that in a Demon Tweeks catalogue.

Middlesex garagiste Hayden Mcasham was the next owner of the Mk5. Being vertically challenged, he stuffed a few volumes of the *Encyclopedia*

*Britannica* behind him in order to reach the pedals, thus giving a whole new meaning to the term 'booking a seat'. Apparently Measham drove the car for an entire season in this manner, no other cockpit arrangement proving as comfortable. Advanced driving instructor Paul Coombs had the car for a while, and it now resides with car dealer Dave Burton in long-wheelbase form.

The Championship-winning Mk 4/5 was sold to Stevenage gas fitter Nev Cooke at the end of 1983, and was later owned by North Country financier Lyndon Foster, Alderley Edge-based, Paradise Baths purveyor Jon Salem, from whom it contracted a nasty case of 'salem-ella' poisoning by being heavily shunted, and Blackburn gas turbine engineer Phil Shepherd who restored it. Tim Cousins is the current owner.

For 1983 Dick produced the Darvi Mk 6. Developing further his thoughts on static weight distribution, this car had a narrow nose to allow air to pass freely to a side radiator, and

inboard rocking arm suspension to facilitate such a small frontal area. This differed significantly from previous Darvis which had incorporated full-width noses and conventional outboard suspension.

The high loadings involved with rocking arm suspension were not fully appreciated by Dick, and several breakages occurred during this car's first season. The excuse to change the arrangement arose early in 1984. Dick's personal suspension system was playing up, and a cartilage operation became necessary. Recovering on crutches, Dick offered Mick Harris a drive in a race on the Brands Hatch Grand Prix circuit, the reigning champion having sold his car and enduring a year off. True to his talent, Mick took an early lead, only for an engine problem to cause him to spin. Unable to restart the motor, he pulled off the track between Stirling and Clearways and climbed out of the cockpit in what appeared to be a safe place. Imagine his surprise, therefore, when,

*Mallory miscellany: Dick Harvey in the needle-nosed Mk 6, complete with rocking-arm inboard suspension and side radiator, leads the more conventional Time 4 of Bill Brown, the Centaur of Bob Savage and the SS Reliant of Bob Simpson around Shaws. (John Gaisford)*

glancing back over his shoulder as he walked away from the car, he saw another competitor run off a straight piece of track and knock the front end off the Mk 6. Duncan 'Captain' Kirk had clearly been overcome by the spectre of the retired Darvi and been drawn to it. Reference to an invisible force field can be found in the ship's log.

The front of the Mk 6 was rebuilt with pull-rod suspension. Working on the bottom of the damper rather than the top, this arrangement transformed the car, and on Dick's return to the fray at Castle Combe he won. This success may of course have been the fruits of physiotherapy rather than revised suspension, but a 30-second win was pretty conclusive evidence of something. Towards the end of the race the leader came up to lap a line of six back markers. As they had been shown blue flags throughout the event, the significance of Dick's supersonic approach escaped them. Five stayed out of the Darvi's path but the sixth pulled across; a friendly tap of wheels put that right, although that may not have been how the back marker saw it.

By mid-season, after a couple more wins, Dick was neck-and-neck with Otford GM dealer Simon Fry and West Drayton electrician Bob Simpson for the championship. Then Mr Fry developed an irritating habit of using the Darvi as a brake, and the season ended with Dick third behind Simon and Bob.

The Mk 6 was sold at the end of 1984 for all the wrong reasons, Peter Nicholl's pile of

*Who was that masked man? Mick Harris had barely removed his helmet when Duncan 'Captain' Kirk became curiously attracted to the Darvi Mk 6 at Brands Hatch in 1984. (Steve Jones)*

greenies proving irresistible. The car was later to prove very competitive in Richard Crossman's hands. But inflation is a maddening thing, and it did not escape Dick's notice for long that the cost of building a new car from scratch was going to far exceed monies received for the old one. Fortunately we can now sleep easily in our beds in the knowledge that inflation is no longer with us.

(What a book this is turning out to be – motor racing and political satire too!)

The next car to roll out of the Harvey garage was the Mk 8. Mick Harris was still building the Mk 7 at the time, of which more later. A development of the Mk 6, Dick's new car incorporated several detail changes, some of which proved difficult to sort out. Falling-rate pull-rod suspension was not a great success. A system whereby the coil spring and damper got softer rather than harder the greater the forces acting upon it, quite understandably resulted in handling inconsistencies. Should there have been any lingering doubt in the driver's mind as to

whether a rethink was called for, the matter was conclusively settled on a cold and damp November morning at Silverstone when Richard Crossman, after several half-hearted attempts, got Becketts seriously wrong in his DNC and wrote off the front of the recalcitrant Mk 8.

The Darvi 86-9 which followed had much more going for it than just state-of-the-art numbering: a needle nose and push-rod inboard suspension, the faithful 748 converted to the by now permitted 848 cc Reliant engine, a stronger 850 gearbox with the latest close-ratio gear cluster, and some of the running gear and rear half of the chassis from the Mk 8.

During 1986 the car showed considerable promise, and during the winter that followed it was fine-tuned. Sitting at his big drawing board in the spare bedroom, Dick made some geometric calculations and concluded that to make the most of the push-rod front suspension, dampers 1 in shorter than those fitted were required. Naturally, such items were neither inexpensive nor readily available, but half an hour with a hacksaw and an arc welder soon took care of that. These home-modified dampers were fitted with the revised geometry and the car's handling was transformed.

Nineteen eighty-seven was Dick Harvey's year. From 14 starts the Darvi 86-9 took ten pole positions, 11 wins and the coveted Goodacre Trophy for winning the PSL/Dellorto 750 Formula Championship. Such domination of a season is a remarkable achievement for any driver, but to do so in a car of one's own design and construction must approach the ultimate motor racing achievement.

The car was one factor in this

success, but there were also two others: Tyres and Motivation. Avon A6 rubber had been used during the previous season and took two laps to warm up, during which time the likes of Ernie Frost and Bob Simpson were well gone. A gentleman by the name of Bob Davis did a deal with Dick, whereby in exchange for a tenner's worth of glassfibre resin the boy Harvey received two Avon A2s, an A1 and an A11 off Bob's

Formula 4 car. These tyres were much softer than the A6s, and despite a season's use were to enable the Darvi to go hard from the moment the lights turned to green.

Davis's other contribution to Dick's success was to suggest, less than subtly, that it was time he stopped being a plonker and did the job of which he was clearly capable. Whether this inspired a new-found confidence in Dick, or a fear of

*Giving the Mk 8 some grief: Dick being made to work hard at Castle Combe in 1985 by the recalcitrant pull-rod-suspended Darvi. The Hague of Ernie Frost, who is languishing behind a sinister dark visor and in his first Championship year, and the Gallard of Richard Stephens, prepare to pounce. (Dick Harvey collection)*

facing the outspoken engineer again should results not improve, is unclear.

# Chapter 4

# THE JACK BRABHAM EXPERIENCE

On the face of it, Dick Harvey's approach to the 1987 season was remarkably audacious.

Oulton Park in March did not appeal to the Harvey sensibilities, and the winter rebuild was still not finished by the Snetterton meeting in April, so it was at Round 3 of the 750 Championship at Mallory Park in May that Dick donned his new Bell helmet in anger for the first time.

Despite the buffeting of high winds and the application of a gentle right foot, there being a motor to bed in and the latest suspension modifications to try, Dick found himself on the front row of the grid next to pole man Ernie Frost in the Hague. A steel fabricator from Canvey Island who had the nerve to introduce an American Dodge motorhome to the humble confines of the 750 Formula paddock, Ernie was the reigning champion and had his sights firmly set on a third title in succession.

At the green light it was Jon Salem's Hague that took the lead with Dick tucked in behind, and as they came out of the hairpin for the first time

the Darvi moved ahead. Revelling in the increased flexibility of the 850 engine, which enabled a higher, 4.2 differential to be used, Harvey won the race with a five-second margin, only suspension set too hard for Mallory's bumps blemishing a near-perfect performance.

Three weeks later Dick was back at the Leicestershire circuit. With suspension suitably softened, pole position was his, but an initial lead was squandered when he outbraked himself into the hairpin and cruised out with a box full of neutrals. By the time he was reunited with some gears Dick was down in ninth place, but within four laps the 87.9 was up to second and pressing Mike Kenny's Marrow for the lead. Then the red flags came out. Newcomer to the formula James Saunders had reduced the ex-Alan Avery, ex-everybody Diablesse to component form through much of the length of Gerrards. On the restart of the race Dick made no more mistakes, pulled away from his pursuers and scored a second win.

Donington Park was next and confidence was high. In

practice the Darvi was more than a second inside Bob Simpson's three-year-old record, and from pole Dick made good use of his soft Avons to take an early lead ahead of Alan Avery's Avalan and Frost's Hague. Then – wham! Just as things seemed to be going nicely a low-flying vegetable displaying awesome straight-line speed blasted past all of them. Mike Kenny had clearly put his engine-building experience at Broadspeed to good use, and Dick had to work hard to keep the Marrow in sight.

Gradually it became evident that the Marrow's advantage was only in a straight line and that the Darvi was quicker through the corners, but several attempts to capitalize upon this at the Esses were met by a firmly closed greenhouse door. So it had to be done at Redgate, to enable Dick to pull away through the series of bends that followed. Taking a deep breath and a slice of grass, he drove around the outside of Kenny, and when he opened his eyes was leading through the sweeping downhill Craner Curves. The development of a misfire on the Marrow's engine

*Leading into Redgate: Dick heads from pole position towards yet another 1987 win, despite a stern mid-race challenge by Mike Kenny, whose striped Marrow is just visible behind Alan Avery's Avalan. Defending champion Ernie Frost's Hague (No. 1), Hayden Measham's Darvi Mk 5 (Spax sticker on nose) and Rod Giles's JGS (No. 15) give chase. (John Gaisford)*

further helped the Harvey cause, and a third win was notched up, together with a new lap record.

Mick Harris debuted his long-awaited new car at Donington. The Darvi Mk 7, or 877 in posh numerics, was a stunning bright red, Group C-style mid-engined racer; and there was little doubt amongst enthralled paddock admirers that here was a future Championship winner.

A sunny Lydden Hill was the scene of the next race. Track-wise racers like to think that hanging around for the green start light wastes time, so they leave the grid when the red

light goes out. Not so. Dick, having set fastest practice time once again, led the field around the short mile circuit to the start line and awaited the pleasure of the BARC starter. With eyes on the light gantry he selected first gear and built up the revs. Out went the red but there was no green. No one moved. On again came the red light, then

*877 debut: Mick Harris unveils the stunning Darvi 877 in 1987. Note Porsche influence and no rear wing. (K.M. Tommey)*

out again, and still there was no green. No bugger moved. The drivers looked expectantly at the puzzled starter, then Ernie Frost set off and everyone followed. On the completion of the opening lap the drivers made to form up again on the grid, only for a marshal to wave them frantically on, and Ernie disappeared into the distance.

Wrong-footed and less than amused by this farce, Dick gave chase, but was unable to catch the flying Hague until the closing stages of the race. Once in the lead and thoroughly confused as to how many laps there were to go, he eased up too early and fell victim to a Frost counter-attack. Side by side into the hairpin the two cars made contact, and locked together slid as one down the aptly named Hairy Hill. Meanwhile the ever-cheerful purveyor of French motor cars, Hayden Measham, was closing on them fast in the Darvi Mk 5. On untangling themselves, Dick found he had the advantage over Ernie, possibly because the ex-kart racer was wearing a Darvi side pod on his head, and win number four was his.

A fortnight later the 750 circus returned to the Kent track. This time Lydden specialist Richard Stephens, son of publisher and Stoneham Special builder Patrick Stephens, put his Gallard (a quick vehicle originally conceived as a Panda by Colin 'Buzby' Robinson) on pole. Dick shared the front row. The novelty value of a green light at Lydden did not escape the 750 men as they left the grid, and after a cracking start Richard took the lead, only to be taken out by Ernie Frost at the hairpin as he still strived to perfect his outbraking tech-

nique there. This was good news for Harvey, and with a clear track ahead of him he won as he pleased.

Returning to the paddock, the Darvi's nearside front tyre went flat. No championship is ever won without a little luck.

Such early season domination incited dark speculation amongst some in the paddock as to what exactly lay beneath the engine cover of the 86-9! But Dick had that one sussed, and suggested casually to a scrutineer that an engine check might be in order. The Reliant was duly sealed, and later found to be entirely kosher.

Now on a roll, Dick's next race was at his favourite circuit, Cadwell. On pole once more, those sticky Avons again launched the Darvi into an early lead, with Richard Stephens, Hayden Measham and Bob Simpson in close pursuit. Then on lap 6 the engine of Stephens's Gallard (named after mentor Jimmy Gallard)

suddenly cut out at Charlies. This caught out the close-following Middlesex garagiste who promptly piled into Richard. The pressure was now off the leader, and barring a mistake, victory number six was his. But it was as if Murray Walker had said the words, for coming out of the final bend for the last time Dick missed a gear. From nowhere suddenly Ernie Frost was all over him like a bad suit, but luck still rode in the Darvi, and it took the chequered flag a gnat's private parts ahead of the Hague.

The Eight Club's August Silverstone meeting had a wonderful tradition which could be traced back to the very first 750 Formula race in 1950. Of course, summers were

*Championship year: the push-rod-suspended Darvi 86-9 leads Jon Salem's Hague into Cadwell's short circuit hairpin en route to an early season win in 1987. Note centre pillar rear wing. (John Gaisford)*

better in those days, policemen looked older, and for half-a-crown you could have a night out at the pictures, a couple of pints and a three-course meal, and still have change for a taxi home. But I digress.

In practice Dick experienced understeer for the first time that season, but still occupied his customary pole position. From the start of the race he was one of four drivers to break away from the pack and fight for the lead. The others were Richard Crossman, a medical journalist who raced a DNC, Mike Kenny in the Marrow, and plumber-electrician Bob Simpson in the SS. On a good day these initials stood for Simpson Special; on a bad day, when the handling was a little awry, Sailing Ship was more appropriate.

Dick, Richard and Mike took it in turns to lead, while Bob lay in wait. Then came the crucial final lap. Richard led out of Becketts, with Dick, Bob and Mike in tow. Approaching Woodcote, Dick slipstreamed into the lead, only to find the dreaded Marrow alongside him. At this point the inevitable backmarker loomed into view,

so Dick dived for the inside while Mike Kenny went around the outside. Unfortunately there was not quite enough track for three abreast, and Dick found himself on some high kerbs. The fast-approaching pit wall looked singularly uninviting, while the escape route up the pit lane was occupied by a couple of old farts shooting the breeze, so back over the kerbing the Darvi bounced. Yet again Mr Harvey's luck held. He hit nothing and finished fourth behind Kenny, Crossman and Simpson, just 0.8 sec covering the four cars.

Back in the paddock the reason for the understeer became obvious: the nearside front tyre was bald. A subsequent search for second-hand replacement rubber proved unsuccessful, so with so much at stake Dick broke the habit of a lifetime and bought a set of new Avon A2s.

A thorough examination of the car prior to Snetterton revealed that the Woodcote adventure had resulted in nothing worse than a bent suspension rocker arm. At the Norfolk circuit, practice was interrupted

*Contrasting approaches: Mick Harris in the Darvi 877 (car 7) takes Luffield at Silverstone in close company with Alan Avery in the Darvi Mk 5-based Avalan. (John Gaisford)*

by Sheffield spring manufacturer Dan White demolishing his Hague-based PC Special at Russell, and when proceedings were resumed the Dick and Mick show got into full swing as their contrasting configuration Darvis chased each other around the two-mile course vying for pole position. The result was Mick Harris's first pole in the new car, just 0.1 sec quicker than Dick.

In the race it was Bob Simpson who made the best start, with the two 'works' Darvis leading the chase. Bob was the Ricardo Patrese of 750 racing by being its longest-serving driver; however, his not inconsiderable experience counted for nothing when the field hit Revett Straight and Dick pulled out of the slipstream of the SS and draughted past. For five laps he held the lead, then Mick made his move, passing Bob coming by the pits, and

*'The bruvver': Jon Harvey at Pembrey in his pristine Darvi 92-J. Mr Simpson in the SS Reliant examines the paint finish from close quarters. (Steve Jones)*

Dick down the back straight. But his glory was short-lived for a misfire set in, and the red 877 dropped to fifth place.

All Mr Harvey had to do now was hold off a determined Mr Simpson, who was showing considerable interest in first place. This was accomplished by a total disregard for the Darvi's rear-view mirrors, according to Simpson supporters, but as Bob later pointed out, Dick always seemed to know where the SS was on the track when it attempted to pass him.

With seven wins and a fourth to his credit, and the best eight scores to count, Dick was now in a position to tie up the Championship should he win at the next round.

The 750 fraternity's third visit of the year to Lydden must have been celebrated in some

style the night before the meeting by the timekeepers, as the formula's practice times bore absolutely no relationship to those actually set. Bexhill accountant Keith McPherson was nominally on pole with the Harrison, but in reality, with due respect to the driver, this was as unlikely as the Pope putting a Minardi on pole at Monza. So for the first time in

his 16-year motor racing career, Dick put in a protest. This threw the organizers into some confusion, and in the end they were forced to ask the drivers what times they thought they

*Even great drivers make mistakes: the 877 of four-time champion Mick Harris turns lawn mower at Brooklands Hairpin, Pembrey. (John Gaisford)*

had done. Not exactly a fool-proof means of establishing a fair grid formation. Whatever, three independent watches had Dick fastest, so onto pole he went.

At the start it was Bob Simpson who got away first, although he only narrowly made it through Chessons Drift without parting company with the tarmac. Second time round he was not so fortunate, the SS getting into a tank slapper as it pointed in rapid succession towards Dover, then Canterbury. This allowed Dick to nip through into the lead. A challenge from Richard Stephens ended in the cheap seats at Chessons, and a spin at Devil's Elbow thwarted Mick Harris's attack. Meanwhile Harvey's Darvi motored serenely on to an eighth win and the 1987 750 Championship.

Savouring the warm afterglow of an ambition achieved, Dick celebrated quietly by leaning on the paddock gate and watching the Formula 1300 race, a can of cold beer in one hand and an Old Holborn roll-up in the other. Jack Brabham must have felt the same way at

Monza in 1966 when he won a championship in a car of his own design. Perhaps he leant on a fence at the Curva Parabolica and got outside a cold tinnie too.

Had Dick Harvey Racing Services been floated on the Stock Exchange, its share prices would have soared following the Darvi's domination of the 1987 750F Championship. The Reliant and Goodacre Trophies for winning driver, the Jem March Trophy for best-prepared car, and the Bill Cowley Trophy for winning the most races in a self-built car all graced the shelves of the Harvey trophy cupboard. The tiny company received orders for 86–9 replicas from Ernie Frost and Keith McPherson, whilst Alan Avery had already based his Avalan (later to be succeeded by the Avalan Mk 2) upon Darvi Mk 5 drawings.

Other cars to receive the Darvi treatment were the ex-Chris Gough Jo Mo of Bob Couchman which, following a dose of involuntary realignment at Snetterton, had the salvaged Jo Mo outboard front suspension grafted onto a Darvi Mk 5

chassis; and the Hague of Rick Goodyer, which benefited from the mating of a Hague front end and a Darvi Mk 5 rear. Interestingly (or perhaps not), Couchman's car raced for some years as a Darvi-JCB, which was either an allusion to Bob's occasional trips into the rough, or alternatively merely stood for Jo Mo–Couchman–Bob. To confuse matters further it is now campaigned as a BCR Special.

Dick defended his title energetically during 1988 in a car essentially unchanged from the previous year. Mick Harris in the mid-engined Darvi 877 was Harvey's closest rival, and a fascinating contest developed between the two contrasting 750 car configurations which had been jointly conceived by the two friends. Ultimately, on an October Saturday at Silverstone, Mick emerged as cham-

*Defending champion: proudly carrying number one on the Darvi 86-9 nose, Harvey leads Mick Harris's Darvi 877 and Peter Knipe's DNC left hooker towards the Snetterton Bomb Hole in 1988. (Fred Scatley)*

pion, and the following day Dick had his horrendous accident at Mallory.

There was never any doubt in Dick's mind that he would race again – 750 racing was too integral a part of his life to be cast aside. Psychologically he was little affected, as he remembered nothing of the shunt. From driving out of the paddock to waking up in hospital there was a blank – the Harvey mental telemetry could print out nothing. Physically things took rather longer, but in July 1991 he was back on a starting grid with a new car, and one leg slightly shorter than the other. The place was Cadwell Park, and after a couple of understandably circumspect early laps he soon found himself moving up through the

*First day back, Cadwell Park, July 1991: helped by Mick Harris, Dick prepares for a return to the track following his horrific accident. (Dick Harvey collection)*

field to finish seventh, which ably demonstrated that the right foot still worked.

The Darvi 91-D was a development of the successful 86-9, and most of the improvements were in the driver protection department. The 'D' denoted Dick, distinguishing the immaculate blue-over-red machine from brother Jon's yellow 92-J built the following year. Dick races the 91-D to this day, ever experimenting with body panel profiles in the quest for optimum aerodynamics, and with other tweaks calculated to attain that illusive winning edge.

To become a 750 racer is neither difficult nor expensive when compared to other forms of motor racing. A season's racing can be undertaken for the cost of a good foreign holiday, whilst a good competitive 750 car and trailer can be had for the price of a small used road car. Accordingly, as many drivers can testify, this is an

ideal formula in which to begin motor racing.

For the newcomer a race licence, motor club membership, helmet and fire-resistant overalls are the basic requirements. A love of motor sport and a sense of humour are also useful attributes. Note that outstanding skill as a driver, technical prowess and an ultra-competitive nature are not included in the list. For although some basic driving ability and proficiency in changing the odd spark plug are helpful, and indeed it is unlikely that you would be contemplating becoming involved without a hint of these virtues in your possession, the object of the exercise is to have fun. To become a part of a sport you have watched, read about and dreamt of from afar. There are no McLaren test drives on offer at the end of a successful season, so relax and enjoy yourself. Ponce around the paddock in the new driving

*Constructor and customer: Dick at the wheel of the 91-D, followed by Keith McPherson in the 86-9-based Darvi CMP. (John Gaisford)*

suit, shoot the breeze with fellow competitors, soak up the atmosphere, and enjoy every minute of being a racing driver.

Although aimed essentially at the impecunious designer, constructor and driver, 750 racing is perhaps best entered with a second-hand car upon which someone else has lavished skilled attention, time and money. Such an approach allows the newcomer to try the sport without too great a commitment until such time as it is decided whether driver and 750 racing cars are compatible. Should things work out, the car can then be developed or replaced by something better, with the ever-available option of a new car being designed and built from scratch. Should things not work out, the driver can bow out gracefully and resell the car with the minimum of lost expenditure.

Rather like horses, second-hand racing cars command prices commensurate with their pedigrees. A well-prepared machine with good-quality components and a record of success will always command a higher price than a car without these qualities. Condition and equipment levels are more important than age, for in a formula which prides itself on rules stability, a 20-year-old car can still be a front runner. Peter Knipe's DNC, Jim Dallimore's Hague and Damon Bland's SS are living proof.

Prices start at £1,000 for old dogs, rising to £5,000–£6,000 for state-of-the-art machinery. £2,000–£3,000 should buy a good competitive car.

A fine example of an affordable and competitive used 750 car appeared in the small ads at the back of the January 1994 edition of the 750 MC monthly magazine, the *Bulletin*. Richard Crossman was offering his Darvi Mk 6 for sale, as raced successfully by its originator Dick Harvey, Peter Nicholls and Crossman since being built in 1983. The advertisement read:

For Sale: Darvi Mk 6, regular F750 front runner. Rebuilt engine, needs running in. Complete outfit with wets, spare gearbox, diffs, loads of spares, body mouldings, lightweight trailer with brakes, tyre rack and winch. Go out and win some cups. £4,250 ono.

Such a car would be very competitive in experienced hands, or could offer the novice a worthwhile introduction to the formula with scope for further development when required. It could even provide the basis for a brand-new racing car, for the mating of an older car with fresh chassis or bodywork is the cheapest way of coming by a new racer. Similarly, an old car bought for perhaps £1,000–£2,000 can provide sound components that might cost more than double that figure to purchase separately, so forming the key ingredients for a new car designed and built from scratch.

The main sources of second-hand 750 cars, and indeed components to fit them, are the aforementioned *750 Bulletin*, the specialist motor sporting press in the form of *Autosport, Motoring News* and *Cars and Car Conversions*, or discreet enquiries around any 750 racing paddock. There is always someone with a car to sell, and never a shortage of candid opinions as to its worth. In fact it is no bad idea to watch a few races and talk with some drivers before launching headlong into any form of motor sport. A 'Wanted' ad can also bring results, with the added bonus of long conversations about motor racing on someone else's phone bill.

Finally, let's look at the comparative costs of buying second-hand and building all new. As already described, good used 750F cars can be bought for between £2,000 and £6,000, with a tired example of use for its components available for a grand upwards. An all-new build would look something like this: chassis and body kit – £1,500–£3,000, according to level of sophistication; race-prepared engine and gearbox – £1,000–£3,000 according to specification; components such as wheels, tyres, springs, dampers, instruments, seat belts, steering wheel, radiators, tanks, exhaust, rear axle and so on – £4,000–£5,000. In other words a brand-new 750 racer could cost as much as £11,000 excluding assembly labour, compared to a second-hand front runner for, say, £6000. By today's standards neither option is excessively expensive compared with other forms of motor racing, but the wisdom of entering the formula with a second-hand machine is clearly demonstrated.

Yet it is possible, using a shrewd mixture of new and used components, hard work, and a little imagination, to design and build your own chassis, bodywork, engine and running gear for sensible money. And in creating and racing the resulting car, you will experience the excitement and satisfaction that is the essence of 750 racing.

# Chapter 5

# GENESIS

The perfect 750 racer goes like the wind down the straights, corners on rails, stops at will, is totally reliable and costs nothing.

To these ends the impecunious designer and builder must strive within the constraints of the formula's technical regulations (Fig. 1). These rules are reproduced in full in Appendix A; however, the key elements are as follows:

1. Reliant 850 cc engine.
2. Four-speed and reverse gearbox.
3. Live rear axle without locking device.
4. Incorporation of two 2 x 2 in square tube longitudinal chassis members.
5. Two-seater body of minimum cockpit dimensions.

As enthusiasts have been constructing cars for more than 40 years to this essentially unchanged formula, there is much to be learnt from tried and tested approaches, particularly as many of these practitioners have been extremely talented. Yet this does not preclude innovation. Rather it suggests that radical thinking is likely to be of more use in the detailed execution than in the fundamental concept of the car's creation, as the major components are fixed by a set of rules that have stood the test of time as a basis for close and relatively inexpensive motor racing. In practice this means that while sequential gearboxes, traction control and transaxles are out, a sideways glance at what is happening to, say, aerodynamics in Formula 3 could be very rewarding. Indeed, if it is accepted that all 750F cars are likely to be blessed with similar power outputs, aerodynamics assume a critical role in allowing one car to go quicker than another. Much can be learnt from the 'professional' formulae and applied, wherever the rules allow, to the design of a 750F car, particularly if that formula produces cars with more grip than power.

Five basic design decisions must be addressed when conceiving the blueprint of a 750 racer: style, weight distribution, chassis type, suspension and body shape. As numerous and weighty tomes have been written over the years concerning all these subjects, it is both impractical and unnecessary to delve too deeply into the complexities of each here. (Appendix B contains a list of recommended further reading.) What is offered is an approach to these issues within the narrow context of a 750F car's design.

## STYLE

In the spirit of the Austin Seven specials for which the 750 Formula was originally conceived in 1949, two-seater sports configuration remains obligatory. Passenger space dimensions are defined in the regulations, and a decapitated legless pygmy can just about squeeze in. As a result, two contrasting styles have emerged in recent years, the 'Clubmans' (Fig. 2) and the 'Sports Racer' (Fig. 3).

The 'Clubmans' is front-engined with the motor set well back in the chassis and wheels outside the body covered by cycle wings, as immortalized by a succession of Mallock, Phantom and Vision 'Clubmans' formula cars.

The more sophisticated 'Sports Racer' reflects the direction professional sports car rac-

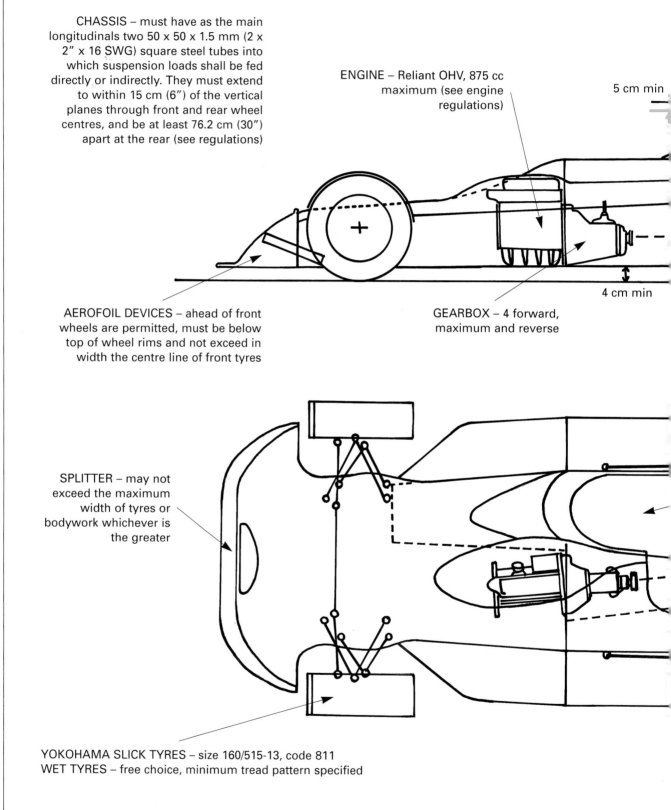

CHASSIS – must have as the main longitudinals two 50 x 50 x 1.5 mm (2 x 2″ x 16 SWG) square steel tubes into which suspension loads shall be fed directly or indirectly. They must extend to within 15 cm (6″) of the vertical planes through front and rear wheel centres, and be at least 76.2 cm (30″) apart at the rear (see regulations)

ENGINE – Reliant OHV, 875 cc maximum (see engine regulations)

5 cm min

4 cm min

AEROFOIL DEVICES – ahead of front wheels are permitted, must be below top of wheel rims and not exceed in width the centre line of front tyres

GEARBOX – 4 forward, maximum and reverse

SPLITTER – may not exceed the maximum width of tyres or bodywork whichever is the greater

YOKOHAMA SLICK TYRES – size 160/515-13, code 811
WET TYRES – free choice, minimum tread pattern specified

**Figure 1** – 750 Formula regulations as demonstrated by the Darvi Mk 5.

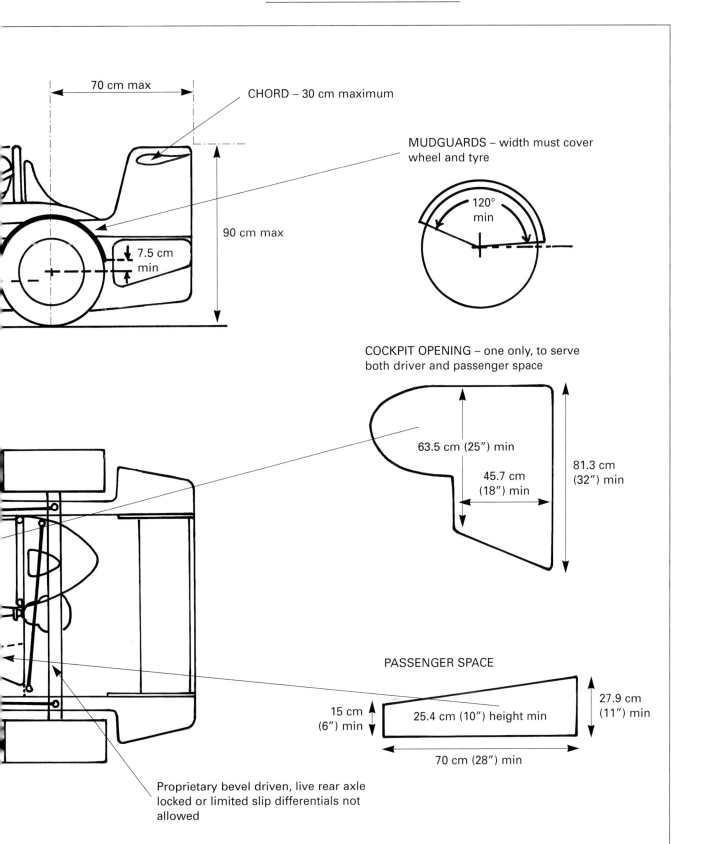

70 cm max

CHORD – 30 cm maximum

MUDGUARDS – width must cover wheel and tyre

90 cm max

7.5 cm min

120° min

COCKPIT OPENING – one only, to serve both driver and passenger space

63.5 cm (25") min

45.7 cm (18") min

81.3 cm (32") min

PASSENGER SPACE

27.9 cm (11") min

15 cm (6") min

25.4 cm (10") height min

70 cm (28") min

Proprietary bevel driven, live rear axle locked or limited slip differentials not allowed

Drawing: Dick Harvey

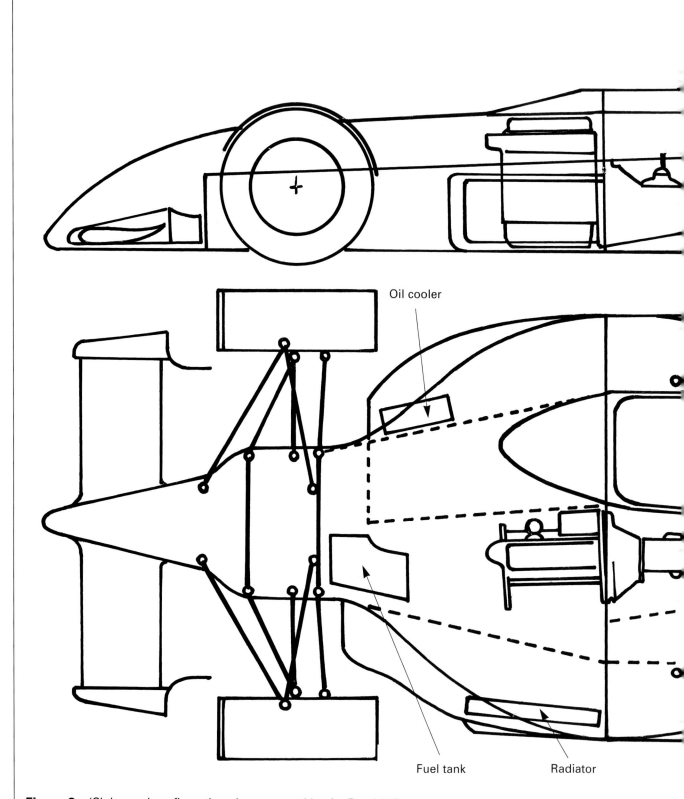

**Figure 2** – 'Clubmans' configuration, demonstrated by the Darvi 91D.

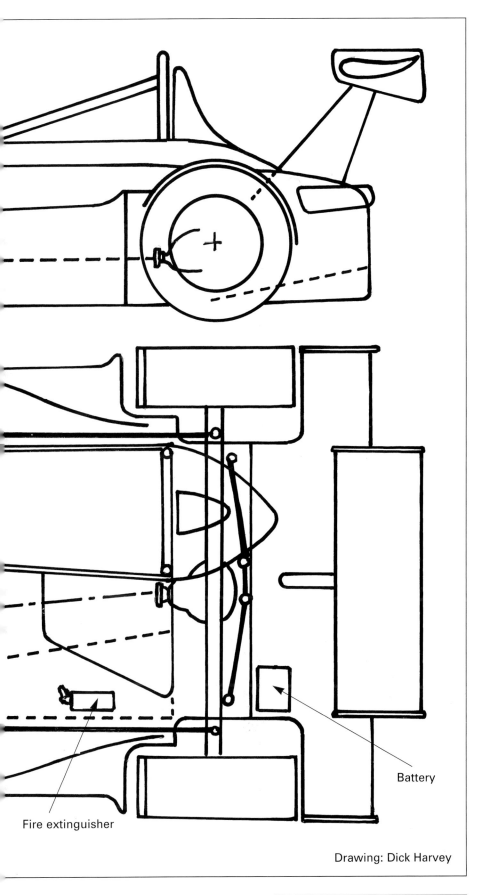

Fire extinguisher

Battery

Drawing: Dick Harvey

ing has been going of late, with mid-mounted engine behind the driver and fully enveloping bodywork. Pioneered by former 750 racer Colin Chapman with the Lotus 23B and John Cooper with the Cooper Monaco in the late 1950s and early '60s, this approach to sports car design reflected the manner in which single-seater racing cars were evolving at that time. Later, international Group 4 sports cars such as the Chevron B8 and Lotus 47, and Group 6 prototypes like the Chevron B19 and Lola 212, refined the style; and most recently it has been perpetuated by Jaguar XJR12, Peugeot 905 and Porsche 956 in the now-abandoned World Sportscar Championship for Group C cars.

At this point it should be made clear that as 750F cars must have a live rear axle, a true mid-engined layout is not possible as the gearbox and differential cannot be combined under the rules to form a transaxle, as is the practice in such major mid-engined formulae as F1, F3000 and F3, and as was the case in the aforementioned international sports cars. Accordingly, the 750 car's gearbox must be connected to, but separated from, the axle-mounted differential by a propeller shaft.

What this means is that the main difference in configuration between front- and mid-engined 750F designs is that in the case of the 'Clubmans' the motor sits in an offset position next to the driver's legs, while in the 'Sports Racer' the engine and driver exchange places. As in either arrangement the power unit sits well back in the car for optimum weight distribution, it could be said, in the interests of total accuracy, that

'Clubman's' approach (CA) no. 1: the smooth-profiled and low-slung SS Reliant driven by creator Bob Simpson. 'Bill Junior' is a reference to Bob's racing father. Note separate tyre-hugging cycle wings, ubiquitous Revolution alloy wheels, and driver's weight close to rear axle. (John Gaisford)

CA2: David Newman's DNC cars have proved popular and successful, chassis once being marketed in kit form. This example is seen taking Becketts corner at Silverstone in the hands of Phil Hoare. (John Gaisford)

CA3: the Richard Scott-designed Centaur was another machine that used to be available as a chassis kit. Here Iain Sclanders psyches himself up in the assembly area prior to a Lydden race at the helm of a Mk 16. (750 Motor Club collection)

CA4: Richard Stephens maintains the family 750 racing tradition in the Gallard. He is seen here powering through Woodcote at Silverstone in 1986. The uncharacteristic expenditure on a set of new tyres was rewarded by a win from pole position. (Harold Barker)

CA5: the Darvi JCB of Bob Couchman holds off Lee Cunningham's Marrow as they sweep through Mallory Park's Devil's Elbow. This car is an amalgamation of the ex-Chris Gough Jo Mo and a Darvi Mk 5 chassis. (Steve Jones)

CA6: another satisfied Darvi customer in the form of Keith McPherson. This needle-nosed, side radiator, push-rod suspension-equipped car is a replica of the championship-winning Darvi 86-9. Known as the Darvi CMP, this example of the Harvey art is now owned and raced by that certifiable shrink, Dr Mike Bott. (John Gaisford)

CA7: built originally by Mike Whatley for wife Linda to race, the left-hand-drive DNC of Peter Knipe is still a front runner despite being well over 20 years old. A dry sumped motor lying virtually horizontally allows a very low frontal area. (John Gaisford)

CA8: the more angular Rapide of Graham Morris demonstrates a further 'Clubmans' interpretation. (John Gaisford)

CA9: Rod Hill demonstrated that less can be more with his diminutive Mystic T3. This race-winner was built with straightline speed in mind, and featured inboard front suspension and a set of ex-Tyrrell, six-wheeler F1 car 10 in diameter wheels. (Rod Hill collection)

both are mid-engine designs – one is forward mid-engined, the other is rearward mid-engined. Whatever, in both instances power is transmitted to the back axle via a prop shaft; only the length changes.

Until the late 1980s the 'Clubmans' approach held sway, mainly for reasons of tradition and simplicity. The rear-engined Warren was the exception, but even it had cycle wing-covered wheels outside the bodywork. Only when Mick Harris's Group C-style Darvi 877 appeared at Donington in May 1987, and went on to win the following year's 750 Championship, did fully enclosed mid-engined cars start to appear slowly in any numbers during the years which followed. Some fully enveloped front-engined machinery had appeared earlier, Dick Harvey's Jeffrey being an example, but the 877 was the first fully enveloped 750 racer to have its motor behind the driver. Indeed, such was the impact of

Mick's stunningly crafted racer at its debut that he immediately received three requests for replicas. Far from being flattered, the Darvi's constructor was actually rather irritated by such approaches, which clearly shows the close relationship that develops between a racing car and its creator. Harris had worked for three years in his spare time to build the 877, and although jointly conceived with Dick Harvey, it was very much Mick's baby. When so much of one's life has been invested in a project, one is very protective of the result, so for someone else to imagine that such an investment can simply be bought may be unwittingly insulting, innocent though the enquiry might be.

The relative merits of the 'Clubmans' and 'Sports Racer' approaches are interesting, not to mention fundamental, to consider. The former has the advantages of a small frontal area, straightforward and inexpensive bodywork in small

*Clubmans miscellany: Hague (6), DNC (17) and Centaur (10) try to outbrake each other into Mallory Park's Shaws hairpin. (John Gaisford)*

manageable sections which can also be a weight advantage, and a 40:60 front–rear weight distribution which aids traction. Disadvantages are more aerodynamic drag than a more slippery-shaped, fully enveloping car, a tendency to lock up the front wheels when hard pressed due to the relatively light nose, and the vulnerability of wheels, suspension and steering arms in a shunt, a mere tap against a barrier seeming to be enough to knock a corner off.

The 'Sports Racer' can boast superior aerodynamic qualities, the ability to brake later as a result of a 60:40 front–rear weight division, more protection to components when biffed, and a state-of-the-art appearance. On the down side it displays a greater frontal area,

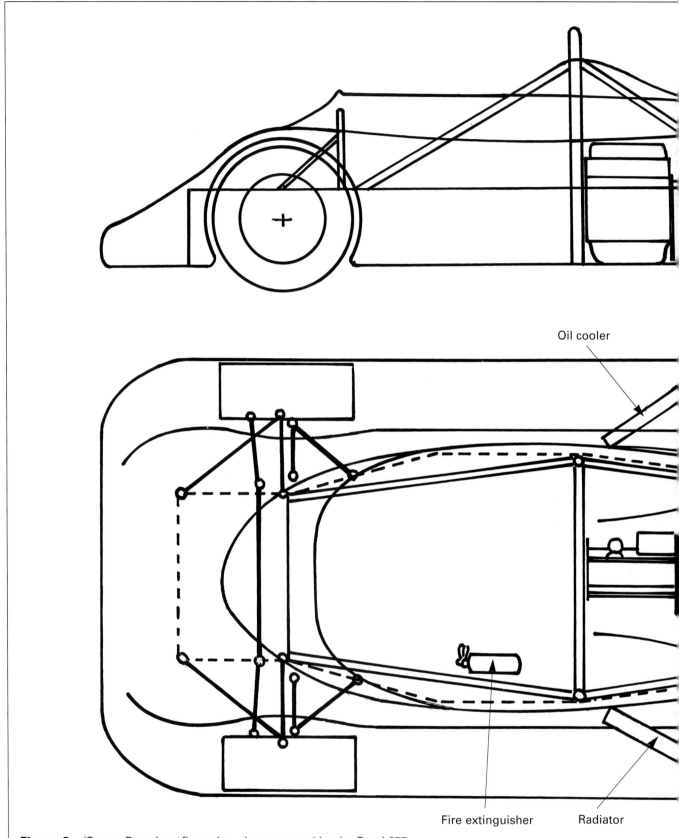

Oil cooler

Fire extinguisher

Radiator

**Figure 3** – 'Sports Racer' configuration, demonstrated by the Darvi 877.

is more expensive and complex to build, has body panels whose size also add weight, and less traction off the start line and out of tight bends due to the comparative lack of weight above the rear axle.

One other point. Nothing delights the 750 racer more than developing his car by experimentation. The 'Clubmans' format allows the simple adjustment or replacement of wings, nose cones, side pods and other manageable-sized panels. The fully enclosed car is less flexible in this respect. Once committed to an overall shape there is no turning back without having to start from scratch again.

On the track the performance differences between the two contrasting configurations are smaller than might be expected. Over the years Dick Harvey with his 86-9 and 91-D 'Clubmans' designs has indulged in numerous experimental 'drag races' during race meeting practice sessions against Mick Harris's 877 to determine the relative straight-line speeds of their differing Darvis, and astonishingly there is very little difference. This may suggest that the aerodynamic superiority of the all-enveloping car is offset by its greater frontal area and weight. Of course, once on the move the slight additional weight is less critical, and its superior braking abilities even things up on a complete lap when up against the superior traction and narrow nose of the 'Clubmans'.

There is of course a third, compromise, approach: a 'Clubmans' front-engined layout which capitalizes upon traction and aerodynamics by having a fully enclosed body.

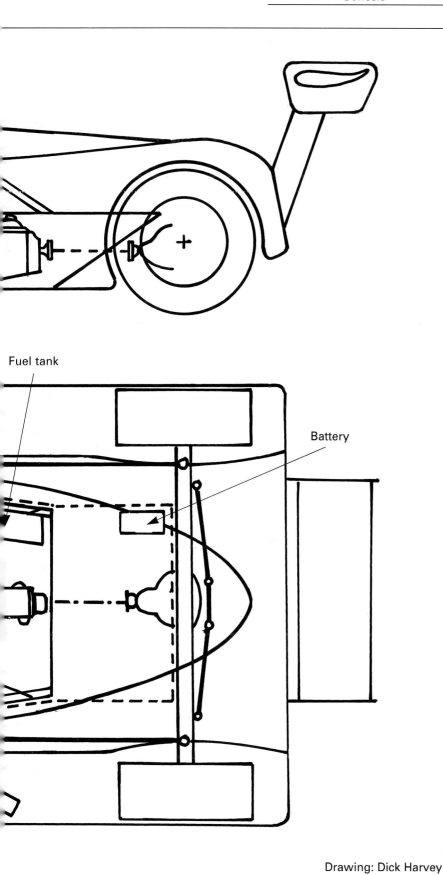

Fuel tank

Battery

Drawing: Dick Harvey

*Sports Racer approach (SRA) no. 1: Mick Harris, winner of more 750 Championships (four) than any other driver, demonstrates that a combination of 7 cwt and 60 bhp is quite sufficient to fly the Darvi 877 over The Mountain at Cadwell Park. (Steve Jones)*

*SRA 2: formula elder statesman (1996 is his 28th consecutive 750 season) and twice champion Bob Simpson is the epitome of the 750 racer. Although influenced by the Darvi 877, the latest SS Reliant was designed and built by Simpson, who is steadily developing it into a winner. (John Gaisford)*

*SRA 3: sneak preview, in February 1995, of Rod Hill's stunning new mid-engined car. Can Am and IMSA influences abound. (Rod Hill collection)*

*Fully enveloped 'Clubman's' approach (FECA) no. 1: the all-conquering Marrow gave Phil Myatt and Andy Jones two championships apiece during the early 1990s. Here Jones holds off Harris's Darvi at Snetterton's Russell Bend. (Steve Jones)*

*FECA 2: the Avalan Mk 2 of Alan Avery leads Harris's Darvi and Gough's CGR1 at Pembrey. (Steve Jones)*

*FECA 3: Chris Gough in the CGR1 seen on The Mountain, Cadwell Park. (Chris Gough collection)*

*FECA 4: Dave Robson in his SDAR fends off a determined-looking Jon Harvey in the Darvi 92-J. (Fred Scatley)*

Once again frontal area and weight penalties apply, as does complexity, so it must be concluded that whichever style is chosen, concessions have to be accepted in respect of some element of the car's performance. It's all a matter of balance, and this is the crux of the formula's regulations. There is room for expression, but no single approach is likely to render

*Closed car approach: the Bill Cowley-conceived Cowley Mk IV GT, now raced by son Nigel, is the only example of this genre to be built since the Forrest Saloon of the sixties. (Nigel Cowley collection)*

*Mid-engine installation: engine turned through 180° and the propshaft belt-driven. (Nigel Cowley collection)*

*Restoration: having stood abandoned in a lock-up garage for six years after leaving the Cowley family and passing through the hands of Trevor Hegarty, Martin Read and Mick Moore, the Mk IV GT was rescued by Nigel Cowley and lovingly restored. (Nigel Cowley collection)*

*Diminutive cockpit and neat instrument panel. (Peter Herbert)*

*Curvatious Cowley awaits action: the stunning Cowley Mk IV GT awaits practice in the Silverstone assembly area. (Peter Herbert)*

obsolete all those that have gone before, thus guaranteeing rela- tively inexpensive close racing.

The last few seasons have seen the exponents of the fully enveloping body come to the fore. The mid-engined Darvi and Simpson Special of Mick Harris and Bob Simpson

*Neat fit: Nigel Cowley prepares himself prior to unleashing the Mk IV GT onto Silverstone's wide expanse of track. Note ingenious rear-view mirror seen by driver through perspex roof panel. (Peter Herbert)*

respectively, and the front-engined Marrows of Mike Kenny, Phil Myatt and Andy Jones, the Avalan of Alan Avery and the CGR of Chris Gough, have been the cars to beat. And yet the 'Clubmans' configuration is far from being dead. Its devotees are led by the Harvey brothers and an army of happy Darvi owners, not to mention a certain Pete Knipe who still on occasion passes the chequered flag first at the helm of a 25-year-old DNC.

Of course the seriously adventurous may wish to consider a closed car. The Forrest first demonstrated the aerodynamic advantages of a 750 racer with a roof when it appeared in the early 1960s, but few constructors have attempted to emulate it. A notable exception was Bill Cowley who produced the strikingly curvaceous Cowley GT. With styling reminiscent of the Group 6 prototypes of the

late 1960s and early '70s, and a mid engine driving a propshaft by way of a chain, this innovative machine was recently resurrected and returned to the track by its creator's son Nigel, with the chain replaced by a rubber belt.

A major problem in constructing a closed 750F car is obtaining a suitable windscreen. No production car yet appears to have one of the required curvature. A purpose-made screen is of course a possibility, but is likely to prove ruinously expensive for the constructor of modest means.

Dick Harvey and Mick Harris originally conceived the Darvi 877 as a closed car based upon the Group C Porsche 956. An early lead regarding the whereabouts of a second-hand 956 windscreen unfortunately came to nothing, so the ever-resourceful duo directed their hunt towards an appropriately-sized glider canopy. But glider

*Dwarfed even by other 750s: Nigel Cowley on track in the Mk IV GT at Mallory Park's Devil's Elbow. (Steve Jones)*

canopies don't grow on trees, despite occasionally landing in them, so again the Darvi design team was thwarted. As a result, the 877 eventually appeared as an open 'Spyder', although the Porsche influence remains in the lines of the nose.

## WEIGHT DISTRIBUTION

The late Arthur Mallock, a gentleman who most certainly knew a thing or two about racing car design, was a great advocate of the importance of static weight distribution; and the argument that it is easier to optimize the balance of the car by the careful positioning of components before it ever turns a wheel rather than having to compensate for imbalances later is hard to fault. So once the style of car has been chosen, and in particular the driver's seating position in relation to the engine, the disposition of all the other items a racing car must carry should be carefully considered.

Whilst it is clearly essential in a low-power formula to keep the overall weight of the car to a minimum so as to ensure as high a power-to-weight ratio as possible, the arrangement of that weight will affect the manner in which the car will react under the forces of acceleration, braking and cornering.

Three fundamental and interrelated concepts influence such behaviour as a direct result of static weight distribution: centre of gravity, polar moment of inertia, and weight transfer.

Were it possible to suspend a car perfectly balanced in mid-air by a cord, the point on the vehicle to which that cord would have to be attached would be its centre of gravity. Thus suspended, no matter in which direction the car was pointing, it would remain balanced. The centre of gravity is the balance point for the entire racing car, and is always found above the ground and between the front and rear wheels.

Far from being an instant of inactivity at an Arctic base camp, polar moment of inertia is a vehicle's resistance to changing direction. This can be calculated by multiplying the weight of each of the car's components by the square of each component's distance from the centre of gravity. So the polar moment depends on both the car's weight and that weight's distribution both inside and outside the wheelbase. The further the weight is from the centre of gravity, the

greater its polar moment of inertia; and the greater the polar moment, the bigger the resistance to directional change. A big American car such as a Cadillac Eldorado is a prime example of this. The smaller the polar moment, the more agile the vehicle, a go-kart being the supreme example of such qualities.

In a corner a car with a high polar moment of inertia will react more slowly to the initial turn-in and tend to understeer, and any subsequent oversteer will start slowly. But once a spin is approached it takes longer for a steering correction to have any effect. Conversely, the car with a low polar moment of inertia will turn into a corner readily but be more nervous and more prone to oversteer. However its quicker reactions will render such tail slides more controllable. The down side of such characteristics is a comparative lack of straightline stability due to less resistance to unsettling forces, and this could be a problem in a small, lightweight racer. Without delving into the mathematics, the basic approach of positioning as much as possible inside the wheelbase and minimizing overhang, particularly at the rear, is the right way to go.

The forces acting upon a car during acceleration, braking and cornering result in weight transfer. When accelerating, a driver is pushed back into his seat by an inertia force reacting to the force accelerating the car. This also transfers weight from the front to the rear of the car. The exact opposite happens under braking. These phenomena are known as fore and aft weight transfer. Under cornering, a car experiences lateral weight transfer through cen-

trifugal forces acting upon it, moving weight from the inside wheels to those on the outside as a bend is entered and negotiated. All these forces, be they longitudinal or lateral, act upon the car's centre of gravity, so its position is critical to the behaviour of the vehicle, particularly when cornering.

In the early days of 750 racing the combination of a practically all-iron Austin Seven power plant well forward in the chassis and a driver sitting almost directly above the back axle allowed a 50:50 front-to-rear weight distribution, and made the achievement of 25 per cent of the total weight on each wheel a possibility. Today's Caterham and West-field derivatives of the Lotus Seven are of similar configuration and weight distribution to those early specials, although a little quicker.

More recently, the importance of rear grip, particularly with increased power, has influenced overall weight distribution, and the latter's effects upon centre of gravity, polar moment of inertia and weight transfer, leading to the engine being set back as far as is practically possible within the chassis, ruling out a 50:50 front–rear weight balance. An all-alloy 850 cc Reliant motor weighs just 100 lb (45.4 kg), or about 120 lb (54.5 kg) with carburettor fitted, whereas an average pilot weighs 12 stone (76.3 kg), so in a 750F the position of the seating has a greater influence on weight distribution than that of the engine. Accordingly, when the driver sits slightly aft of the power unit in a 'Clubmans' configuration, the ratio front to rear is about 40:60. In the case of the 'Sports Racer', where the driver sits slightly forward of the engine, it is about 60:40. In such a lightweight machine there is little that can be done to alter these figures to any great extent.

The achievement of lateral balance is both possible and highly desirable, particularly in a car with an offset driving position. By weighing the driver, then the components to be accommodated within the chassis, side-to-side equilibrium can be achieved by their careful distribution. Movable feasts, at least in the design stage, include engine, gearbox, propshaft, differential, fuel tank, radiators, oil tank if fitted, and battery. With careful positioning, the driver's weight is largely offset. There are also smaller items such as fire extinguisher, fuel pump, fuel pressure meter, instruments and various piping which, when added together, can make a significant contribution to the equation. In the case of a featherweight driver, those items left over when lateral balance has been created may be positioned fore or aft of the pilote for greater weight on the front or rear of the car. The optimum weight distribution above each wheel is therefore likely to be 20:20 front/30:30 rear for a 'Clubmans' design, and 30:30 front/20:20 rear for a 'Sports Racer' if the driver is balanced laterally, although it verges on the impossible to avoid some lateral weight bias towards the driver.

Dick Harvey is a self-confessed 'big awkward sod' who would consider himself ill were his weight to fall to 12 stone. Therefore on his most recent creations, the Darvi Mk 6, 86.9, 91D, 91J, and the replicas built for Ernie Frost and Keith McPherson, the water radiator was moved to the left side

within a pod, taking air from its leading face. Such a radical move necessitated a narrow nose in order to allow cooling air to reach the radiator, and this in turn obliged Dick to use inboard suspension. Most professional single-seater formulae are now designed in this way, and this is but one illustration of how the amateur constructor can follow, or on occasion lead, the experts.

By concentrating the weight of the driver and running gear near the centre of the wheelbase, a low polar moment of inertia and a responsive, manoeuvrable racing car is created, which can be further enhanced by a low centre of gravity by positioning components as low as possible in the chassis. But beware of burying items such as fuel pumps, which occasionally require urgent attention, in inaccessible places.

Highly regarded Brabham and McLaren Formula 1 car designer Gordon Murray once said, 'All things being equal, the car with the lowest centre of gravity will win.' So learn from an expert.

## CHASSIS

A direct link with the formative years of 750 racing, when Austin-based specials with timber-framed bodies sat on top of steel 'A'-shaped chassis, is the current requirement to incorporate a pair of 2 in x 2 in x 16 swg (standard wire gauge) square steel tubes as main longitudinal chassis members. These must be a minimum distance apart at the rear, extend to within a certain distance from each of the four wheel centres, and be fed suspension loads directly or indirectly.

Such constraints would suggest little alternative to a spaceframe chassis, but in fact it is possible to build a monocoque and lay it on top of the stipulated longitudinal tubing.

A spaceframe is an open steel structure comprising a lattice-work of tubing, triangulated for strength. A triangle is the ultimate two-dimensional rigid structure, and a pyramid its three-dimensional counterpart. A spaceframe chassis is largely a series of pyramids. To this framework all running gear is attached, to be covered eventually by body panels. It is impossible to have a chassis that is too stiff. A chassis that flexes is right up there with chocolate fireguards and canoe handbrakes in terms of usefulness, for the best suspension and tyres cannot possibly compensate for movement in the frame to which they are attached.

When the pyramid is constructed of thin sheet rather than tubing it becomes a monocoque. The chassis and body are one, as is the case with most of today's passenger cars.

Simplicity and strength are the spaceframe's main attributes, and in terms of cost and weight the best design has the fewest number of tubes without prejudicing rigidity. Driver safety should also be built into the design at this stage, with the roll-cage an integral part of the frame, together with side impact protection and a degree of impact absorption within the front and rear extremities of the chassis.

The monocoque is said to have superior strength for any given weight when compared with a spaceframe. Developed in the aircraft industry, it carries loads in a stressed skin which forms the outside of the structure. Whereas the triangle is the basic geometrical unit of a spaceframe, a monocoque takes its strength from sheets which form rectangular or trapezoidal boxes.

The monocoque is the more difficult chassis form for the home builder to deal with, particularly when it comes to accident repair. A man on a galloping horse with a patch over one eye can normally spot a bent tube on a spaceframe, but it could take more than a beady-eyed battalion of bodyshop guys at walking pace to check out the structural integrity of a shunted monocoque.

## SUSPENSION

As many learned tomes have been devoted to the subject of suspension design, it may be safely assumed that it has a considerable bearing upon the drivability and subsequent success of any racing car. Whilst the complexities and subtleties of suspension theory are extensive, a number of basic principles are of relevance to the embryonic 750F car.

Wheel control under all conditions is of paramount importance. The car's outer wheels, which do most of the work during cornering, must maintain the largest possible tyre contact patch with the track surface; no wheel should undergo significant camber-angle changes (the angle the wheel makes with the vertical) under heavy acceleration and braking; and track variations, in other words the wheel following a weaving line down the road, should not occur during wheel travel. Furthermore, the car's roll centre, which is the point about which it leans under centrifugal cornering forces, should not vary during entry, negotiation and exit of a bend.

In reality this is all about a car's ability to remain stable under a variety of extreme conditions, and the confidence such predictability instils in its driver. An experienced or talented pilot may be able to drive around handling deficiencies, but the car will never be truly competitive. For the less experienced or talented, the series of confusing and contradictory messages an ill-handling car can impart will upset that driver's composure and trust in the machine, making it impossible to race another car effectively.

An example of how a handling difficulty can catch out even a skilful competitor occurred a few years ago at Cadwell Park. Mick Harris was experiencing traction difficulties with the Darvi 877. An inherent forward weight bias of

*Front wishbones and push-rod on the Darvi 91-D. (Dick Harvey collection)*

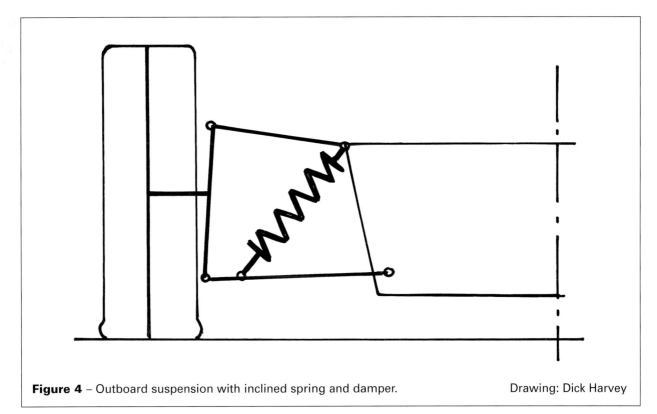

**Figure 4** – Outboard suspension with inclined spring and damper.   Drawing: Dick Harvey

the mid-engined configuration was causing a torque reaction from the engine through the rear axle, which in its turn was causing the comparatively lightly loaded right wheel to lift and the car to step sideways in tight right-hand corners. Torque, in chassis terms, is the effect of a force applied in such a way as to cause rotation. What was happening to Mick's car was that under acceleration the rotation of the propshaft in the direction of the left rear wheel was causing the axle to rotate around that wheel which then lifted the other.

Despite starting the race in pole position, Mick's problem resulted in a tardy departure off the grid due to excessive wheelspin. However once on the move it only recurred when exiting the short circuit's tight right-hand hairpin. By mid-race the Darvi had taken the lead and on each lap its driver would anticipate the sudden

oversteer out of the hairpin by applying some opposite lock. But on one lap towards the end of the race, as a result perhaps of tyre wear or the ever-increasing temperature of the rubber, the inner wheel failed to spin. This left Mick with a handful of unnecessary left lock and a quick trip into the Cadwell banking.

Virtually all modern racing cars have their front wheels located by wishbones. These consist of an upright carrying the hub to which the wheel is attached being connected to the chassis at two points, one at the top and one at the bottom. Each of these two links is 'A'-shaped, not unlike the forked bone found between the neck and breast of a bird, and is known as a wishbone, with the apex attached to the hub and the two legs attached by a pair of rubber- or metal-mounted pivot points to the chassis. The upper and lower wishbones are

not necessarily parallel nor of equal length, giving the front wheels camber characteristics which vary according to vertical suspension movement and lateral body roll. Such characteristics can be tuned to achieve the optimum compromise for cornering.

The simplest form of front suspension on a wishbone-equipped car is the outboard-mounted inclined shock absorber and coil spring (Fig. 4). This is attached to the chassis at its top, and to the outer end of the lower wishbone, where the latter meets the wheel hub upright, at its base.

Simplicity is the inclined outboard unit's main asset. The limitation of such an arrangement is that the dampers' angled position causes the forces being fed into it to vary. As a result, damping is not linear, with resistance diminishing as force increases. This is known as decreasing or falling rate suspension to the *aficionado*. Linear damping could be sought by mounting the shock absorber in a vertical position by means of a top bracket cantilevered out from the chassis, but this would result in additional aerodynamic drag, a restriction upon steering lock, and a feature that would look bloody awful.

By mounting the shock absorber inboard – that is, within the framework of the chassis – greater flexibility of damper positioning is possible, particularly in the push-rod arrangement which allows the unit to be located almost anywhere on the car and at any angle. Then, by directing the forces generated by wheel movement more directly into the shocker, the desired damping characteristics can be obtained. Additional inboard mounting advantages are the removal of the dampers from the airstream (although this might lead to them getting

hot if not cooled in some way), the use of a low-drag narrow nose being possible, protection in a minor shunt, increased steering lock, the opportunity to position the dampers as a contribution towards the car's overall weight distribution, and a reduction in unsprung weight. The latter is of some importance. The fewer the parts on the car uninsulated from track irregularities by not resting on springs, the less the car will be disturbed by undulations and trips across kerbs. This is because the comparative weight of the sprung body will be less upset by the relatively light unsprung wheel, tyre and associated components bouncing up and down.

The three most common forms of inboard suspension are rocker arm, pull-rod and push-rod.

Simplest is the top rocker arm (Fig. 5), a lever connecting the outer end of the upper

wishbone to the top of a vertically positioned shock absorber, pivoted within its length. By a basic rocking action wheel movement is fed directly into the damper. This system affords good wheel control, but the bending forces acting upon the lever are considerable. To avoid flexing or breakage, a lever of robust dimensions is required, which can mean a beefy piece of metal that is less than beautiful hanging in the airstream. When a Darvi first used this type of front suspension, Dick Harvey employed 300 lb (136 kg) springs as he unknowingly compensated for a bending rocker arm in his efforts to achieve the desired damping. However, after a series of beefing-up measures on the arm, 160 lb (72.5 kg) springs proved quite adequate.

Pull-rod suspension (Fig. 6) acts upon the base of a vertically mounted shocker via an

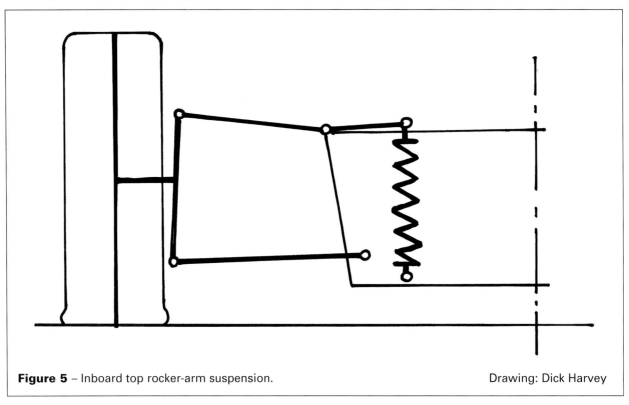

**Figure 5** – Inboard top rocker-arm suspension.

Drawing: Dick Harvey

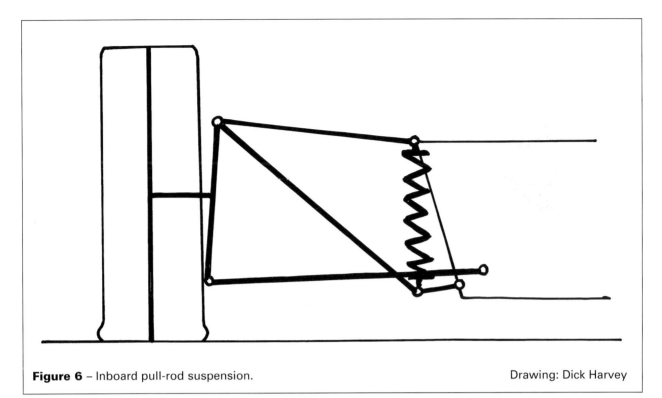

**Figure 6** – Inboard pull-rod suspension.

Drawing: Dick Harvey

arm attached to the outer end of the top wishbone. A rising wheel pulls on the arm, which in turn causes a lever at the base of the damper to com- press it. Like the rocker arm arrangement, this allows linear damping and good wheel con- trol, but the linkages can be cumbersome.

Most flexible is the push-rod (Fig. 7). Acting directly upon the top of the shocker by means of a bell crank connect- ed by tubular rod to the outer

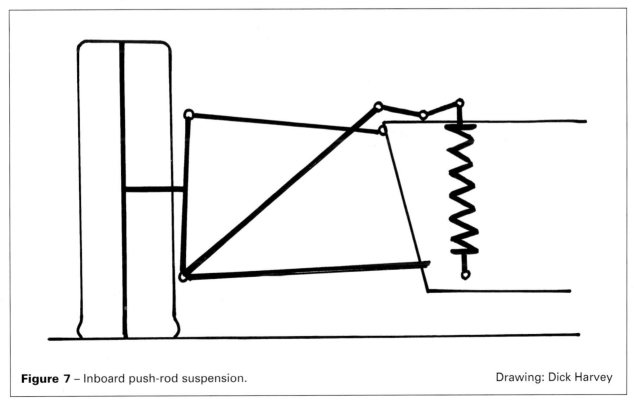

**Figure 7** – Inboard push-rod suspension.

Drawing: Dick Harvey

end of the lower wishbone, this device enables the shock absorber to be placed in almost any position. Now the bell crank is a cunning tool. Essentially a three-cornered piece of metal, one corner is connected to the push-rod, another to the shocker, whilst it pivots on the third. This allows force from one direction to be transferred to another. Subtle variations in

*Inboard push-rod front suspension on the Darvi 91-D. Note linkage to roll bar. (Peter Herbert)*

bell crank size, position, and locating points can obtain whatever damping characteristics are required, the system operating through a series of arcs. For instance, by altering the pivot point, the directness of the damping action can be increased or reduced – useful for differing circuit or weather conditions. No surprise therefore that push-rod suspension is favoured by the majority of Formula One designers.

At the rear of the car the obligatory use of a solid axle precludes independent suspension, so the choice of rear suspension design focuses accordingly upon effective rear axle location. Vertical movement of the axle is usually controlled by a pair of upright or inclined coil springs and shock absorbers, while fore and aft axle travel is eliminated at each extremity by a pair of forward-reaching radius arms (Fig. 8). These arms, linking both top and bottom of the axle to the chassis, also prevent its rotation under acceleration and braking. However, there remains the problem of preventing side-to-side axle movement during cornering, a sensation calculated to disturb even the very coolest of drivers.

The Panhard rod and Watt's linkage are the most popular techniques employed to locate axles laterally, and it will not have escaped the notice of students of early motoring and steam engines that both devices have been around for some time. Each operates in a similar manner, providing horizontal linkage between axle and chassis.

A Panhard rod runs across the full width of the car, pivoted on the axle at one end and on the chassis at the other. Vertical axle movement is accommodated by the rod moving in an arc about the chassis mounting. As the rod arcs it will of course try to shorten and allow horizontal axle movement, but provided that the rod is mounted horizontally when the car is at normal ride height and is as long as possible, lateral movement will be minimal. This is particularly true on a racing car where vertical movement of the axle will be small due to stiff springing.

Such an arrangement is

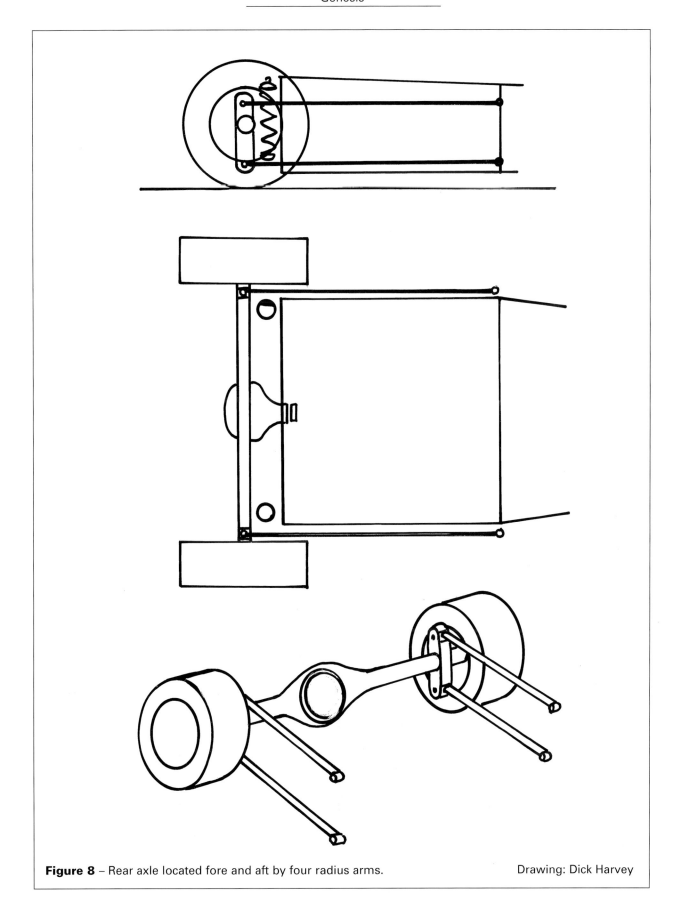

**Figure 8** – Rear axle located fore and aft by four radius arms.

Drawing: Dick Harvey

simple and cheap (the 750 racer's favourite words). The down side is that it is directional, for, being located to one side of the chassis, the axle will respond slightly differently in left-hand bends than in right-hand bends. This is a result of the car's rear roll centre altering through a corner. The roll centre is the point about which body roll takes place, and on a Panhard rod-equipped car this is approximately where the rod crosses the vehicle's centre line. Cornering in one direction, the rod will move slightly downwards as the chassis mounting dips with body roll, lowering the roll centre. This is generally considered to be a good thing. Cornering in the opposite direction will cause the chassis mounting to lift with body roll, raising the rod and the roll centre, leading to a cornering imbalance.

Let's be clear that we speak of extreme conditions here, and in almost all respects the Panhard rod has much to commend it. But motor racing breeds extreme conditions, therefore any design feature that calls for a compromise is worth noting.

British motor racing circuits are tackled in a clockwise direction, so there must be more right-hand corners than left. Accordingly, even the slightest cornering imbalance should be fashioned to favour right-handers. A Panhard rod should therefore be located on the left side of the chassis and right side of the axle, then as the body and chassis dip to the left under centrifugal force through a right turn, the rod and roll centre will move down with the chassis location point. The Kent circuit of Lydden is one place where a Panhard

rod's directional characteristics can be felt. Coming off Canterbury Straight there is a long right-hander through Pilgrims followed by an even longer one around Chessons Drift. Devil's Elbow, which is arrived at next, is the only proper left-hand bend on the course, therefore the manner in which a car goes round it is most noticeable. A 750 car with Panhard rod will oversteer here despite having shown no tendency to do so during the rest of a lap.

The Watt's linkage provides lateral location without any horizontal movement by employing two horizontal links between axle and chassis, one to the left and one to the right. The two rods, one running above the axle from one side of the chassis and one running below from the other, are parallel, and are joined together at the centre of the axle by a vertical link pivoted on the centre of the differential casing. Vertical axle movement results in equal lateral movement in the two locating rods, provided that they are parallel and of equal length, rotating the vertical link upon its axle centre-point location. This allows true vertical movement of the axle as the pivot point, which is also the roll centre, cannot move laterally.

The main advantage of this arrangement is that it prevents any sideways movement, however small, yet it is still relatively simple, cheap and light. However it occupies more space than a Panhard rod, the rear roll centre is higher, and suspension travel is more limited.

The Mumford link is in essence two Watt's linkages. In theory it cannot work, as vertical axle movement would appear to be completely inhibited, but, perhaps through minimal compliance in the bushing, this system does in fact function, and function well. The Darvi stable's current state-of-the-art 'Clubmans' 91D and 92J cars and 'Sports Racer' 877 all use Mumfords.

*A Mumford-linked race axle on the Darvi 91-D. Note cantilevered battery tray to optimize static weight distribution. (Dick Harvey)*

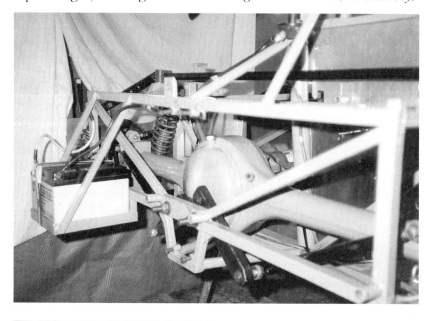

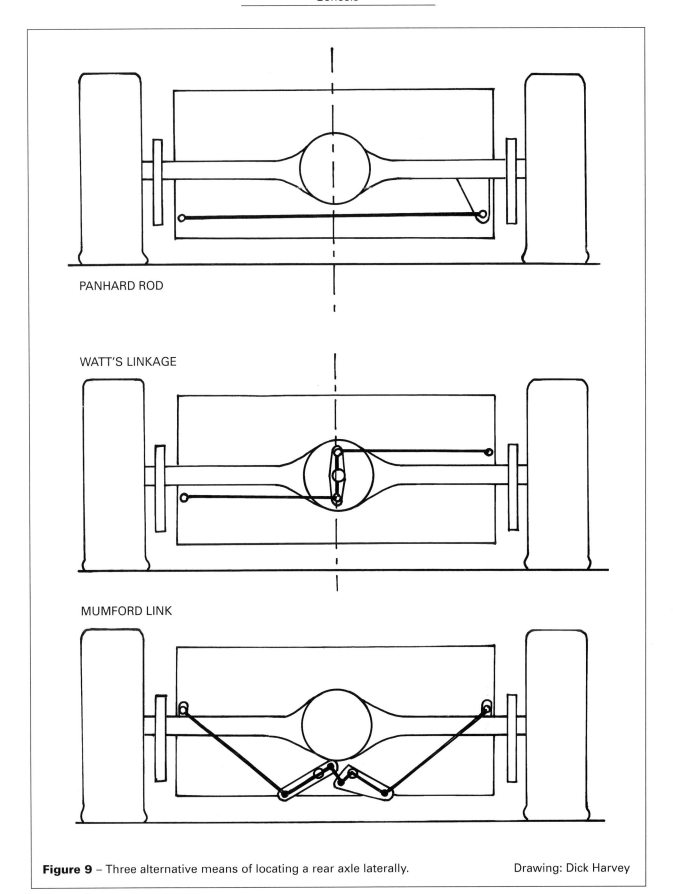

PANHARD ROD

WATT'S LINKAGE

MUMFORD LINK

**Figure 9** – Three alternative means of locating a rear axle laterally.          Drawing: Dick Harvey

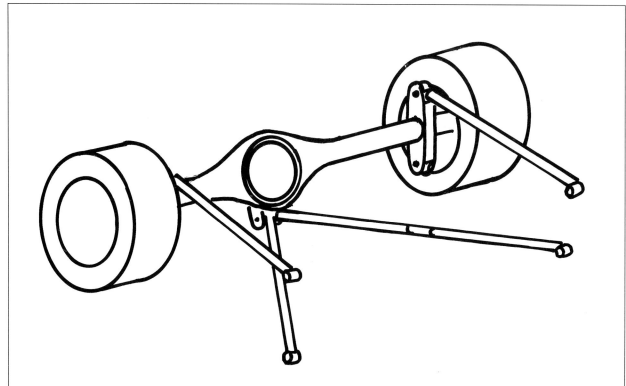

**Figure 10** – The use of an 'A'-bracket with two radius arms for both fore and aft and lateral axle location.

Drawing: Dick Harvey

A low roll centre and very positive axle location are this arrangement's advantages, it also appearing to act as a large anti-roll bar. This is most apparent when a Mumford-equipped car inadvertently drops a wheel onto the grass. In such a situation the Panhard rod-endowed machine, for instance, will often spin. Yet the Mumford car appears to transfer its weight to the opposite wheel and pull out of the situation without a trip into the cheap seats. Clearly Michael Mumford knew what he was doing when he designed this one, even if no-one else actually understands what he knew. The down side is that this is quite a complex arrangement to build with lots of joints, and the forces acting upon the chassis mountings are considerable. Breakages are not unknown.

An A-bracket is a fourth alternative (Figs. 10 and 11). Much favoured by Colin Chapman in his formative years, and even used on early production Lotus Cortinas until its incompatibility with standard Cortina leaf springs caused problems, this means of axle location comprises an A-shaped arm fixed to the axle centre by a spherical bearing at the arm's apex, with the two other ends attached to the chassis. The A-bracket is horizontal when the car is at normal ride height. The bracket allows the axle vertical movement, whilst when the car is rolling the axle pivots about the spherical bearing and transfers side loads into the chassis. The pivot point is the roll centre, so if for example it is located at the base of the differential housing, it can be kept low. The A-bracket also resists axle twisting under acceleration and braking.

Simple and non-directional, the only disadvantage of this system seems to be a lack of resistance to torque reaction during racing starts and under-acceleration out of slow corners which causes the right rear wheel to lift and lose drive. As seen from head-on, the prop-shaft rotates clockwise into the front of the differential, so there is a tendency for the axle to lift in its efforts to rotate about the left rear wheel. Other forms of lateral rear axle location appear to be more effective in their suppression of such tendencies, an observation supported by Mick Harris's unsuccessful attempts to outdrag fellow competitors off various start lines around the country prior to his A-bracket being replaced by a Mumford link.

Finally, we have the intriguingly named Woblink. Developed by our old pal Arthur

Drawing: Dick Harvey

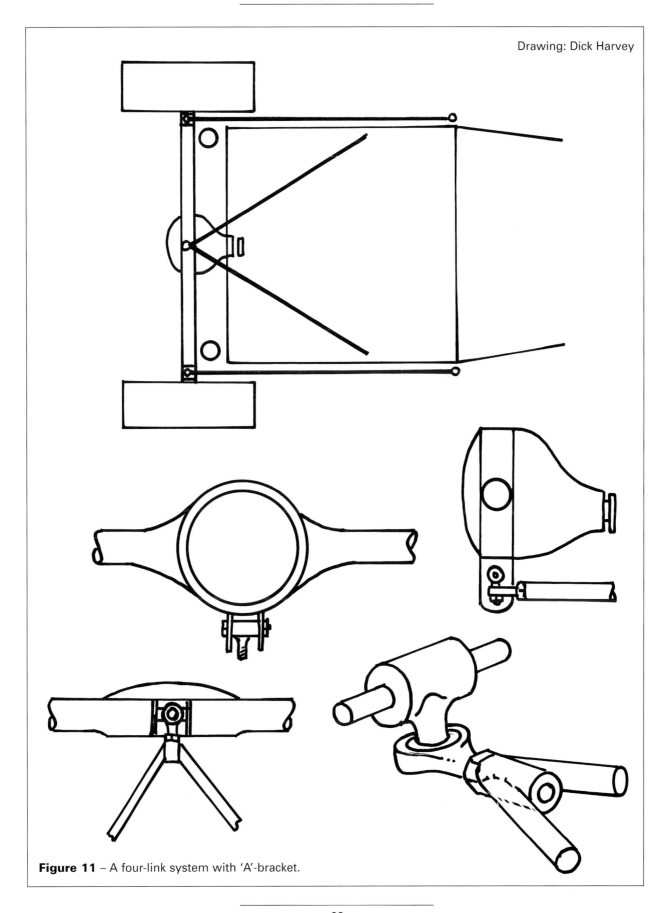

**Figure 11** – A four-link system with 'A'-bracket.

Mallock, a man devoted to the advancement of the solid rear axle due to his dedication to 'Clubmans' car racing, and christened as an amalgamation of this arrangement's influences (James Watt, Maurice Olley and Donald Bastow), it combines elements of the Watt's linkage and A-bracket to achieve a very low roll centre. This is done by dropping an arm vertically from the centre of the axle to a point below it, and pivoting that arm at its central point which will be close to the base of the differential case. The top of the arm is linked by a short rod to a point on the back of the axle to the right, while the centre of the arm is linked by a longer rod to a point beneath the axle to the far right. The bottom of the arm is chassis-mounted. The arm's top link is allowed to move in an arc with axle movement and body roll as it is fully floating, but as the other two location points are secured to the axle and chassis, effective lateral axle control is guaranteed. Furthermore, as arm movement is pivoted from the low chassis mounting, an extremely low roll centre results. The only disadvantage to this design seems to be its minimal ground clearance and vulnerability to trips across kerbs. Finally, as proof that innovation still thrives in the 750 world, Mick Harris actually combined a live rear axle with wishbones on his Darvi 877 during the 1995 season.

## BODY SHAPE

Aerodynamic efficiency, it may be argued, is by far the single most important consideration when designing a racing car. This does not mean that style, weight and its distribution,

chassis structure and suspension design, as already discussed, are less relevant, but that they should always be considered in context with their contribution toward aerodynamic efficiency.

The difference between a good car and a winning car may not be very great in terms of aerodynamic performance, but a more powerful car does not have to lose out to a less powerful one in respect of aerodynamic efficiency by very much before dropping behind on the track.

750 Formula racing is all about getting a relatively low-powered car through the air, and as power outputs will not vary a great deal between the engines used, aerodynamics must play a critical role in any 750F car's success.

As the nearest thing to a wind tunnel the impecunious 750 driver is likely to have, will be the draughty gap between his house and his garage, the contours of his racer will have to be determined by observation of what is already being raced in the formula, and what is happening in the professional formulae. Formula 1 has traditionally been the pace-setter in aerodynamic research and application due to its vast financial resources and engineering talent, and the resulting design solutions have then percolated down through Formula 3000, Formula 3, Formulae Renault and Ford and so on. Look, for instance, at how Tyrrell pioneered the high nose with wing supported on plates beneath, which not only spread to most F1 designs but also soon found its way into Formula 3 attached to a Dallara. So there is a certain logic in relevant ideas finding their way into 750 racing

from such elevated sources. Don't be afraid to copy – everyone in motor racing does it.

Like electricity, airflow is normally invisible. Without a wind tunnel and sophisticated equipment it is difficult for the amateur constructor to visualize what happens to airflow when a car passes through it. Crude experiments with hair dryers and paper tabs loosely fixed to body moulds, or smoke tablet emissions fanned gently across wings by gas heaters, are likely to be inconclusive at best, therefore a rudimentary understanding of aerodynamic theory will be invaluable.

A car's resistance to passing through air is known as drag. A function of this resistance is a tendency for the car to try to lift. All aerodynamic forces increase as the square of speed, so twice the speed, four times the drag and lift, triple the speed, nine times the drag and lift. Clearly, neither drag nor lift are good news, therefore the aim must be to minimize drag and reverse lift into downforce. The relationship between drag and downforce is expressed as a ratio, and this is known as the drag co-efficient. A ratio of 1:1 indicates that for every 1 lb of downforce there is 1 lb of drag. More encouraging in terms of keeping a car firmly on the ground at speed would be a ratio of 5:1 – 5 lb of downforce for every 1 lb of drag.

The total drag to which a car is subjected is the sum of the drag on its individual components. Bodywork, wings, tyres, suspension components, air intake ducts, mirrors, roll-over bar and, of course, the driver all produce drag due to the positive air pressure acting upon them. However, certain areas of the car such as tyres and radiators within side pods

develop positive pressure in front and negative behind, so it is the sum of these forces that determines the drag of an individual component. Generally, positive pressure is developed against the front of a car, negative pressure against the back. Another name used (not too accurately) for negative pressure is vacuum, and it is into such a low-pressure area immediately behind a car that another competitor enters when slipstreaming. Wings create considerable drag, but their capacity to give downforce is much greater. Accordingly their contribution to a car's overall aerodynamic efficiency is huge. For instance, a rear wing may display an individual downforce-to-drag ratio of 6:1 on a car of overall downforce-to-drag ratio of 2:1.

When air flows over a surface, the molecules in contact with that surface adhere to it. Those molecules that do not adhere slip over those that have, but at reduced velocity

due to friction. As the distance away from the surface increases, the flow increases due to reduced friction, and at some point the airstream made up of these molecules returns to its natural speed. This area of reduced speed airflow is known as the boundary layer, and the thinner the boundary layer, the lower the drag.

Surfaces with a front edge tilted downwards tend to have thin boundary layers, while those tilted up tend to have thicker ones. Interestingly, if a surface – particularly a wing – is too steeply inclined downward the boundary layer will not form properly. Conversely, if a surface is too steeply inclined upwards the boundary layer becomes so thick that the airflow becomes sluggish and separates and lift disappears. In such a case, a wing is said to stall. We speak here of an aircraft wing; when reversed, these principles can be applied to keeping a car firmly on the ground.

*Fresh air – the poor man's wind tunnel: Chris Gough takes his CGR1 for a spin with tufts of wool stuck in strategic places to monitor wind flow across the body. (Chris Gough collection)*

So much for drag; what about downforce, the vehicular equivalent of lift on an aircraft? To understand this it is necessary to understand air pressure. Basically, there is static atmospheric pressure, which only varies with altitude and temperature, and dynamic pressure, which results from velocity. A very clever Swiss mathematician answering to the name of Daniel Bernoulli discovered that the sum of the static pressure and the dynamic pressure equals a constant. In other words, any increase in the dynamic pressure will result in a drop in static pressure, and vice versa. This means that air taking a longer path around an object speeds up and has lower pressure than slower air taking a shorter way around it. Hence lift takes place, and this is the principle of flight when applied to a wing. When reversed, downforce occurs.

When air passes over, under and around a shape such as a car, streams of air molecules separate. However they will all take the same amount of time to negotiate an object. Accordingly, those taking a longer, more tortuous path, say under the curved surface of a front wing, will have to travel quicker than those crossing the smoother upper surface, and so a pressure differential results. A wing of aircaft design will naturally create lift, and it is this principle that gets aircraft into the air. As the higher air speed and thus lower pressure can, by turning an aircraft wing design upside down, be made to occur beneath the wing, downforce results.

To maintain the desired pressure differential between air flowing across the upper and lower surfaces of a wing used on a car, end plates are used. These prevent air spilling off the area of high pressure on the wing's top surface as it tries to equalize pressure by occupying the low-pressure area beneath. Such attempts at pressure recovery by spillage can be clearly seen on any damp or wet day as a vortex of airborne water droplets spiral from racing car rear wings.

Appreciating what happens beneath a racing car at speed is as valuable as knowing what happens above. By reducing drag and encouraging airflow to accelerate towards the low-pressure area to the rear, underside pressure is itself reduced and further downforce produced. This is commonly known as 'ground effect'. A flat smooth floor will both reduce

drag by maintaining a thin boundary layer and, if allowed to rise gently towards the rear, direct airflow to the area of low pressure which exists in the car's wake and beneath the rear wing. To maximize the benefits, needless to say, a fair amount of sophistication is required. The quality of air admitted to the underside from the front must be of low turbulence or 'clean', there must be minimal leakage of air during its journey from front to rear by virtue of a low ride height and some form of horizontal floor extension, and channels, dams and 'diffusers' (the curved upswept panels below and behind the gearbox on single-seaters) must be introduced to optimize the velocity and direction of airflow exiting the underbody to the rear. Designers work on the principle that the key to airflow velocity and its associated reduced pressure is to channel as much of it as possible through the smallest available gap over the greatest possible distance. In fact, the creation and maintenance of pressure differentials, high on top of a car and low beneath it, are what racing car aerodynamics are all about.

A Formula 1 car is said to produce so much downforce that at certain speeds it is in theory capable of driving upside down across a ceiling. It is doubtful whether a 750F car will ever be capable of generating such suction, but every little bit helps. And remember, children, don't try this trick at home.

So where does all this leave the stout yeoman sitting at his drawing-board and about to embark upon the design of his first 750 racing car? Inspired? Confused? Or a combination of both?

Unless you are blessed with the imagination of a Colin Chapman, John Barnard or Gordon Murray, it is both likely and sensible that you will base the shape of your masterpiece upon a car already racing. However, here is a list of useful ingredients:

1. As small a frontal area as possible, although it is said that total surface area is equally important.
2. A frontal area as smooth as possible to minimize friction with the air to be penetrated, and capable of directing clean air free from turbulence beneath a flat floor, and into radiators and brakes.
3. A nose shape, with or without wings, able to produce downforce onto the front wheels and shield the front tyres in order to lessen drag and retain rubber heat.
4. Smooth, flowing body lines that allow air to pass over with minimum friction.
5. Flat underside sloping gently up towards the rear, vertical or horizontal air barriers, and low ride height to allow air to accelerate as it passes beneath the car to form a low-pressure area.
6. Cut-off tail to reduce drag and air disturbance, with any fence or wing positioned in such a way as to minimize drag and maximize downforce.

There are those who say, possibly after 12 pints in the clubhouse, that rear wings don't work on 750F cars as they fail to reach high enough speeds. However, there is evidence to the contrary.

A couple of years ago at Silverstone, Pete Knipe spun

his DNC at Brooklands whilst dicing with the leaders of a hard-charging 750 field. Amazingly, everybody managed to avoid the DNC, now stationary in the middle of the track, except Jon Harvey, whose Darvi knocked off Knipe's rear wing. Once the dust had settled the bold Peter, blissfully unaware of his loss, stormed after the rapidly disappearing pack. He got as far as Copse when, without the benefit of accustomed rear downforce, he turned into the corner and promptly spun like a top. Until a marshal put him wise, Knipe was convinced he had suffered a puncture.

When Mick Harris debuted his fully enveloped Darvi 877 at Donington it had no aerodynamic aids at the rear, and swooping downhill through the Craner Curves in practice the car was going disconcertingly light at the back as front downforce increased with little or nothing at the rear to balance it. Clearly, rear downforce was in short supply. So, after pondering the problem in the paddock, a piece of $1/2$ in (12 mm) diameter rope was produced by Mick and tank-taped across the upper edge of the tail. This formed an approximately 1 in (25 mm) high fence which allowed air pressure to build up in front of it and create downforce. Stability in the race was noticeably improved.

The front-engined but fully enveloped Marrow appears to work well without a rear wing, but the rear bodywork is tapered in such a way as to allow air to flow over it and create downforce without spilling off the sides. (It should also be remembered that the driver sits well back in the 'Clubmans' position to lend more of his weight to the rear of the car.) When designing the Marrow, John Morris made it narrower than normal to gain a straightline speed advantage over his rivals by having less frontal and total surface area. On fast circuits this objective was achieved, the Marrow being capable of 127 mph (204 km/h). But as is so often the case, an advantage in one area of racing car design led to a trade-off in another. A narrow body meant a narrow wheelbase, and handling was at least to some degree compromised. As downforce, by increasing the sprung weight, effectively decreases the ratio of unsprung weight, it is useful to control more than a hundredweight of live rear axle bouncing up and down in a car weighing no more than seven times that figure. This is perhaps one of the main reasons why a rear wing is particularly effective on a 750F car.

One more thing. Should you come up with a new angle on producing a winning 750 racer, first check out the idea with a 750MC scrutineer. Club officials are always pleased to advise on questions of eligibility, and it could save you much wasted time and money.

# Chapter 6

# OUTSIDE IN THE GARAGE SOMETHING STIRRED

**S**o the momentous decision to build a 750 Formula racing car has been taken. You have chosen its configuration, settled on a bodywork design, and have summoned the enthusiasm and determination to construct, then race, such a machine. You are Colin Chapman trapped inside the body of Ken Average.

Let us take things step by step.

## DESIGN

Once it has been decided whether the car is to be front- or mid-engined, inboard- or outboard-suspended, where the major components are to be deployed, and what the bodywork shape is to be like, and you are satisfied it will fit within the formula rules, it is wise to pen some drawings from which to work once construction begins.

From these drawings you should build an $1/8$th scale balsa-wood model. This will tell you if the chassis is likely to be rigid, and if there is sufficient space for all the running gear.

A carefully crafted model of the proposed racer can save an invaluable amount of time and frustration, not to mention money, in the avoidance of such basic cock-ups as the steering column going through a driver's foot, or there being insufficient space for the engine to be inserted, as well as indicating the chassis' ability to withstand major twisting forces without flexing.

An $1/8$th scale chassis frame can be modelled quite easily using $1/8$ or $1/16$ in square balsa to represent square steel tubing (or hollow section to the purist). Twelve sticks arranged as a rectangular box will represent the chassis outline, with triangulation added as necessary. The mandatory 2 in x 2 in members may be formed from four $1/8$ in sticks bonded together in parallel, available as $1/4$ x $1/4$ in, from your local model shop, while a cardboard or wooden block can represent the engine, gearbox, fuel tank, battery, and so on. Basic though such a mock-up may be, it will certainly demonstrate whether everything fits between the tubes, and if the necessary chassis stiffness is likely to be present. Uncon-

vinced? Well, just imagine how a wooden matchbox will become lozenge-shaped if squeezed, then how relatively undistorted it remains if modestly reinforced by a little balsa triangulation.

Were further proof of the importance of the model as a constructional tool required, consider this: most professional race car manufacturers employ people who do nothing else but build models for checking purposes prior to the creation of the real thing.

## WORKSHOP

The basic requirements for the workshop within which your masterpiece is to be built are that it be dry, secure, and has electricity. One of the beauties of a 750 car is its ability to fit easily into a domestic garage, with room to spare for the proud owner to walk around it.

An elementary set of tools plus an electric drill will provide a good start, with more specialist equipment such as welding gear being scrounged or hired later. Obtaining welding gear has become much easier during the last few years, with BOC for example supplying small bottles known as Portapac. Mick Harris built his Darvi 877 using just one set.

Good lighting and plenty of storage shelving are also useful, both being major contributions towards avoiding the aggravation of losing things.

Finally, a level floor is good news, as we will see later.

## CHASSIS CONSTRUCTION

A chassis' function is to link all the car's components together. In doing so, it must be strong, stiff, and as light as possible. The formula's regulations dictate certain dimensions and metal gauges; the rest is up to the constructor's ingenuity.

In the early days, when 750 racers were Austin Seven-based, chassis were made from cold-drawn seamless steel (CDS), this being solid metal drawn over a die to form a seamless tube. With the development of modern electric welding techniques, such tubing can now be formed by folding flat steel sheeting into a box section and electric resistance welding (ERW) a seam along the meeting faces. While CDS remains stronger than ERW, its strength far exceeds what is necessary for an effective chassis frame, and in virtually all applications ERW is strong enough. Exceptions are the roll-over bar, where the regulations require the use of CDS, and the suspension anti-roll bars. The latter undergo considerable twisting, a form of stress for which ERW is not intended, particularly at the rear of the car where the solid axle allows considerable wheel travel.

Today's electric welding is so good that it is often virtually impossible for the naked eye to detect whether tubular steel is solid or seamed, and Dick Harvey's horrendous Mallory Park shunt bears witness to the strength of ERW steel, no chassis tube breakage occurring.

ERW tubing is not a new concept, but it has only become popular in recent years due to the high-quality welds appearing. Prior to such advances, ERW would split along the weld if hit hard enough.

Professional manufacturers often use high-quality Reynolds alloy tubing, which is both strong and light. However, it requires skilled electric welding which, once set, is most arduous to remove, rendering accident repair uneconomic. Therefore, if damaged, it's a throw-away item. Accordingly, such tubing is an expensive and impractical option for the impecunious home builder and is unlikely to be pursued.

A visit to your local steel stockist will reveal two interesting facts: (1) CDS can be as much as five times as expensive as ERW; and (2) steel comes in less-than-manageable 20 ft lengths known as randoms (possibly because the till receipt will show 6.09 m now that the metal trade's machinery has gone metric!). To avoid cutting charges you will have to go equipped with a truck, a trailer, or a hacksaw, although if only short sections for, say, a roll-bar or a piece of triangulation are required, it may be cheaper to buy from a specialist racing supplier.

Desirable steel thickness is dependent upon its intended function, and the smaller the gauge number, the stouter the metal. The roll-over bar should be 14 gauge (g), the mandatory 2 x 2 in longitudinal members 16 g, and the remainder of the chassis 18 g. For localized stiffening, where full triangulation is not possible due to the obstruction of a key component, 16 g tubing is advisable. An increase in tube section in such circumstances will be more effective than an increase in gauge, and any weight penalty easily offset by the bracing benefits.

Tube sizes will also vary. In this regard it can be useful to work in multiples of 1 in, where appropriate, so that calculations are made easier. Apart from the obligatory 2 x 2 in tubes and $1^3/8$ in minimum diameter roll-over bar, most of the framework can be assembled in 1 in square, this being a good compromise between strength and weight. For triangulation, $3/4$ or $5/8$ in members may be used, although if space does not allow, $1^1/2$ x $3/4$, 1 x 2 or $1^1/2$ x 2 are alternative sizes for frame member sections.

With steel cut to size and a framework designed, the next stage, before it is all fixed together, is to find a substantial level base, hence the earlier reference to a flat garage floor. Should you be blessed with such a phenomenon, it is possible to mark out the outline of the chassis base, bolt blocks of wood at each side of the outline in strategic positions, then clamp the tubing in position ready for welding. The only shortcoming of working on the floor is that it involves a sizeable amount of crawling about on cold concrete, which is about as much fun as a poke in the eye with a burnt stick.

Perhaps a more practical approach is to use a blockboard base. This is done by

*Chassis grows in garden: Chris Gough's race-winning CGR1 takes shape. (Chris Gough)*

taking an 8 x 4 ft sheet of inch-thick blockboard, reinforcing it from underneath by a grid of 2 x 2 in wooden battens, then screwing the board onto wooden trestles. The chassis outline can now be scribed upon the board's upper surface, locating blocks made of more 2 x 2 screwed into place, and the tube laid between them on top of the markings.

The importance of reinforcing the blockboard with timber cannot be over-stressed. Garages are inevitably damp, and if the board absorbs the moisture it will bend. A base in such a condition will form a very effective foundation for a banana-shaped car, and they do not perform well.

A third alternative is to use a professional-style metal jig, which is a ladder-like structure on adjustable legs. The chassis is built up on top of the outstretched ladder, with each

section held in place by a series of clamps. Some jigs are like a large spit which can be rotated. As building such a jig may take longer than building the chassis itself, this is not a frequently used option unless more than a single chassis is contemplated.

Of the current crop of distinguished constructors, Bob

(known as Bill Junior to some after his 750 racing father) Simpson took the cold-knee route when building the Simpson SS by putting the chassis together on the workshop floor. Four-times 750 champion Mick Harris chose a substantial blockboard base secured to massive trestles when creating the chassis of his two-time championship-winning Darvi 877, Mick's choice of wood no doubt influenced by his carpenter father. Apparently one gets used to the smell of burnt wood which accompanies welding metal on a blockboard base and it is not unpleasant. Meanwhile, at Darvi's High Wycombe HQ, Dick Harvey uses a metal jig, all cars since the Mk 2 and 3 having been fabricated in this way.

Before delving into the weird world of welding, some final thoughts on the format of the chassis frame. A three-bay lay-

*The cockpit, Darvi 91-D. Note driver protection, engine and gearbox position, and instrumentation. (Dick Harvey)*

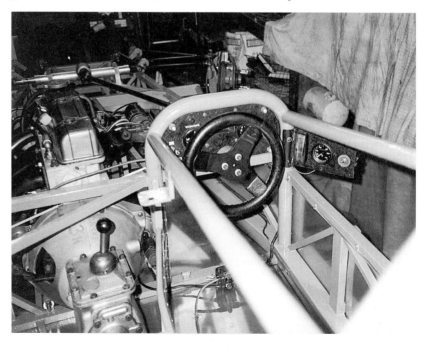

out formed by four sub-dividing bulkheads is the usual arrangement, with the forward-most partition behind the nose, the second dividing the footwell and pedals from the steering rack and front suspension, with master cylinders mounted on the cross member, a third bulkhead a little way back separating the engine and driver, with instruments and switches mounted on a cross member-supported fascia, and a fourth barrier between the driver and back axle, usually supporting or including the roll-over bar.

When building the 91-D following the demolition of his 86-9 at Mallory, Dick Harvey built as much driver protection as possible into the new chassis – because, as the man says, 'If a driver needs it, he needs it badly.' This was done by continuing the 14 g, 1½ in round-tube roll-cage down to the bottom chassis members, fitting a similar hoop as a dashboard bulkhead, then joining the two hoops by a pair of side tubes, one to each side of the driver, which continue forward beyond the bulkhead into the bottom chassis rails, thus creating a kind of survival cell which should absorb impacts from any direction.

# WELDING

Once all the chassis tubes are assembled in the desired shape, it is time to weld them together. In the case of 750 car construction, weld is perhaps not strictly the correct word, for the form of fusion usually advocated is brazing. Welding is when two pieces of metal, and filler rod of similar metal, are heated at high temperature to become molten and then flowed together, bonding as one when cooled; brazing is when two pieces of metal are heated enough to become red hot but not to melt, then are fused together by a brass or bronze filler rod, rather like soldering.

Brazing has a number of advantages for the amateur racing car builder. Without an inordinate dollop of skill it is possible to do a good braze, and even a poor one will be better than a poor weld, save only that all angled joints need to be made with as good a fit as possible. The nickle-bronze alloy fused between the joined steelwork has in fact a higher tensile strength than the steel being joined, and such a joint should withstand all that club racing is likely to throw at it. Less heat is required to braze a joint than to weld it, therefore less metal distortion is caused. Finally, it is far easier to repair a brazed chassis that has been bent in an accident than a welded one, for it is just a case of applying heat and a wire brush to open a brazed joint, whereas a welded one must be cut apart with a hacksaw or ground open with a grinding wheel, neither of which are easy instruments to insert between complex triangulation.

Prior to the chassis tubes being finally joined together and brazed, they should first be lightly 'tacked' into place with just a small blob of filler rod. The golden rule in doing this is: Proceed With Caution. Set the lengths of tube up carefully with spirit level and set-square to ensure they are level and at right angles, then proceed box by box throughout the length of the frame. Once each box has been 'tacked', check again for squareness by measuring diagonally across the rectangles formed. Triangulation may now be added, but again constant checks should be made to ensure the boxes remain square.

Where bushes are to be inserted into chassis tubing suspension, this should be done prior to assembly only when drilling is impossible once the chassis is welded up. Ideally, holes should be drilled after the chassis has been welded, and necessary suspension pick-ups added so that any slight distortion can be compensated for by an adjustment in the position of the hole or mount. This is also the point at which consideration should be given to the location of threaded bushes for seat belt mounts, using tubing that is as beefy as possible.

The other point to note is that tube lengths should always be accurately cut. Do not be tempted to fill gaps with braze: the joint will be weakened and the braze will shrink, causing distortion. It is best to cut the tube slightly too long then file it down, though this is a job not without its hazards. The wearing of heavy-duty or even chain-mail gloves will protect your delicate Steinway-playing digits from razor-edged tubing with an attitude.

Once the framework has been tacked together to your satisfaction, with all angles and distances checked and double-checked for squareness, it is time to braze the chassis together properly. And, as with tacking, Proceed With Caution. As one element of the frame is brazed into shape, another will move, so it is constantly necessary to check, not only angles, but also diagonal and longitudinal distances. A chassis is of such length and width that a small error at one end can be compounded incrementally to such a degree that by the time the other end is reached, a significant bow has been built into the structure.

To ensure absolute accuracy in the checking of right-angles, don't rely upon a plastic set-square from a long-forgotten school geometry set, or even a small joiner's metal set-square; instead make your own from a substantial corner of plywood or aluminium off-cut, and make it large enough to check two converging tubes over a significant amount of their length.

Tape measures too are important. Use metal ones, and have plenty of them, for they get lost and damaged. They are particularly susceptible to the flames of a welding torch. Some years ago a 750 car constructor took his impecuniosity to outrageous lengths by riveting the tip back onto a tape measure that had had its end inadvertently cut off. Unfortunately, the first foot of its length was now only 10 in long, and when a friend later borrowed said tape whilst building his own car, a less-than-square chassis resulted.

There are three basic methods of applying flux – the substance mixed with the metals to promote fusion – to the brazing rod. The first, and most common, is to dip the heated rod into powdered flux before beginning the joint, but this calls for a degree of judgement as to how much flux will be needed. Frequently this leads to an excessive flux scale on the joint, a singularly laborious and difficult job to clean off later. Then there is rod which is already flux-coated. Sounds great, but the amount of flux needed will vary from one application to another, so in many cases there will not be

enough on the rod. This leads to the use of more rod in order to get more flux, or dipping an already-coated rod into some flux, and I think you begin to get the picture as to the wastage which can result, and the great dollop of bronze that you don't need. The third option is the all-singing, all-dancing gas fluxer. An attachment in the acetylene pipe to the welding torch feeds a gas flux into the flame, so allowing just the right amount for each application of the heat, and avoiding the need for continually dipping into a flux tin. With its distinctive green flame, rather than the more usual blue, gas fluxing is the professional way of brazing, leaving only a little white powder around the joint which can be easily pressure-washed off when cool. Normally it is necessary laboriously to chip and file the hard bead-like flux deposits off joints. Gas fluxers may be hired, and are certainly more expensive to operate than the alternative methods, but their ease of use during a large job such as a chassis fabrication makes it well worth considering the extra expenditure. The only other point to note is that there is a tendency for the flux to eventually clog up the pipes bringing acetylene to the torch, so it is wise to disconnect the flux supply when small jobs which do not justify its convenience are tackled. Once clogged, the most desperate solution is to replace the pipes, but the deposit is soluble in water and a decent soak submerged in a bucket of water may do the trick.

Rather than trying to braze the whole chassis in one hit, it is better to do no more than two hours' work at a time. The

job requires care and concentration and inevitably flux fumes are inhaled as you lean over the subject of your attentions, so you begin to develop the symptoms of a heavy cold combined with a hangover if you spend too much time in such an atmosphere. Wear a proper mask if possible and work diagonally to minimize distortion, as you would if tightening wheel nuts.

The best approach is to braze section by section, then once the flux has cooled, chip it off and clean up the joint with a file or wire brush. The longer the flux deposit is left, the harder it is to remove. But removed it must be, for the best paint job in the world will not last five minutes if it has been applied on top of flux deposits. What happens is that the flux absorbs water, this gets under the paint and causes it to fall off, and you are left with a white furry mess.

Bead-blasting, a process that peppers a metal component with fine glass or similar beads, is useful for cleaning up small manageable parts such as wishbones or radius arms, but there are not too many cabinets around large enough to accept something as large as a chassis. When such a cabinet is found, it is more likely to be used for shot-blasting, a far more abrasive process whereby coarser grades of grit, aluminium oxide, or brick dust are sprayed at quite high pressure at a component. Needless to say, 18 g lightweight chassis frames do not take kindly to half house bricks being tossed at them.

Should a large enough bead-blasting cabinet be found, it is important to remember that if a used chassis is being treated, all holes, say from aluminium panelling rivets, must be filled with self tappers or similar to keep the beads out, otherwise you will acquire a clean chassis twice as heavy as was the case before it was bead-blasted.

In welding, as in so many things, there are little tricks to ease the way and make a better job. Here are a few of them:

1. When a section of tube, say 1 in square, is to be brazed at right angles to a larger-section tube, say 2 in square, it is far better to cut and file the large tube and slot the smaller one inside it to its full depth than merely butt against it and braze in place. This ensures a far stronger joint which, in the case of a roll-hoop fitting on a 2 x 2 member, could make all the difference between having to buy a new helmet and walking away without a scratch, were the car to flip, should the member collapse and allow the hoop to drop by 2 in on impact. Drilling a hole large enough to accept a tube is not a simple job, and a square hole is even worse when dealing with a piece of, say, 16 g metal. Therefore it will be necessary to drill a circle of small holes then, once weakened, knock the centre out with a ballpein hammer, and file smooth the edges of the hole. The smaller-section tube is then pushed right through and brazed at both sides of the larger tube, thus effecting a very strong joint (Fig 12). When being cut, the thinner tube's length must take into account the extra amount needed to sink into the other member, while the piercing should be done prior to assembly as it is unlikely to be too accessible later.

2. Where it is necessary for a number of tubes to meet at one point, perhaps for triangulation purposes, braze that junction as one, rather than adding to it as you go.

3. Typically, the mandatory 2 x 2 members will lie at the bottom of the chassis to form the basis of the frame, but as fully triangulated lighter tubing is added above, it will ever so slightly bow upwards at each end as it loses out to the strength of the ever-increasing superstructure. To compensate for this disturbing tendency, a piece of $1/8$ in deep packing should be inserted under the centre, so creating a bow. By the time the chassis is completed it will have pulled itself straight.

4. Where it is necessary to butt a piece of square-section tube up against the side of another, similar-sized section, a good tweak is to heat the tube to be added, then squeeze in two or four sides by approximately $1/8$ in with a pair of pliers. This allows additional braze to be contained within the concave faces when the end is hard up against the other tube, making a stronger joint. This wheeze is attributed to aeronautical engineer and Formula 4 champion Bob Davis, a man who knows more than most about such matters.

5. Next we have 'backing up'. When a piece of metal tubing a foot or more in length and supported only at each extremity is subjected to heat, say when a tube is brazed into the side, it will expand and bend. To prevent this, substantial lengths of tubes should be positioned parallel to the unsup-

ported section and clamped to it, so lending resistance to distortion. Once brazing is completed and the metal has cooled, they may be removed.

6. Where holes in separate sections of tubing will later be required to line up, say to accept bushes on which a suspension rocker arm must pivot, a dummy bar or length of tube should be passed through them prior to the tubing being brazed in place. Once lined up, the bushes are tacked into place, and the dummy bar is then removed while the chassis is fully welded. On completion, should the bushes have moved slightly out of line, a device known as a 'boggling bar' (pointed and tapered) may be inserted to persuade them back into alignment with each other. They should then be rechecked with a dummy bar prior to being finally brazed into position.

7. Finally, an appreciation of the disparate qualities of square- and round-section tube is fundamental to chassis design and construction. Square-section is more resistant to bending than tube or round-section due to its having four corners. Thus it is highly suitable for chassis frame construction because it will not readily flex. Square-section is also easier to measure for flatness and squareness, and happily accepts panelling, bodywork and components being mounted onto its flat faces. Round-section tubing's curved surface makes it resistant to twisting, hence its suitability for suspension roll-bars, wishbones and radius arms.

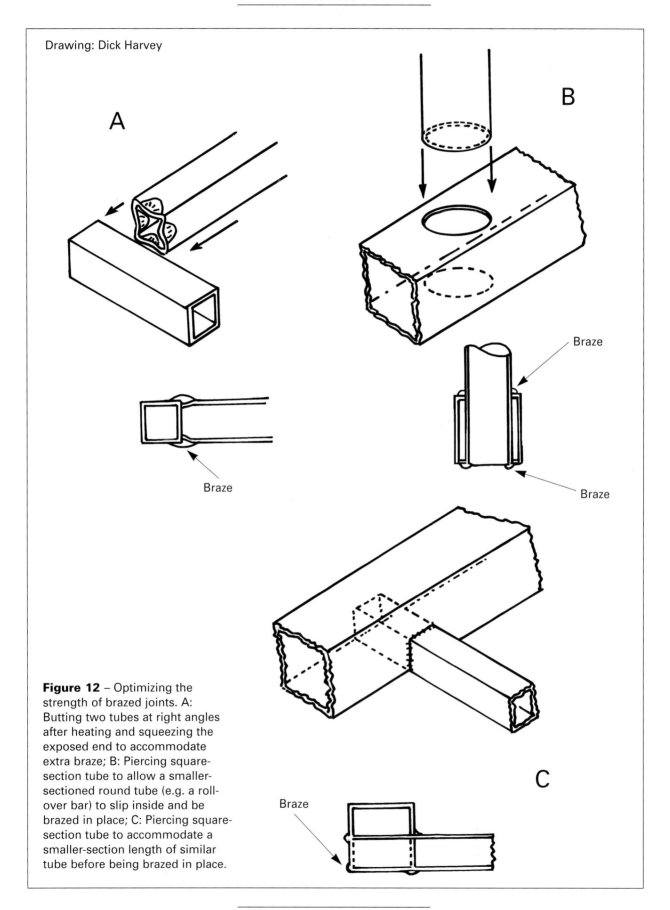

Drawing: Dick Harvey

**Figure 12** – Optimizing the strength of brazed joints. A: Butting two tubes at right angles after heating and squeezing the exposed end to accommodate extra braze; B: Piercing square-section tube to allow a smaller-sectioned round tube (e.g. a roll-over bar) to slip inside and be brazed in place; C: Piercing square-section tube to accommodate a smaller-section length of similar tube before being brazed in place.

The craft of steel spaceframe construction is the management of distortion. All braze shrinks to some degree, but by proceeding carefully step by step and constantly checking angles and measurements, a flat, square chassis is within the capabilities of the home constructor.

On completion, the framework should be rubbed down and painted. A single coat of enamel is sufficient, then bends, corrosion or cracks will cause the paint to flake and be easily spotted. A salutary tale regarding the down side of carrying out too good a chassis paint job concerns former 750 driver and, more recently, Renault Clio pilote Hayden Measham. Being a garagiste, Hayden had the paint shop lovingly coat his chassis in the latest two-pack paint. Unfortunately he subsequently rolled the car at Cadwell, and although well bent it was impossible to assess the extent of the damage as the paint was unblemished. It took two YTS lads a week to remove the paint with thinners, brushes and scrapers before a repair could be carried out.

Although black or white may look good when new, a light grey chassis is more practical in the longer term, and is the colour favoured by most professional constructors, although Vision for one used to supply chassis in glorious blues or scarlet. Black PVC powder-coated chassis are also gaining popularity, but are rather impractical when it comes to accident repair.

## KITS

Whilst design and build is the essence of 750 racing, not everyone has the facilities, ability or inclination to start a car from scratch. For such enthusiasts the kit once existed – DNC, Centaur, JoMo, Harrison and Jeffrey, to name a few – but today only Dick Harvey or John Morris would be able to supply one, at a price. As essentially a one-off, a kit is expensive to produce, yet the production of more than a couple would flood the market, particularly when it is considered that, if the buyer is an existing 750 racer, the purchase would release another car for sale. Were, say, ten to be produced, it would merely be a case of dispatching chassis drawings to a company such as Arch Motors, and body moulds to a glassfibre specialist, and a run of cars could be produced at reasonable cost. But, at the moment, 750 Formula racing does not quite have that following.

There is of course the chassis kit, and Dick Harvey has supplied essentially Darvi Mk 5 LWB chassis to both Rick Goodyer (Hague) and Bob Couchman (JoMo), onto which they put all their existing running gear.

## PANELLING

Once the chassis has been assembled and painted, the floor panel may be fitted. As this is stressed, and adds strength to the chassis, it should be made from a single piece of aluminium of decent thickness and specification. In reality, however, the first time you drive over the surface of a less than billiard-table smooth paddock and a few dents are acquired, that stress is somewhat less than absolute. Structural grade NS4 hard or half-hard aluminium sheet of 18–20 gauge thickness is required, and if you happen upon a redundant DC10, L72 is a seriously superior aeronautical equivalent. For additional protection, 22 g stainless steel sheets may be added beneath such vulnerable areas as the footwell and fuel tank, or be used to replace the aluminium entirely.

A well-proven method of making the floor for the chassis is to lower the latter onto a single sheet of aluminium, mark the chassis outline on the sheet, then cut to shape with a pair of tin-snips. Using a black felt-tip pen, the outlines of all the chassis tubes onto which the floor is to be riveted may now be marked. Removing the chassis from the aluminium, the tube outlines should be drilled along their centre lines at 1 in intervals to accept $1/8$ in rivets, though at this stage the holes will be put in undersized (3 mm is ideal, or $3/32$ in). As an added safety measure, consideration should be given to doubling up on the driver's side rivets, and in any case this should be done along the 2 x 2 members by having two lines of holes side by side, $3/4$ in apart and staggered, the effect being that all holes are no more than $3/4$ in from one another.

Turning the chassis upside down and placing the drilled aluminium floor pan back onto its up-ended base, the chassis can be drilled to align with the floor holes, once chassis and floor have been temporarily clamped together. Holes should first be drilled undersize, then the correct size to take an $1/8$ in rivet. With drilling completed, the floor pan should be taken off and deburred to remove all drilling swarf, then cleaned with thinners. The chassis tubing should also be deburred, then when all mating surfaces are smooth and clean, the aluminium is ready to be clamped back onto the upturned chassis base for the final act to begin.

Before riveting begins, each corner of the floor pan should be temporarily secured to the chassis by a removable device known as an 'Avdel', or 'Grippernicker' if you happen to be serving in the RAF, later to be replaced by permanent rivets once all the others have been fitted. If this is not done, the aluminium has a habit of trying to do a rumba as the rivets go in which will inevitably lead to the misalignment of holes somewhere along the line. Aluminium rivets tend to be favoured as they are easily drilled out for repairs, however stainless steel are available and strong but hell to work with.

Riveting must be carried out like a medical operation, with the severed stem of every rivet accounted for after each insertion. No easy task when perhaps 600 of the blighters could be used, but infinitely preferable to a sharp piece of metal finding its way into a tyre. Air rivet guns can be hired, and are worth every penny on a job of this size if you ever wish to play the violin again.

Lastly, when riveting, work from the centre of the floor outwards in order to keep the aluminium sheet taut.

Side panelling should be in thinner 22–24 gauge NS4 or SIC aluminium, using as few pieces as possible in order to add further strength to the structure. Bends can be moulded around anything hard that happens to be lying around: a dustbin, a post box, a garden roller. The driver can be surrounded by double-skinned inner panelling for protection and comfort, and all bulkheads should be panelled and sealed. Where a panel is exposed it should be painted before being riveted to avoid having to mask the surroundings if it is to be painted after fitting. If a panel may need to be removed on occasion, it should be secured by rivnuts which are rivets internally threaded to accept small screws or bolts.

## BODYWORK

The simplest method of cladding a chassis is by panelling it in aluminium, but unless you can live with something that looks as if it's come out of the Fisher Price catalogue, or have served an apprenticeship with Touring of Milan, curves mean glassfibre. Now known as GRP – Glass Reinforced Plastic – this form of bodywork begins life as a buck, from which a mould is taken. The mould is filled with glass matting mixed with resin which is allowed to set, then out pops the body shape. Simple as buying a lottery ticket? Not quite.

'Clubmans' configuration cars can be moulded in sections of manageable size, but a mid-engined design with its fully enclosed bodywork is a much bigger proposition. Mick Harris took more than two years to make the front and rear sections, two sidepods and two cockpit sides of his Darvi 877.

Whatever type of bodywork you choose, the steps towards its construction are as follows:

1. A 'buck' or 'plug', which is the solid version of what is to be made, is shaped from wood, aluminium, glassfibre, or anything else that is cheaply available. In a perfect world where money is no object it would be great to use new timber and make a buck easily dismantled once the mould has been produced. The reality is that the last couple of bodywork sections made by Dick Harvey involved bucks shaped from steel frames covered with old aluminium sheet and hardboard, then smoothed with cheap bodyfiller before being rubbed down.

Some 'experts' suggest plaster as a cheap and easily shaped material from which to make a buck, but unless you enjoy the luxury of a heated garage the plaster will never be persuaded to dry out. Although the finished body may be in several sections, and a number of bucks will be needed, it is wise to build the bucks as one to ensure continuity of lines and fits. The separate bucks are therefore linked together, rubbed down as one, and then separated for moulds to be made. Any required returns or fences are added before the mould is formed. A smooth finish is essential as the mould surface will be a reverse copy of the buck, and time spent now will be saved later when the mould is rubbed down.

2. The finished buck is polished with several coats of a release wax (five is typical) and buffed to give a good shine. Use the real thing – it's expensive but it works. Beware of wax polishes, especially those containing silicones – they seem to aid adhesion rather than prevent it. Once waxed, the buck should be treated with a release agent to enable,

hopefully, the completed mould to be separated easily from the buck.

Mould-making can now start. The buck is covered with a layer of pigmented gel coat suitably catalysed. If extensive rubbing of the mould is anticipated, a useful trick is to apply a second coat in a different colour once the first has been allowed to 'go off'. Then, when rubbing down the mould, you will be able to gauge when to stop before rubbing through the gel coat and into the laminate proper.

Once the gel coat has 'gone off', layers of matting and activated resin, applied by brush, are built up on the buck. The use of brushes and rollers consolidates the laminate and forces out air bubbles. Up to four layers may be applied at one time – more will cause excessive shrinkage and warping. When the mould has been built up to the required thickness, it is allowed to harden and cure for a day or so dependent on temperature. As this is a typical winter job, and British winters are not unknown for their sub-zero termperatures, 3–4 days may not be uncommon.

The mould can be released from the buck once fully hardened, but this is not the work of a moment. A vacuum frequently forms between the buck and the mould, so they must be eased apart carefully. Sometimes it is necessary to break up the pattern inside the mould to avoid possible damage to the mould itself which is still 'green' and fairly weak.

3. Once released, the mould should be allowed to harden or cure. Ideally it should be placed back on the buck so that it is fully supported. If this is not possible, it must at least be well supported in some other way, as at this early stage it will easily twist and warp.

When fully cured the mould should be rubbed down with gradually smoother grades of wet and dry paper, then polished with rubbing compound. A highly polished finish to the mould will not only ensure a good finish to the moulding, it will aid release. Perfectionists now spend countless hours polishing, the finish they obtain reflecting their efforts.

The mould must now be polished with several layers of release wax, preferably over a couple of days, then buffed to a smooth finish. An application of an additional release agent is always carried out for the first moulding from a new mould, which may seem something of a belt-and-braces approach but is well worthwhile. This is not usually necessary for well-used moulds, these normally being washed out with soap and hot water to prevent build-up of material. The fully prepared mould is now ready to produce the body shape of your choice.

4. The mould is painted with activated pigmented gel coat and allowed to 'go off'. Next, two layers of matting coated with activated resin are added with brush and roller. Localized strengthening or the addition of inserts or fittings may require extra layers to be applied. For example, when building the Darvi 877 Mick Harris used corrugated cardboard glassed into place on top of the GRP laminate within the wheel arches to reduce damage from stones. This was done once the laminate had cured, and was replaced during the racing season as necessary.

5. Front cycle wings on 'Clubmans' configuration cars can be neatly fixed to their supporting stays without the use of untidy-looking nuts and bolts. The wings are first applied with a little bodyfiller on the underside and sat on the stays. Then, whilst held in place by the filler, a layer of glassfibre is run over the stays and underside of the wing to bond them together.

6. Unless you are contemplating using self-coloured mouldings which will require trimming and polishing before use, it will be necessary to rub down the freshly moulded glassfibre panels with wet and dry paper with hot water and detergent prior to painting. This process not only enables the paint to adhere, as with metal panels, it also removes the release agent from the panel surfaces as some always gets transferred to the panel from the mould. Careful preparation is the key to a good paint finish. Cellulose or two-pack paint may now be applied.

# AERODYNAMIC WINGS

Front wings may be made from glassfibre or aluminium. Endplates are fine in glassfibre, but are better in 'poor-man's honeycomb' – corrugated cardboard in a two-layer sandwich – to stop them flapping about.

Because of their size and complexity, rear wings are made from aluminium so as to

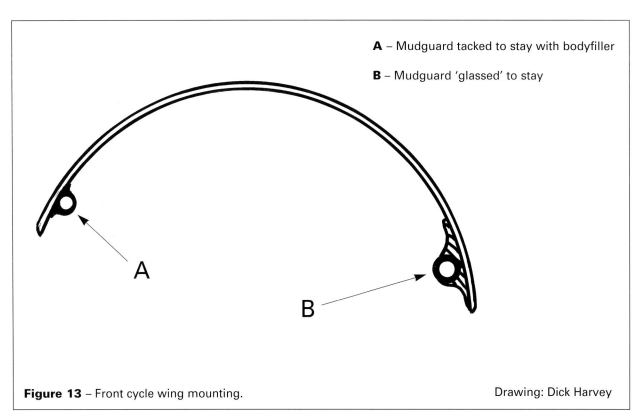

A – Mudguard tacked to stay with bodyfiller

B – Mudguard 'glassed' to stay

**Figure 13** – Front cycle wing mounting.                    Drawing: Dick Harvey

be flex-resistant. It is possible to make them at home by rolling alloy around a vice-held tube, but for the modest cost

*Rear wing, Darvi 91-D. Note stout roll-over bar. (Dick Harvey)*

involved it is usually better to have the metal rolled into shape professionally, as it is quicker and gives a superior finish. Endplates and formers, which are the transverse, wing-strengthening members, can be

made from steel cut from sheets and returned at 90° then welded, or from aluminium beaten from 22 swg sheet over a solid former, or moulded in GRP from a single mould so each is identical in size and shape. The outermost formers may be part of the endplates.

Of course, as rear wing design and construction is such a complex affair, you may consider buying a second-hand wing. Look for one with a narrow chord, a flat profile with adjustable flap, and preferably a visible form of mounting. Then you can direct your energies into some really good brackets to stop it flying off as you approach a first victory.

## HUBS AND UPRIGHTS

Triumph Herald, Spitfire and Vitesse 3¾ in PCD hubs and uprights are popular, but if Vauxhall Viva hubs and uprights

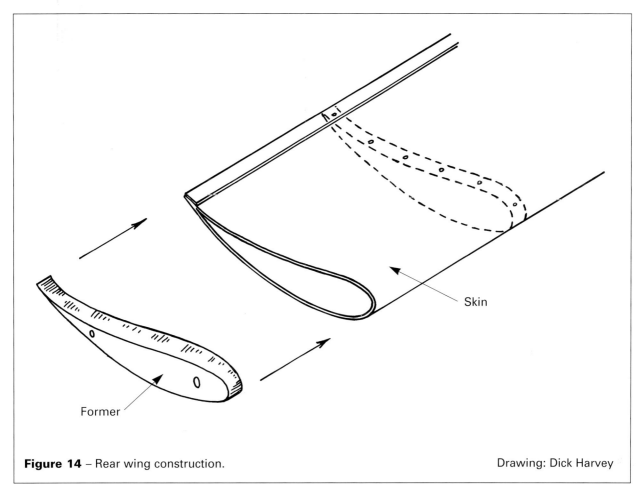

Skin

Former

**Figure 14** – Rear wing construction.                    Drawing: Dick Harvey

are used, they share 4 in PCD hub centres with those of the BMC rear axle. This means that the same-centred wheels can be used all round. Of course there are others; it is all a question of availability, and there is nothing to stop you grafting on a live stub axle, for example a Mini front without its driveshaft, or even one from a formula car, in order to have the convenience of centre-lock wheels. These sit on four pegs and are retained by a single nut. The first time you have to change wheels in a hurry in a wind- and rain-swept

*Single-seater steering rack on the Darvi 91-D. Note neat petrol pipe routing, chassis triangulation, brake master cylinders and pedal arrangement for balance adjustment. (Dick Harvey)*

paddock, you will realize the full joy of such an arrangement.

## STEERING ARMS AND RACK

Once again Triumph Herald

and Vauxhall Viva racks are the choice of many, and steering arms should be made from 5/8 in diameter 10 g cold-drawn steel. The rods are threaded in opposite directions at each end to screw into drilled and

85

tapped female rose joints. Adjustments can then be made merely by loosening their locking nut at each end of the arm and twisting it in one direction or another. The rack should be positioned if possible in line with the top wishbone to eliminate bump-steer. This phenomenon, as the term suggests, is changes in direction caused by suspension movement rather than steering input, and needs to be eliminated from the car's handling characteristics completely. Ackerman effect (or angle), although desirable to some degree, should originate from and be controlled by the angle of the steering arm viewed from above. This makes the inner wheel turn more sharply than the outer one in a corner, and is generally the cause of amiable disagreement among builders and drivers as to whether it is needed or not.

## WISHBONES

Fabricated from 18 g EWR tubing, top wishbones are typically 3/4 in in diameter, bottom wishbones 7/8 in. Bead-blasted, painted matt black, then waxed, these prominent suspension parts, at least on a non-fully enveloping bodied car, can look extremely smart. But use a minimum amount of paint so that flaws can be detected quickly.

At the rear, radius arms may be made of 18 g EWR tubing of 7/8 in diameter. Panhard Rods are made in 16 g at 7/8 in diameter, or 18 g at 1 in diameter.

## ANTI-ROLL BARS

In motor racing there are two kinds of roll-bars. This can confuse a simple person, and often has. There is the roll-over bar, designed to protect a driver should he be unfortunate enough to invert his machine, and there is the anti-roll bar, designed to control a car's body and chassis movement, or lean, when cornering.

An anti-roll bar takes the form of a solid steel or tubular round-section rod running across the chassis in bearings, with a blade or lever arm at each end. The blades are connected to the wheels, so when one rises relative to the other the rising blade exerts a twist into the bar. The bar resists the twist, and so controls the wheel lift and resulting chassis movement.

The strength or resistance within the bar is determined by its length and diameter, while the length and leverages of the blade are what govern its effects. Adjustment can be made by pick-up holes, slides, or twisting blades. Accordingly, the lever arms are often drilled in several places or have a slide

*Rear roll bar on the Darvi 91-D. Note adjustment holes along blade, radius arms and rear disc brakes. (Dick Harvey)*

adjustment in order to vary the strength of the bar according to conditions. Blades are rotated from vertical (hard) to horizontal (soft). For instance, in the wet, when grip is at a premium, a softer roll-bar setting with less roll-resistance may allow a driver more feel as to what the car is doing through roll. Adjustments between front and rear bars can also fine-tune handling characteristics. But some roll must always be allowed to remain, otherwise it may as well be running solid without suspension movement. At the front of the car this will prevent the suspension geometry from functioning effectively, with the result that the wheels will be unable to follow the road surfaces properly, and grip will diminish.

Anti-roll bars should be made from CDS, as the forces acting upon them are considerable. They should also be solidly mounted with no compliant rubber, and such specialists as Merlin Motorsport can supply polypropylene blocks with steel mounting-plates, onto which socket cap screws secure the blocks. The

blocks come in five sizes for different diameter bars. However, if a stiffer bar is required once a certain diameter has been tried, a heavier gauge of the same diameter can be used without having to change mounting blocks.

Bar diameters and thicknesses are a personal choice, depending upon the design of car and handling characteristics sought, but as a guide, after much experimentation, Dick Harvey uses 3/4 in 18 g tubular CDS front and rear on his 92D. However, this is of purely academic interest to the owner of any car with leverages and pick-up points different to those on the Darvi.

On outboard suspension the roll-bars are connected directly, via rose-jointed drop-links, to the wishbones at the front of the car, and axle at the rear, and the connections should be as close to the wheel as possible. On inboard suspension a much shorter bar has its blades connected to the rocking arms acting on the damper. In theory, by rotating the blades from flat, when they are quite compliant, to on edge, when they are at their most resistant, roll-resistance can be adjusted. But to be effective the blades must be well located, otherwise they may bend rather than twist. In the more professional formulae, this can be done by the driver via a long cable and, were he about to do a Grand Prix distance, it might be a worthwhile modification for the 750 man. But in reality it is hardly worth it for a ten-lapper, and in any case there will be plenty of other things to hold his attention.

# Chapter 7

# MAKING THE ROBIN FLY

First a short history lesson: between 7 October 1962 and 16 June 1968, 55,914 600 cc all-alloy, three-bearing, wet-linered ohv Reliant engines were produced to propel the three-wheeled Regal. Developed from the 750 cc side valve Reliant that had been based on the 750 Austin unit, these were the direct spiritual descendants of the original Austin Seven.

On 17 June 1968 it grew by 100 cc, and by 11 January 1973, 65,798 700 cc versions of the Reliant motor had been made, to be found beneath the glass-fibre bonnets of three-wheeled Bugs and Regals, and now four-wheeled Rebels.

A further 50 cc took it to 750 cc between 12 January 1973 and 8 September 1975, 25,844 editions finding their way into the sharp ends of three-wheeled Bugs and Robins, and Rebels. And yet more power came when another 100 cc were squeezed out of this plucky little device for the three-wheeled Fox, Kitten and Rialto models, and by 15 November 1978, 29,532 had hit the streets. Another 40,000 or so have since followed, under the direction of Bean, Reliant's

new owner. Sadly, Bean went bust in November 1994, but that is not necessarily the end for either car or engine.

As Michael Caine is so fond of saying, 'not a lot of people know that', and nor perhaps would want to. But for the racing engine builder of modest means but the right knowledge, this is a bargain price goldmine. However it is essential to be aware, not only of the best bits to use, but also of their least expensive sources. Some components are better suited to competition application than others. Once identified, then traced to the Reliant model within which they are to be found, it is a matter of stalking the correct dead vehicle to its final resting place.

Most Reliants have three wheels, with the single one up front, and admirable as they may be in weight, price, and rust defiance, these plastic projectiles can share some of the more tricky handling characteristics of an overloaded wheelbarrow if given some grief, and have been known to fall over. Bad news for George and Mildred on a day trip to Bognor, but good news for racing types.

So a visit to your local auto dismantler or scrap-yard will be the rewarding route to your first racing engine, and for forty quid a decent motor could be yours. To secure the lowest possible price, be prepared to do your own dismantling, so bring along tools, hacksaw, metal cutters, scissor jack, heavy boots, wet suit or thick overalls, and a plastic sheet to lie on. Seven Fifty Motor Club members are another source of engines, normally substantially modified already, whilst if all else fails, the world-famous emporium of Dick Harvey Racing Services usually has a few previously owned units in stock.

So which is the engine to go for?

As the 750 Formula regulations allow the use of the largest of the available power units, the 850 is clearly the one to have. Although that's not quite the full story. When first admitted to the formula, few cheap second-hand 850s were available, so enthusiasts built hybrids by attaching 850 rods to modified 850 cranks and fitting them to 750 blocks. With supplies of inexpensive 850

*The Reliant block. (Dick Harvey)*

*Top view of block. (Dick Harvey)*

*Underside of block. (Dick Harvey)*

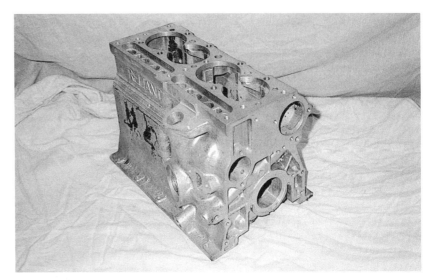

engines now more plentiful, and good-quality 750 main bearings rarer than pork pies at a barmitzvah, this ruse is no longer necessary. There are plenty of Glacier White bearing shells about as they fit 600, 700 and 750 cranks, but they are only suitable for road use in an 'Arnold' (a term of endearment for the Reliant three-wheeler much favoured in the South of England, and derived from the steady sort of chap who drives one).

However, early motors do remain of value for their cylinder heads. Having thicker decks, and smaller ports and chambers than later 850 heads, these older articles have more metal with which to play. They allow more shaping to improve gas flow, and more shaving to help raise the compression ratio.

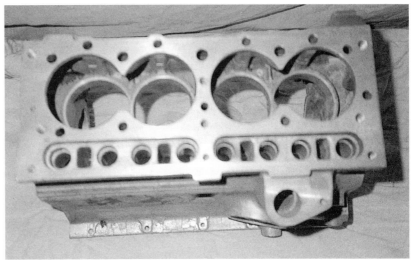

The 850 cylinder head is in fact relatively efficient, and requires little work to bring it up to semi-race specification. But the steady rationalization of manufacture has resulted in less metal being used, and while kidney-shaped chambers are built at the factory they have square corners between chamber roof and walls. No doubt these speed up production, but they also trap end gasses which is bad technical news. Filling them up with weld is not only a difficult, highly skilled and expensive job, it is also illegal as the regulations of the formula expressly forbid the addition of material, other than for the replacement of valve seats or guides. Accordingly, the

*Rotatable engine stand with drip tray. (Dick Harvey)*

combination of an early head and an 850 block is recommended.

Once a suitable engine has been acquired, the step-by-step transformation into a racing power-plant runs as follows:

## LUBRICATION

The standard Reliant lubrication system relies upon what is basically a Mini pump, deep within the sump, driven by a

6–8 in long shaft rotated by the camshaft by means of 'skew gears', which also activate the distributor. Repeated high revs and the heightened oil pressure needed at racing speeds result in the 'skew gears' first wearing thin, then failing, with totally disastrous results. There follows a loss of oil pressure, ignition timing

*Underside of block with crank in place. (Dick Harvey)*

slipping, and a big bang, often accompanied by vital engine parts strewn across the track.

Fortunately there are several reliable ways of averting such a disaster, but all involve fitting an external oil pump.

The first option is to use a Ford Fiesta or Escort pump driven off the front of the camshaft. This requires a purpose-made timing case, available from Dick Harvey for around £130, while for an additional £60 a self-aligning drive dog enables even the most mechanically challenged to line up the pump drive and camshaft accurately. This arrangement is straightforward, efficient and popular.

Second option is to dry sump

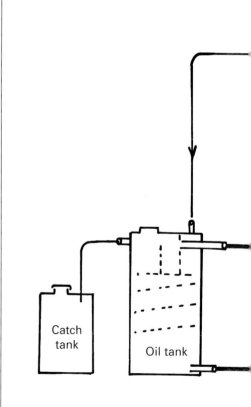

**Figure 16** – Dry sump lubrication system.

Catch tank

Oil tank

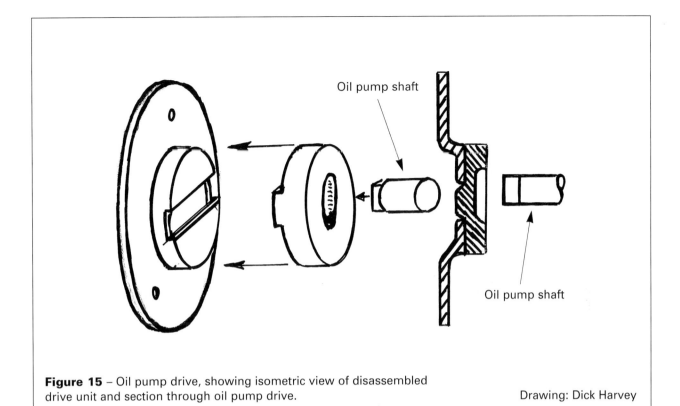

**Figure 15** – Oil pump drive, showing isometric view of disassembled drive unit and section through oil pump drive.

Drawing: Dick Harvey

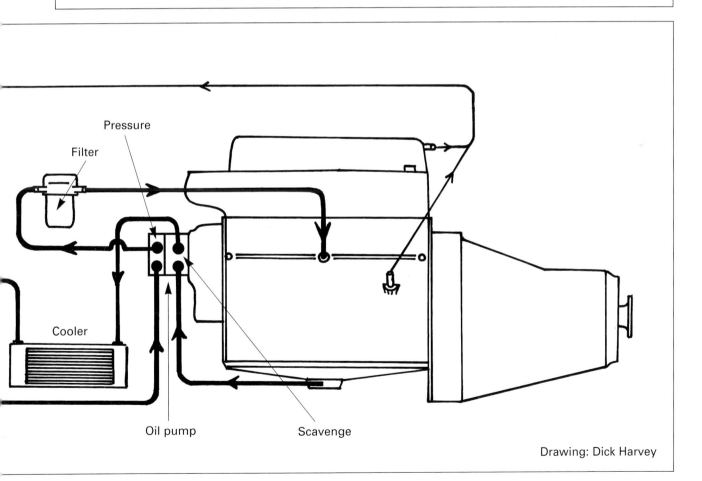

Drawing: Dick Harvey

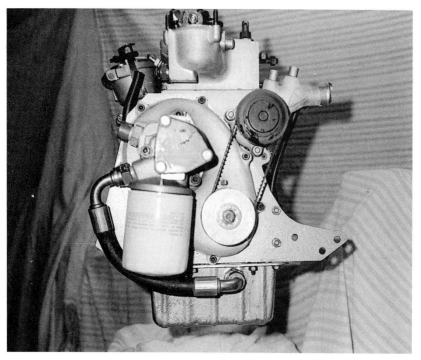

*External oil pump. (Dick Harvey)*

the motor. This involves storing the lubricant in a remote tank rather than in the sump beneath the engine, then pumping the oil out of the tank

through the engine and back into the tank (see Fig. 16). The dry sump pump is again

*Breather pipe running from original fuel pump drive opening to rocker box. (Dick Harvey)*

mounted on a modified timing case and driven off the front of the camshaft, although it is possible to adapt the standard case by fitting a 1 in thick alloy plate to the front of it, but of course this adds weight and looks rather untidy. (Such a plate may also be used on the Fiesta pump wet sump set-up.) Once popular, dry sumping is less so now, for although it is very efficient and eliminates surge under hard cornering, the system is relatively heavy, involves bulky pipework, and is more expensive than wet sumping. Competitive front-engined campaigner Pete Knipe for one remains a devotee of the dry sump, but when it is considered that in his quest for speed and balance his DNC is left-hand drive with motor lying virtually on its side, the benefits of this form of oil feed become obvious.

A third option is to use a wet sump arrangement (Fig. 17) with a dry sump pump's pressure section, but with the scavenge section blocked off, mounted on a special timing case. As with a full dry sump system, a remote filter is necessary. These need to be plumbed in carefully and correctly, as many have found to their cost (see Fig. 18). Otherwise oil pressure, although fine in the garage and when warming up in the paddock, will take a dive when the engine is fully extended, and then it's blow-up time.

Finally, where space does not allow a pump to be mounted on the front of the engine, as is the case on the mid-engined Darvi of Mick Harris and SS Reliant of Bob Simpson, it is possible to employ a Mini oil pump fitted to a Reliant pump housing and driven off the

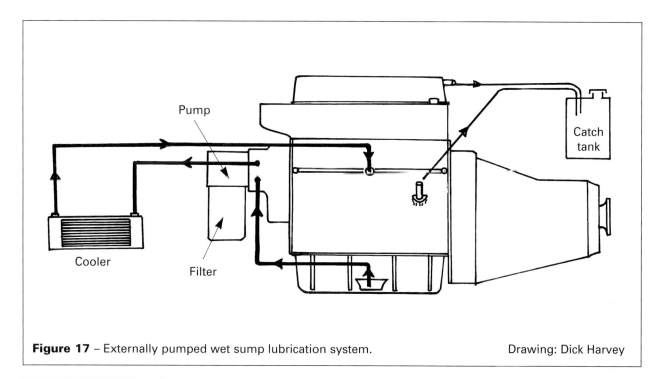

**Figure 17** – Externally pumped wet sump lubrication system.          Drawing: Dick Harvey

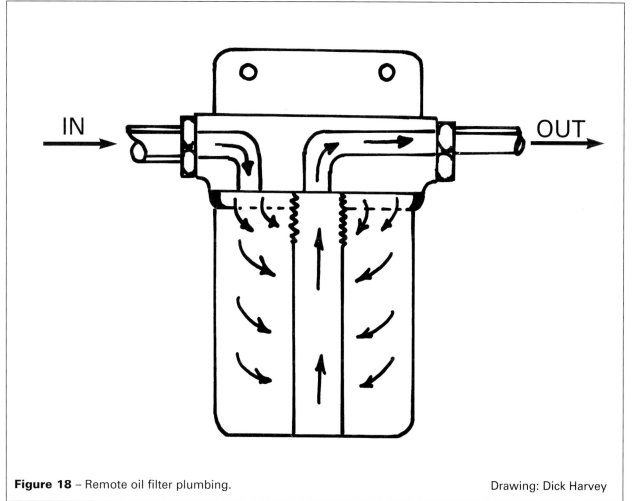

**Figure 18** – Remote oil filter plumbing.          Drawing: Dick Harvey

front of the camshaft or crank-shaft by a toothed belt via a modified timing case. The gearing will differ between cam or crank drive, it generally being a 1:1 and 2:1 reduction respectively. Purpose-built oil pumps are also available, at a price, from Pace Products, and they too can be belt-driven. A remote filter and suitably adjusted pressure-relief valve within the block complete this technique.

For most engine builders the front-mounted Ford pump makes most sense. However it is important to decide upon the lubrication system before any other work is ever begun.

# CYLINDER BLOCK

Whilst Reliant have never looked unfavourably upon the competition user, 850 blocks are not cheap items. Hence a used example is the common basis for a racing engine build, and is often to be found lurking beneath a coating of dirty oil in a muddy corner of a breaker's yard.

Once you have carried it triumphantly home, the first step in its preparation for the rigours of competition is to steam-clean and bead-blast it, having first removed everything removable, including cylinder liners, studs, and oil way and gallery plugs. Then, once stripped and clean, the block must be carefully examined for corrosion and cracks. Figure 19 shows common trouble spots.

## Block trouble spot no. 1

Viewed from the back of the block, it will be noted that the rocker-shaft oil feed from the camshaft bearing is very close to the tapped hole for the top right-hand gearbox mounting

bolt. If the thread strips or has been helicoiled, oil leaks can occur here. Occasionally the thread is sound but it still leaks, as cracks can appear between the threaded hole and the rocker-shaft oil feed drilling, and being under pressure, a little oil goes a long way. The trick fix is to drill down from the block face to just above the camshaft bearing and press in a length of small-bore aluminium tubing.

## Block trouble spot no. 2

Viewed from within, the rocker-shaft oil feed can be seen towards the top left of the block's rear face, and this is prone to corrosion. Again, drilling and the insertion of an aluminium tube is the cure. The first time Dick Harvey and Mick Harris experienced such corrosion was a rather messy affair. Whilst giving a freshly built engine an initial run in the garage, they lifted the swirl-pot cap to check water circulation. To their horror the duo were confronted with grey-brown froth which proceeded to pour out everywhere, even when the engine was switched off. Oil under pressure mixed nicely with water by the action of a water pump forms a wonderful emulsion. Add a little steam and you have froth, lots of it. It took two days to clean out the car, and this was the result of corrosion in a second-hand block.

## Block trouble spot no. 3

Taking a section through the block, there are two problems to look out for. The first is corrosion in the water-jacket. As the oil feed to the centre main and camshaft bearings is just below the jacket, such corrosion, often caused by a lack of anti-freeze in the system, can

**Figure 19** – Block trouble spots. A: Viewed from gearbox end of block exterior, arrow shows where thread may strip or cracks may occur, causing leaks from rocker-shaft oil feed; B: Block rear face viewed from inside, with arrow showing where corrosion may occur and cause leakage of oil from rocker-shaft feed into water-jacket; C: Section through centre of block with upper arrow indicating main oil feed just below water-jacket. Corrosion here will allow water into oil. Lower arrow points at an area to be checked carefully for cracks, which can result in uneven or no oil pressure; D: View through block showing where liner locates in bore. Arrows indicate danger areas where corrosion can occur leading to water seeping into the oil.

Drawing: Dick Harvey

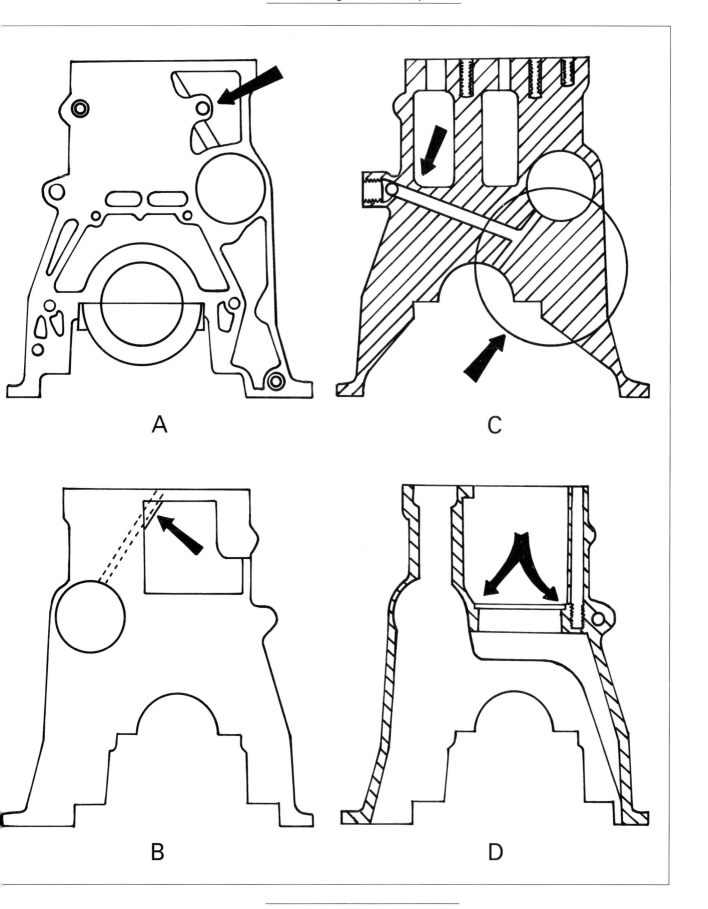

A

C

B

D

result in oil under pressure entering the water. Once again, sleeving with a tube can be the answer, or better still fill the base of the water-jacket with Devcon epoxy, which is a strong metal filler.

The second problem which can occur is cracking between main and camshaft bearings, which can spread up into the water-jacket. This is usually a result of the block flexing, quite common with 750s which employed bent-wire crankshafts. It is less so, but not unknown, with 850s. They have counter-weighted crankshafts but bigger main-bearing journals than earlier engines, therefore there is less metal about at this point in the block. A cracked block is scrap.

## Block trouble spot no. 4

Taking a section through the bore, which houses the liner within the block, corrosion can occur actually within the bore itself. As this will allow water into the sump, and there is no effective cure, the block should be scrapped. Corrosion is quite common in second-hand blocks around the top of the bores. This causes the liners not to seal properly and again water will enter the sump. This can be rectified by building up the spigots with Devcon. This epoxy-filled compound is immensely strong, and can even be machined when cured. Whether there is corrosion present or not, it is quite a good idea to fill the water-jacket up with Devcon to just below the liners. This not only prevents corrosion, it may also add to block stiffness. Not a cheap material, but it certainly works.

Other items worthy of scrutiny are all threads, to be repaired with helicoils if neces-sary. Main-bearing threads should not be helicoiled: when they have been, variable oil pressure and other problems have been observed, most probably as a result of thread flutter. A favourite thread for stripping is the one above the water pump. This is a blind hole into which a $3/8$ in UNC threaded stud is inserted of shorter length than the other head studs, rather than the longer $3/8$ in UNC used elsewhere on the top of the block. If a longer stud is used in error it bottoms out and wrecks the thread. Camshaft bearings should be replaced where needed, and the main bearing alignment checked and the block line-bored if required.

To improve oil circulation, lubricant is re-routed back into the engine mid-way along the main gallery through the side of the block, rather than through the front as standard. This provides the main bearings with a more direct feed. An aluminium boss for oil unions should be welded to the block because, whilst it is perfectly possible to drill and tap $1/4$ BSP (British Standard pipe) in the side of the block and use a $1/4$/$1/2$ in double male fitting as a union onto which the $1/2$ in BSP fitting from the $1/2$ in oil pipe may be connected, it takes two spanners, one on the union nut and the other on the oil pipefitting nut, to tighten the joint. It is tempting to use just one, on the outer nut, and this can tear the fitting from the block. Safer by far is to weld a drilled and tapped $3/8$ in aluminium boss to the side of the block onto which a $3/8$/$1/2$ BSP male fitting is screwed to take an oil hose. This offers far more resistance to the affections of one-span-nered apes; and whilst you are

at it, have the hole in the block for the now redundant oil filter housing welded up.

Finally, the compression ratio should be raised. There are two ways of doing this: removing metal off the top of the block or from the bottom of the cylinder head. A combination of both is better still. Compression ratio is calculated thus:

$$\frac{\text{swept volume of one cylinder} + \text{cylinder head combustion volume}}{\text{cylinder head combustion volume}}$$

In standard form the Reliant 850 has a compression ratio of 9.5:1. This is typically increased to anything from 11–11.5:1 up to 12:1. As a matter of interest, as much as 14:1 was not unknown when 22 mm restrictors were mandatory. When 750 cc motors were raced on good quality five-star fuel, such a compression ratio was a possible advantage, but today, unless illegal 'rocket fuel' is contemplated, this is no longer the case.

The cylinder liners project .004 in proud of the block deck in standard form, with the pistons .025 in down the bores at Top Dead Centre (TDC). The block and liners should be machined or 'decked' in such a way that the pistons sit higher relative to the top surface of the block, but the liners remain .004 in proud. Typically, about .040 in is removed from the top of the block to allow the piston crowns to sit .015 in above the deck, but the experienced have skimmed as much as .060 in off, to bring the piston .035 in above the deck. This produces a very healthy compression ratio, but a less-than-healthy crunch when piston makes contact with head if the engine is either over-revved or suffers bearing failure, and it allows no margin for repairs.

Any piston position at TDC above deck level requires the use of a competition head gasket. This is .069 in thick rather than the standard .040 in, and costs around twenty quid.

To obtain required racing clearances, the cylinder bores must be honed. In standard form the Reliant piston-bore clearances are pretty tight, and at serious revs, as the pistons expand with heat, seizure will occur very quickly. A gap of .002–.003 in minimum, measured at the skirt, needs to be created between piston and bore liner to avoid such unpleasantness. Honing also ensures that the bores are round. When stored on their sides, one on top of another, 365 days per year, it only takes a distortion of .0001 in per day for an annual deformity of 3–4 thou in old stocks of liners.

## CRANKSHAFT, FLYWHEEL AND CLUTCH ASSEMBLY

Formula regulations require the standard Reliant crankshaft to be retained. Even if brand new, the crank should be crack-tested and carefully examined prior to assembly. Check in particular the radii on the journals, that all oil holes are clear and in the correct places, that big-end and main journals are precisely the size they ought to be, and that the crank is perfectly straight. Mass production is a wonderful thing, but not infallible.

Turning to the flywheel (if you will excuse the shameless pun), it is highly desirable to prevent it coming adrift at serious revs. This is of particular concern to gentleman drivers of 'Clubmans' configuration machinery, whose 'meat and two veg' may well lie directly in the flight path of a flywheel being launched into orbit. Chassis tubes and perhaps a right-hand starter motor of course offer some protection, and an alloy shield inside the transmission tunnel can also be fitted, but it is better to make sure a low-flying lump of metal does not come loose in the first place.

In stock form the flywheel is secured by three setbolts threaded up to their heads and without shanks, and a dowel. When angered, these can shear. Conversion to a six-bolt fixing is the answer, whereby the dowel is replaced and two additional holes are drilled and tapped, to be fitted with three high-tensile shanked bolts.

The flywheel is already quite light, therefore further weight reduction should be limited to the shaving of metal from below the ring gear to remove the step (see Fig. 20). Have the clutch face refaced while you are at it. As the item is cast

*Flywheel six-bolt fixing. Note replacement core plug welded in back of head. (Dick Harvey)*

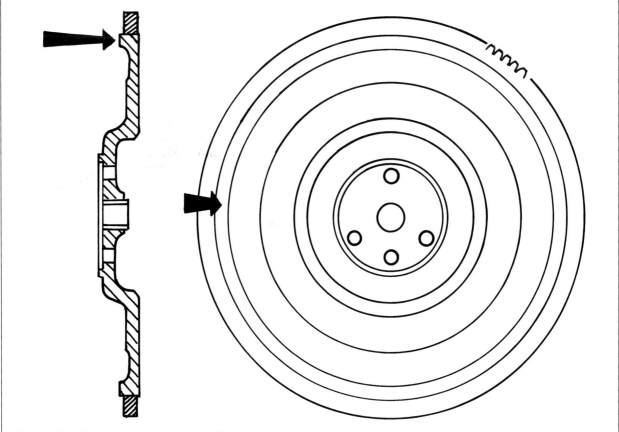

**Figure 20** – Lightening the flywheel. Section through wheel shows, by arrow, the only area where metal may be removed. Drawing of flywheel face again shows the area of the circumference from which metal may be removed. Note the standard three bolt holes and single dowel hole.      Drawing: Dick Harvey

steel, the kind of hole-drilling and slot-cutting associated with the lightening of steel-billeted flywheels is neither advisable nor necessary. Cracking occasionally occurs in two areas – along the clutch face where 'Arnolds' have been riding the clutch, and from the standard bolt and dowel holes outwards. In either case the flywheel should be scrapped.

Over the years, both spring and diaphragm clutch mechanisms have appeared on Reliants. For racing purposes, Imp diaphragm 6¹/₂ in diameter clutches have proved effective and popular. Recently Reliant have been using Ford Fiesta clutches; their employment for racing presents no

problems provided the latest Reliant release bearing is fitted at the same time.

Finally, the complete crankshaft, flywheel and clutch assembly should be professionally balanced.

## CON RODS

Although complete freedom is allowed by the formula rules in the choice of connecting rods, the standard components have proved fully capable of dealing with the enormous acceleration and deceleration loads from the pistons at racing speeds. Straight off the shelf, con-rod sets are reasonably well balanced, but beware of the odd unmatched rod that has found

its way into the parts bin. There can be as much as 40–50 grams difference between a rogue rod and those from a matched set, and it is not possible to remove that amount of metal safely in order to balance such a rod with the others.

Whether the rods to be used are new or second-hand, they do of course require extremely careful checking before use.

Crack testing is worthwhile, especially when using second-hand rods – see Figure 22. A particular area for attention is the shank just under the small-end eye, as one or two have broken at this point over the years. The rod should be checked for straightness and

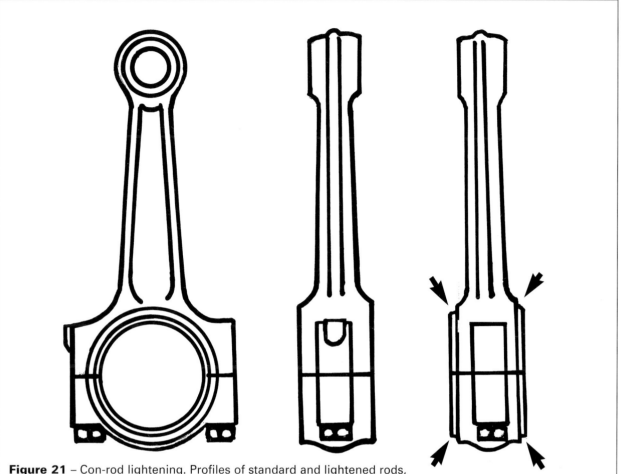

**Figure 21** – Con-rod lightening. Profiles of standard and lightened rods, with arrows indicating where metal may be removed from around big-end eye.                        Drawing: Dick Harvey

**Figure 22** – Checking con rods. For straightness, a big end-sized mandrel is inserted into the big-end eye, then rested vertically on a pair of 'V' blocks, whilst a gudgeon pin is inserted in the opposite end. Distances are now measured with a dial gauge. Rod is then laid between two pairs of 'V' blocks to check for twist.

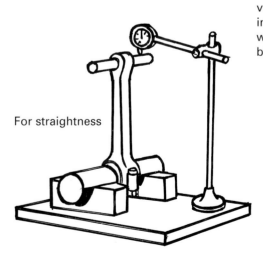

For straightness

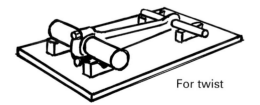

For twist

Drawing: Dick Harvey

*Rods and pistons. (Dick Harvey)*

twist, and all threads must be examined. If less than perfect, the rod should be consigned to the dustbin. Big-end bolts should be new when building a fresh engine, or following bearing failure on a campaigned one; otherwise it is generally safe to re-use bolts. Make sure the threads and the radius between shank and threads are up to scratch. Small-end bushes must be replaced if worn, and in doing so always hone to the correct size. Adjustable reamers don't work. They leave steps which quickly flatten down with use, leaving the new bush looser than the one replaced. As for tab washers, if they can be bent easily into position, what is stopping them being bent out again? So forget them. Instead use turned and chamfered heavy-duty washers under big-end bolt heads.

Rods should be balanced end to end as well as overall, but metal must not be removed from the shanks as this will cause serious weakness.

Finally, should a rod have suffered heavy bearing failure, or show signs of 'blueing'

through previous overheating, you should throw it as far away as your strength will allow.

## PISTONS

As with con rods, pistons are free, and once again the stock items are perfectly adequate for racing. Some people remove too much of the skirt to lighten them, which results in excessive rock and piston slap, particularly as racing clearances allow some movement anyway. Sets tend to be reasonably well balanced off the shelf, but when balancing is carried out, metal should be removed from inside the skirt, definitely not by spot drilling under the piston crown as this causes pistons to crack across the crown. Standard piston rings are satisfactory provided the piston ring grooves are in good condition, otherwise ring flutter then breakage will occur. Circlips must be fitted correctly with sharp edges out, and eyes to the bottom of the groove in the piston. For added security PTFE discs are added to prevent the circlip jumping out of its slot and scoring the bore. See Figure 23.

Piston failure is a fairly rare

occurrence within the formula, which is quite remarkable considering the standard Reliant component is being required to go up and down and stop in between much faster than normal, with a bigger bang and bonfire on top than it was ever designed to withstand. Pistons are very much in the front line of the battle. For this reason many experienced competitors replace them after each season, for when pistons do fail they have a tendency of taking the rest of the engine with them, and pistons are cheaper than engines.

When failure does take place, breakages and cracking occur along the piston surface between number 2 ring and the oil ring, or between numbers 1 and 2 rings. Occasionally pistons have also been known to crack around the crown. Finally, seizure of rings in pistons, and pistons in bores, or at the very least heavy scoring, will result if bores are not honed out sufficiently for racing purposes.

## CAMSHAFTS

We now enter the realms of serious myth and bullshit.

Many are the cams that are available for use in a race-prepared Reliant motor, and provided the cam remains in the manufacturer's original position, retains chain drive, and is the sole means of operating the push-rods and valves, the choice is yours. DNC, Dick Harvey, Mike Kenny, Kent, Piper, Philspeed and others are able to supply race camshafts at a wide range of prices. All of them work perfectly well; only experience can determine whether the characteristics of a particular cam suit

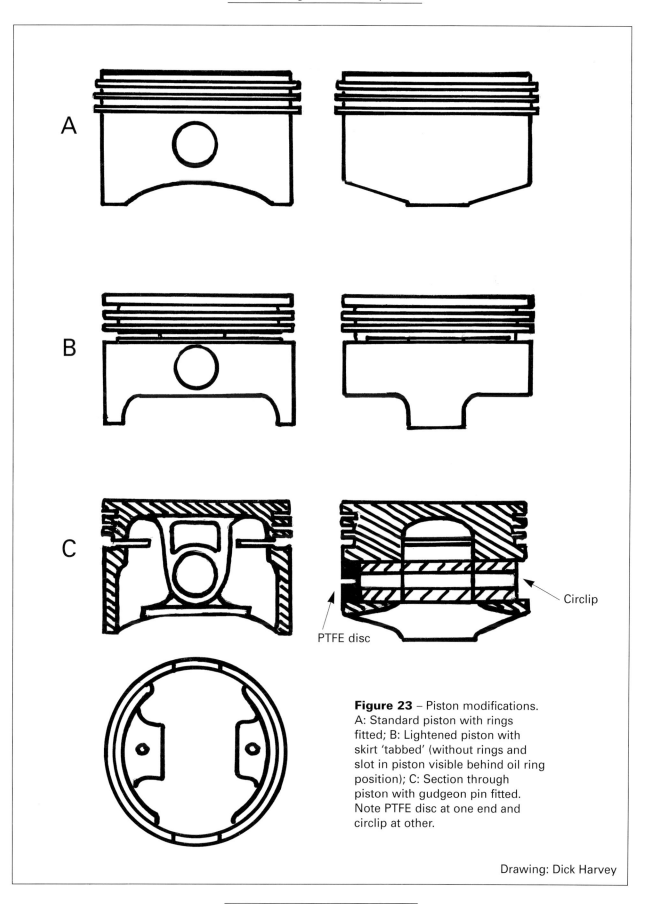

**Figure 23** – Piston modifications. A: Standard piston with rings fitted; B: Lightened piston with skirt 'tabbed' (without rings and slot in piston visible behind oil ring position); C: Section through piston with gudgeon pin fitted. Note PTFE disc at one end and circlip at other.

Circlip

PTFE disc

Drawing: Dick Harvey

your car and you as a driver.

Standard cam followers are fine, but a good tweak is to bore them out to 9/16 in to reduce weight. Some claim the basic Reliant follower to be too small in diameter for racing application, and indeed it is necessary to use the larger BMC 'A' series items if DNC 713 or 714 cams are doing your valve lifting, but in all other applications the stock followers work well. 'A' series followers, as with standard ones, can be lightened. The block will require drilling and reaming to take the bigger diameter, and the camshaft centre-bearing journal must be reduced in width to avoid numbers 4 and 5 followers hitting it.

The standard cam sprocket bolts are 1/4 UNF with 5/16 in diameter shank, fine threaded, and into cast iron – a disaster waiting to happen. These are rather vulnerable so should be replaced by 5/16 UNC HT cap-head bolts, which also have the advantage of extra clearance when the self-aligning drive dog is used.

The regulations require the retention of Reliant's single-row timing chain, and the cam should be timed in accordance with the maker's specifications. If you think you know better you are on your own, chum. To ease timing adjustment it is common to slot the sprocket holes at the front of the cam, around which the chain sits, then secure with a rawl or dowel pin once the timing has been set. Alternative approaches include off-set dowels, as used in Ford tuning, redrilling the sprocket to coincide with its optimum

*Early head with pedestal kit. (Dick Harvey)*

position for a correct setting, or reslotting the groove in the crankshaft sprocket (the slot that locates on the woodruff key).

# CYLINDER HEAD

Head modification is all about improving the breathing of the valves within the combustion chambers, enhancing the flow of gasses through ports, and increasing the compression ratio.

The accompanying illustra-tions (Fig. 24) demonstrate the combustion chamber shaping and porting necessary to achieve maximum efficiency from a Reliant cylinder head. This is a tried and tested approach, but may not be the only one. David Vizard's book *Theory And Practice Of Cylinder Head Tuning* is worthwhile further reading on the subject, containing lots of good formulae. It is a question of deciding

*Modified and standard heads. (Dick Harvey)*

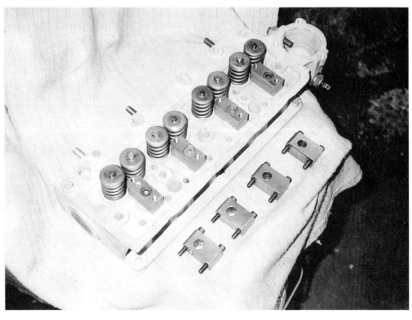

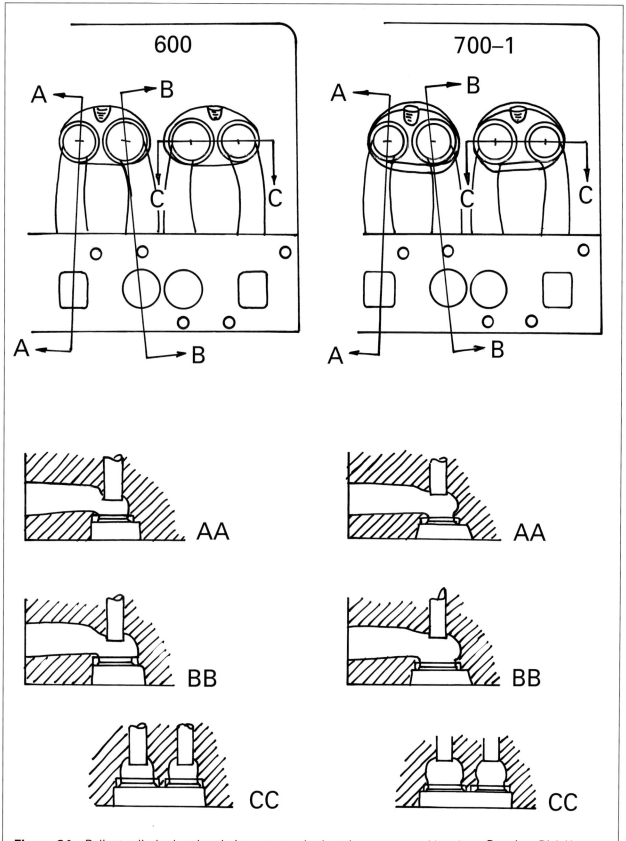

**Figure 24** – Reliant cylinder head variations as standard, and race-prepared head.     Drawing: Dick Harvey

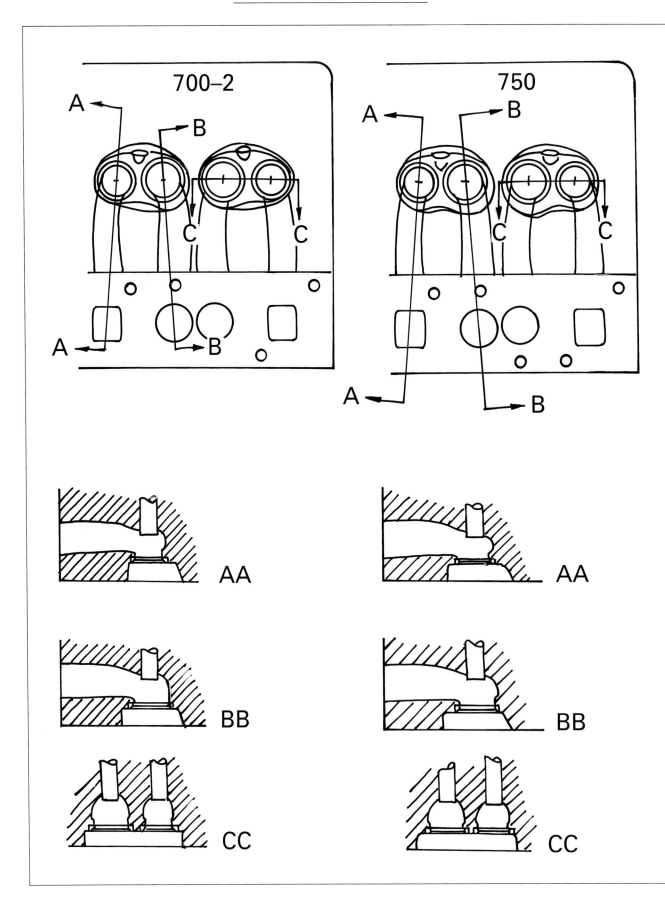

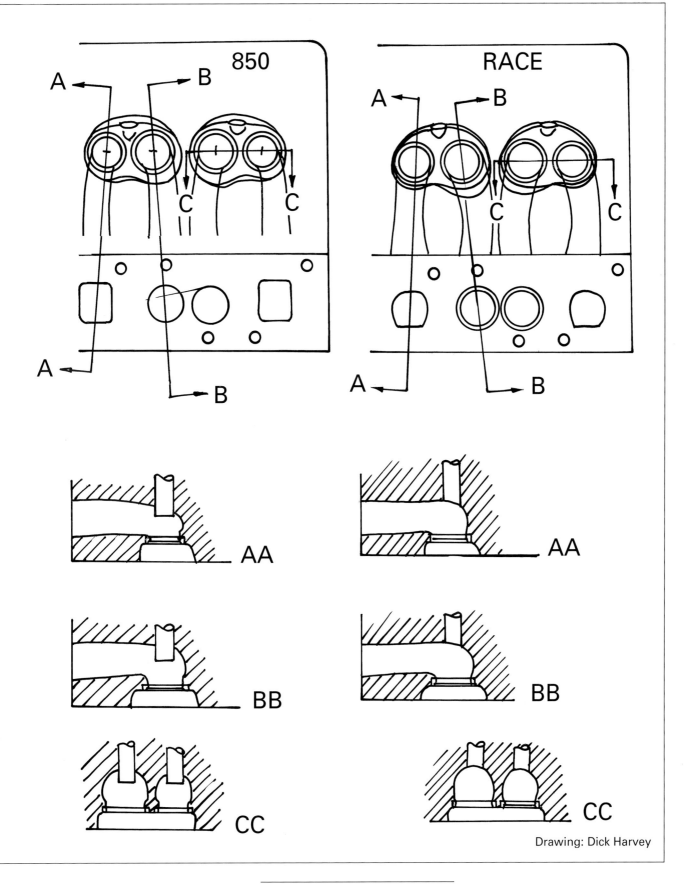

Drawing: Dick Harvey

at what revs you want it all to happen. *Gas Flow In The Internal Combustion Engine* by Annard and Roe is another rich fund of advice, if perhaps less of a right-riveting-read, and contains a valuable discourse on valve seat and port shapes, and valve seat widths.

To raise the compression ratio it is necessary to skim metal from the underside of the head. As mentioned earlier, the removal of metal from the deck of the block also contributes to this process.

As will be explained in more detail when we come to the engine's induction system, a change in the formula's regulations introduced at the beginning of the 1995 season abolished the obligatory 22 mm restrictor.

With a restricted engine, when the regulations permitted only a 22 mm inlet hole to be fitted to the induction system, a 12:1 cr was about right, which probably equates to about 10:1 on a derestricted engine. This is due to the formula for calculating such things, as described earlier, assuming perfect breathing and an ability to fill the combustion chamber fully – an unlikely occurrence on a first-class unrestricted engine, but a virtual impossibility with a restrictor in the inlet manifold.

When valve sizes are considered, big is not necessarily best – a further consequence of a restrictor. Therefore the standard 850 valves at 1.125 in inlet and 1.030 in exhaust were often argued to be large enough to cope with what came at them after being first forced to squeeze through a 7/8 in hole. If the preferred earlier 600 or 700 head was utilized, these valve sizes were actually reduced to 1.100 in and 0.980 in respectively to avoid the need for valve seat replacement. Valve seats can easily be replaced, but 750 guys don't like spending money, and in any case valves that are too big mask valuable breathing space.

With the elimination of the 22 mm restrictor, it might be thought that bigger valves would be beneficial, but only time would tell, for the 1995 season at least. However, at the 750 Motor Club's Annual Formula Discussion in November 1994 it was suggested that standard 850 valve sizes (1.125 inlet and 1.030 exhaust) be the maximum allowed in order to contain costs, and this might perhaps become a part of the formula's regulations.

Bronze valve guides are found to be stronger than the standard cast-iron guides, used to wear better prior to the use of super leaded petrol, and may be combined with Ford-sourced double-valve springs. These work one inside the other, and are wound in opposite directions. The stronger outer spring combined with the softer inner spring provides a system which is strong and resistant to bounce, up to engine speeds in excess of 9000 rpm. Bronze guides also allow a step to be incorporated at the top to prevent them falling down into the combustion chamber.

Rocker gear also differs between early and later heads. On the 850, valves open to a greater degree relative to the push-rod – 1.25:1 – than is the case with the 600 and 700 heads' 1.06:1. This represents 19 per cent more lift on a given camshaft, and mounting holes for the rocker assembly at variance, so fitting later rocker gear to an earlier head is not the work of a moment. Unless, that is, you are the proud possessor of a Dick Harvey pedestal kit which, for the paltry sum of £55, will perform this miracle of modern engineering for you. Prior to the use of the pedestal kit it was necessary to drill and plug an early head to move the 850 rockers over. But if that head later became damaged, all this hard work was wasted.

The free-revving nature and generous clearances of a racing engine require the crankcase and its internals to be able to breathe well, thus ensuring free oil drainage, a happier life for various oil seals, and the elimination of power loss from pistons working against an air-oil pressure build-up. To achieve this a 1/2 in internal diameter rubber pipe should be run from the left side of the block, where the original mechanical fuel pump drive opening is located, up to the rocker box, both to ventilate the crankcase and to return displaced lubricant to the engine, and a 1/2 in bore pipe run from the side of the crankcase to the catch tank. From the rocker cover a 3/4 in rubber or clear plastic pipe must discharge into a clear plastic catch tank, minimum capacity 2 litres, for which a windscreen washer bottle or DIY store turps container are popular choices. The proficiency of such an arrangement is a favourite target for eagle-eyed scrutineers, rightly concerned about oil finding its way onto track surfaces.

Finally, don't forget to weld in place a 1/8 in thick replacement aluminium core plug at the back of the cylinder head. Made of steel, the original's expansion rate differs from that of the alloy head, and it has

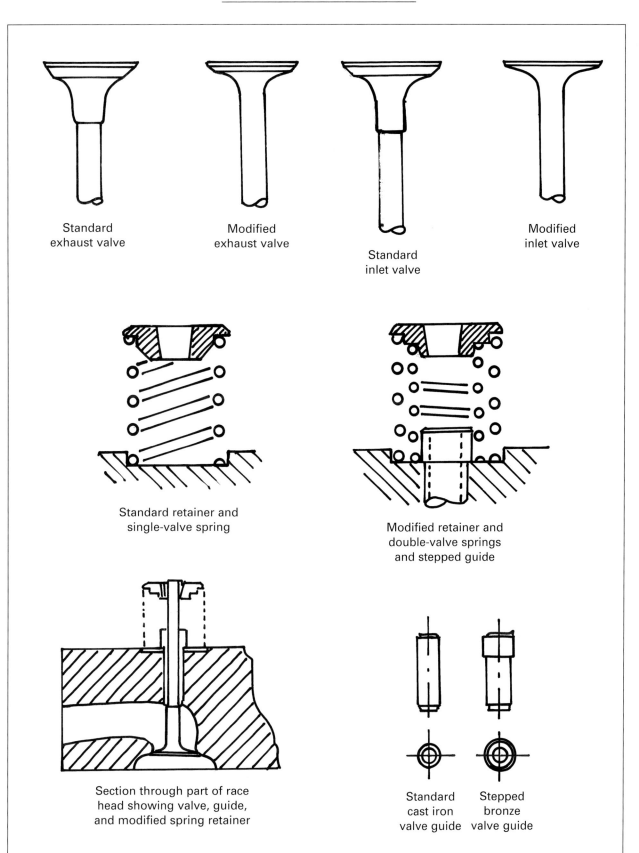

**Figure 25** – Valves, guides and springs.

Drawing: Dick Harvey

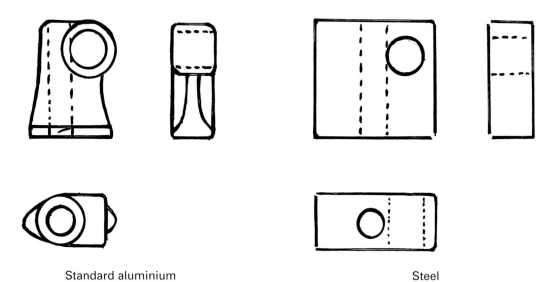

Standard aluminium

Steel
(straight replacement)

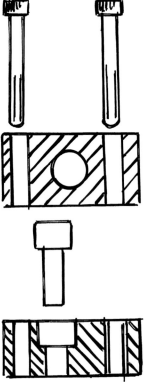

**Figure 26** – Pedestal
modifications and rocker
gear lightening.

2 Piece steel
(for use with 850 rockers
on earlier heads)

STANDARD

Side view

View from above

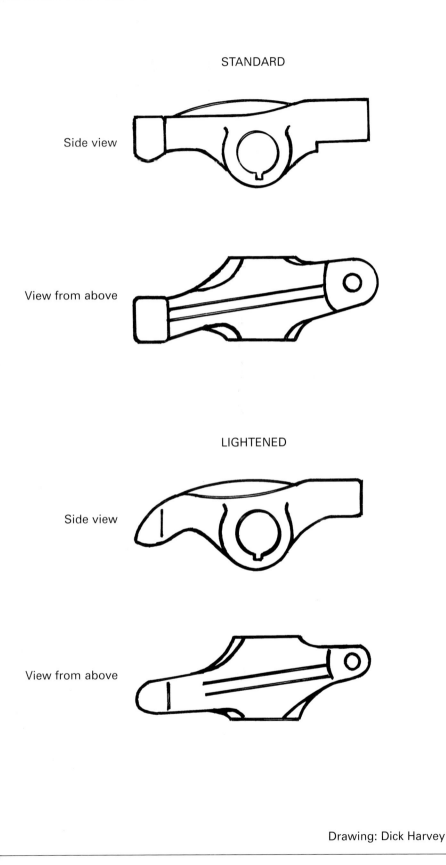

LIGHTENED

Side view

View from above

Drawing: Dick Harvey

been known for the plug to pop out in the heat of combat. Experience suggests that a driver's lap times are detrimentally affected when a sudden surge of very hot water hits him directly in the nuts.

When, in 1966, Reliant power units were first allowed into the 750 Formula, the rules required them to run with 22 mm restrictors in their air induction systems to limit power and thus equate them with the Austin-powered cars still much in use. In time, Reliant engines became mandatory, but the restrictor remained, it being now argued that this curb upon horsepower led to reliability, people with bottomless pockets being unable to build demon motors, and inexpensive and close racing.

Whilst the restrictor may have achieved some of its objectives, it also introduced an element of 'black art' into getting the most out of the strangled Reliant motor, with success on the track frequently rewarding those who had got their inlet manifolding absolutely spot on. Now it is only fair that such labours should be rewarded, but of late the gap between those in the know and those who were not was widening to such an extent that it was not unusual for there to be a nine seconds a lap difference between the times set by those on the front of the grid and those at the back.

This situation was not good for 750 racing, as an engine that did not respond to conventional tuning methods due to the artificial restriction of its air intake was leading to disillusionment amongst many of the drivers, and little encouragement for new competitors to enter the fray. Following lengthy and passionate debate over a number of seasons, the 750 Motor Club took the momentous decision to discard the restrictor in February 1995, and the notice amending the regulations appears in Appendix A.

## CARBURETTORS

In the early days, 600 cc and 750 cc Reliant engines were typically raced with a down-draught 321MPE Weber on a down-draught Reliant manifold, although others, including SU, were used by some. Then the Dellorto FZD semi-inclined, single-choke, side-draught car-

*Side radiator, Darvi 91-D. Note cooling system piping to swirl pot and carburettor air box. (Dick Harvey)*

burettor, mounted on a cast-alloy manifold, was 'essential wear' among 750 racers for some years, with a 22 mm restrictor in the carb. Then onto the scene came the Marrow, complete with Weber 40 DCOE carburettor with one of its twin chokes blanked off, and it flew. So everyone followed suit, and now most people use either a Weber or Dellorto equivalent.

As yet it is too early to evaluate the impact of derestriction fully. Only a couple of seasons' racing will do that. However, it is likely that experimentation with larger-choke carburettors and different cams and valve sizes will have only a modest effect upon power output due to rev limitations and realistic valve size constraints remaining unchanged. In other words, the airflow bottleneck has merely been moved from the area of

the carb/inlet manifold along to the cylinder head porting, and it is physically impossible to make that much bigger. The traffic jam has moved further down the road.

Initial impressions are that a derestricted engine is more eager to rev, and delivers its power more readily in the low to mid rev ranges. But caution must be exercised as the revs build up in top, for although the power will keep on increasing, so will the likelihood of serious damage, should the same rev limits respected in the days of the restrictor not continue to be observed.

## COOLING

A standard water pump may be used with heater outlet blanked off and the standard V-belt replaced by a toothed belt and

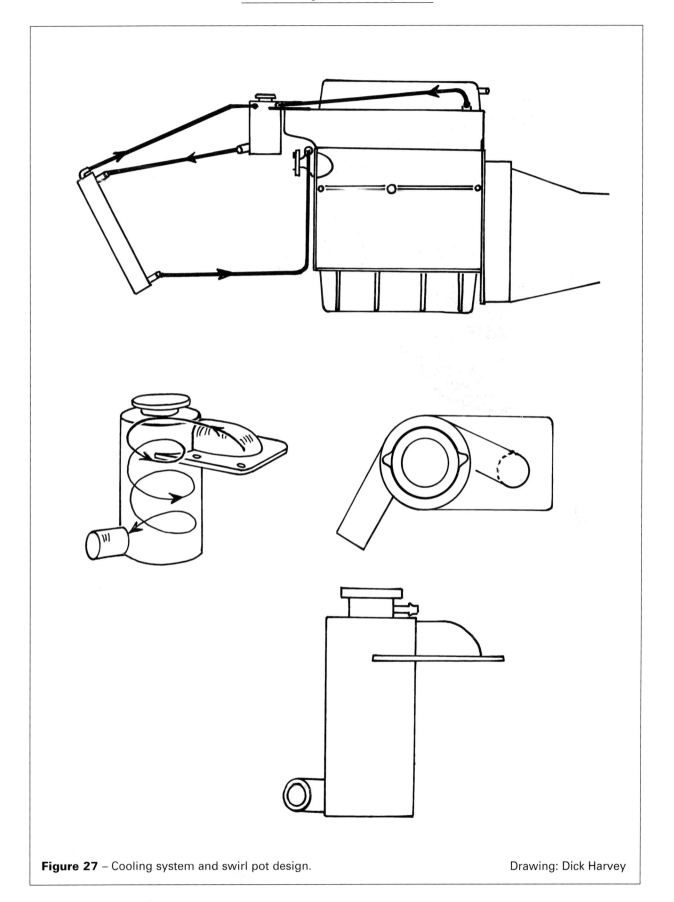

**Figure 27** – Cooling system and swirl pot design.                    Drawing: Dick Harvey

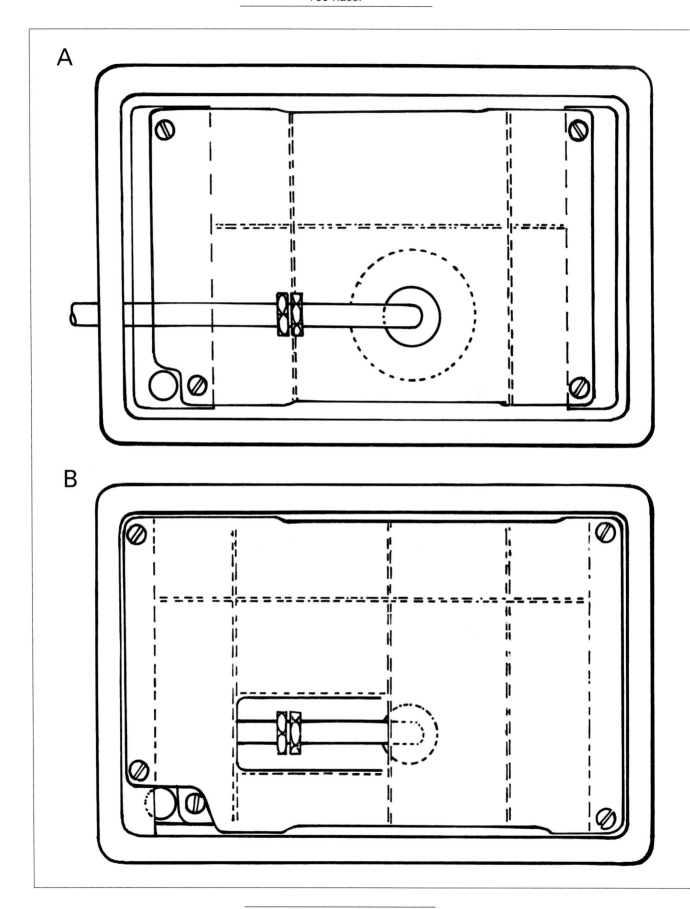

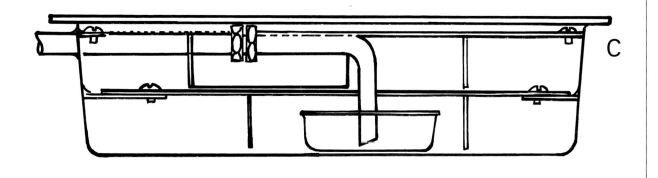

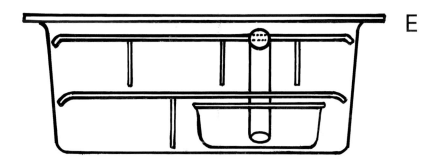

A – Plan view of sump with pick-up and lower baffle plate fitted
B – Plan view of sump with upper baffle plate fitted
C – Side view of baffles and pick-up
D – Side view of sump pan showing permanent mounting plates for baffles (fully welded and sealed to sump to prevent passage of oil)
E – End view of baffles and pick-up

**Figure 28** – Wet sump baffling.                                    Drawing: Dick Harvey

pulley driven by the toothed belt pulley from the crankshaft (see Fig. 27). The pump is slowed down by choice of belt sizes, a 10–20 per cent reduction being necessary when crank-driven to reduce the possibility of cavitation (the introduction of air pockets) into the water system. To bleed the head a pipe should be run from the heater take-off at the back of the head to the top of the swirl pot.

Mini radiators are popular when a nose location is chosen, though aluminium rads from Metros, Golfs, etc., have also been used. But a word of warning. Many have an open matrix, as they are fitted in the donor vehicle in a shroud with cooling fan, and are designed to allow air to pass freely through them under normal operating conditions. This does not provide sufficient cooling when racing. A way round the problem is to incline the rad. forward by approximately 30 per cent so that air must slow to pass through it and thus absorb more heat. Side radiator locations, as used on the Darvis of Messrs Harvey and Harris, are more appropriate for open-matrix rads as the airflow is slower when it comes in contact with them. Dick and Mick favour aluminium Fiesta units.

## SUMP BAFFLING

The standard Reliant sump is as much use as a chocolate teapot, and serious baffling is needed to prevent oil surge. See Figure 28.

## EXHAUST SYSTEM

Most popular is the four-pipes-into-one arrangement, it being argued that this is the least restrictive. A 4–2–1 system is generally considered to be more suited to road or rally use where torque is of greater importance. Yet a high-revving 850 can always use some help in the torque department, particularly as most circuits contain some slow bends, therefore the use of a 4–2–1 should not be discounted.

Until the last few seasons the popular sizes for the 4–1 system were 28 in long primaries of $1^1/8$ in OD 18 swg running into $1^1/2$–$1^5/8$ in OD 18 swg tail pipes, but the tendency now is to go for 28 in long, $1^1/4$ in OD 18 swg primaries running into $1^5/8$–$1^3/4$ in OD tail pipes. A 4–2–1 system can be quite effective with $1^1/8$ in OD primaries, $1^1/4$ in OD secondaries, running into a tail pipe of $1^1/2$–$1^5/8$ in OD.

Noise is one of the key targets for the invective of those who criticize motor sport (sadly they appear to be increasing in number). Therefore the sport's governing body in Great Britain, the RAC Motor Sports Association, imposes strict rules upon silencing, and tests are carried out regularly at race meetings. Club racing cars, with the exception of certain Historic machinery, are not expected to exceed 110 decibels (measured on the A scale) when a reading is taken at a distance of 0.5 m from the exhaust outlet, with the engine at three-quarters of maximum revs.

To meet these requirements a reasonably large-diameter silencer is necessary, and a 5–6 in diameter, 10–12 in long box with $1^3/4$ in diameter tail pipe, is about right. The silencer should be repackable, and filled with Rockwall insulation material. Silencers are commercially available but you can also build your own – see Figure 30.

Many are the wheezes that have been employed to outwit the innocent noise inspector, and one of the more imaginative was successfully executed some years ago on the speed hillclimb scene by future British champion David Grace. Young Mr Grace, then in his formative years and at the wheel of a Mallock, hit on the idea of having two tail pipes, one a dummy prominently exiting from one side of the car, the other more functionally but less obviously exiting from the other. For much of the season this stratagem worked a treat, officials dutifully pointing their microphones at the dummy pipe and taking impressively legal readings. Then one day, at the Hitchings brothers' farm course of Gurston Down in Wiltshire, the noise test was conducted in the middle of a straw-strewn farmyard, where the marshals were bemused to witness hay being hurled mysteriously into the air from the opposite side of the Mallock to the one which had the testing equipment trained on it.

## BATTERY AND IGNITION

Though battery and electrically powered starter motor are mandatory, an on-board charging system is not. Therefore both weight and power-sapping pulley drives can be saved by not carrying an alternator. A motor cycle battery of at least 18 amp hours and preferably 24 amp hours, positioned to optimize weight distribution, should see a car through a full race meeting if properly charged in advance, and is significantly lighter than a car bat-

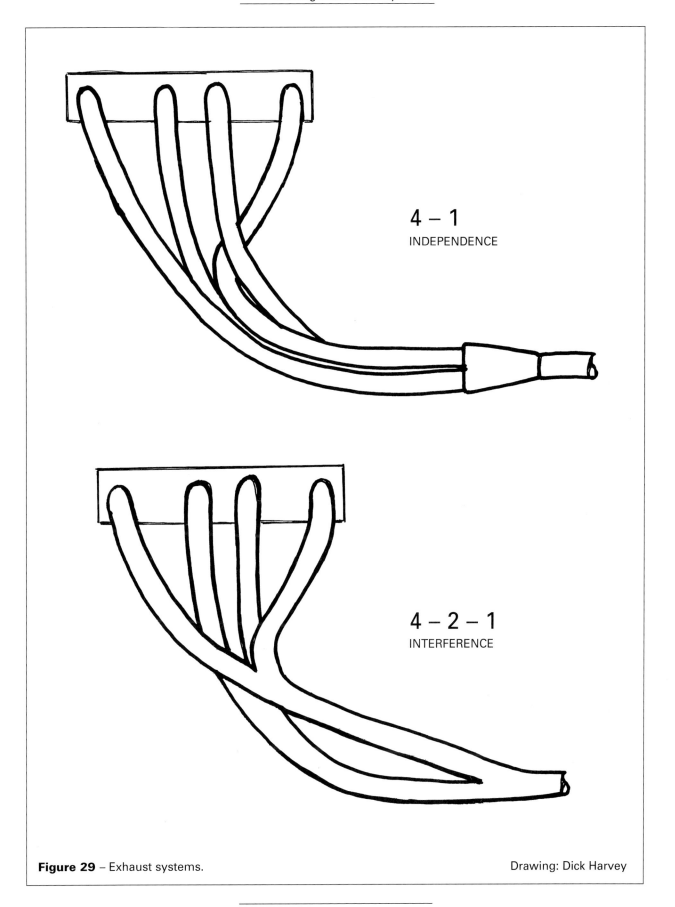

4 – 1
INDEPENDENCE

4 – 2 – 1
INTERFERENCE

**Figure 29** – Exhaust systems.

Drawing: Dick Harvey

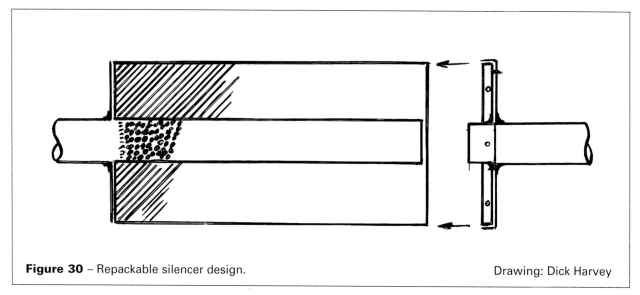

**Figure 30** – Repackable silencer design.                    Drawing: Dick Harvey

tery. Sealed gel versions are best, as enthusiastic kerb-hopping during hot laps can loosen plates inside wet-cell models, leaving the hapless driver suddenly halted out on the circuit with no electrics. They are also lighter, and do not require the acid-proof sealing boxes often required for lead-acid type batteries.

The standard Reliant distributor is Mini-derived, therefore upgrading it to Cooper S specification is advisable for race use. Some convert to an electronic system and this works well, but if it ever stops working, it's curtains. Good old-fashioned points are simple and repairable, and best of all they are cheap. There are also strong off-the-shelf versions with a wiser spring allowing 10,000 rpm, should it be required!

NGK plugs cannot be accused of being cheap, but they are very good and last forever in a 750F car. The B8EV is the grade to use.

## LUBRICANTS

And here is your starter for ten: What has a racing Reliant engine in common with a diesel? Harvey, High Wycombe, reading 'Autosport', presses his buzzer. 'Both have high compressions, run at high temperatures and exert high loads on their bearings.' And he gets a bonus point for adding, 'So why pay exotic prices for exotic racing oils when what goes into Farmer Giles's tractor will work equally well in a racing 750?'

One such oil is the 20/50 XHD (Extra Heavy Duty) Ringfree from the Shropshire-based family company of Morris Oils, available direct or from motor factors. There are of course others, Shell Rotella being one.

With the recent disappearance of five-star petrol from garage forecourts, Super Unleaded has of late been the chosen tipple for pump-fuelled racing cars due to its octane superiority over leaded four-star. Apart from allegedly being bad for your health, it is also unkind to bronze valve guides subjected to a constant flow of fuel without a lead lubricant, and they eventually suffer wear. Therefore a substitute such as RedeX should be added

to each fill-up.

Two gallons are normally sufficient for a 10–15-lap race. The tank should be made of light alloy, and positioned advantageously within the chassis to optimize its weight contribution. A remote, rubber-mounted, solid-state electric fuel pump – generically known as a Facet – should be employed to pump the go-juice to the carburettors. As these are capable of pressures as high as 6–7 psi, an adjustable pressure regulator may be necessary, to be installed in-line. Typically, a side-draught Weber DCOE or equivalent Dellorto DHLA will require 3–3$^1/_2$ psi.

## POWER OUTPUT

Off the shelf, a Reliant 850 produces around 40 bhp, and can be revved to a safe 6,000 rpm, with a daring 7,000 not out of the question. A healthy racing unit will push out about 65–70 bhp, rev safely to 8,500 rpm, and occasionally see over 9,000 in the heat of combat.

Now 65 horses – and we speak of flywheel figures – are hardly going to rip chunks of tarmac from the track when the rear wheels make contact, but in a car weighing 7 cwt (356 kg) or less, we are still talking 186 bhp per ton, which makes even a Sierra Cosworth look sick.

With the frontal area of a starved budgie and the lines of a well-groomed panther, a 750F car can hit 100 mph (160.9 km/h) and beyond along a suitable straight. This velocity, combined with downforce-inducing aerodynamics and slick tyres, allows lap-speed averages of 83.96 mph (135 km/h) around the Silverstone National Circuit, 83.66 mph (134.6 km/h) at Snetterton, and an amazing 93.1 mph (149.8 km/h) at Mallory Park.

To put a 750 racing car's capabilities into perspective, let us compare sample Pembrey circuit lap times, as published below in 1994 *Autosport* race reports.

Yes indeed, speed freaks, the motor from the modest Robin can really be made to fly.

| | |
|---|---|
| 750 Formula | 1 min 4.80 sec |
| Formula Vee | 1 min 4.90 sec |
| National Saloon Car Cup | |
|   Class A Ford Escort Cosworth | 1 min 4.11 sec |
|   Class B BMW M3 | 1 min 7.52 sec |
| Pirelli Porsche Production Championship | |
|   Class C | 1 min 8.70 sec |
|   Class D | 1 min 12.20 sec |

## Chapter 8

# RUBBER, LEATHER AND OTHER RUNNING GEAR

**O**ne of motor racing's sad truths is that the little things cost the most. Fifty quid may buy a running motor, but a set of decent instruments, a top-quality safety harness, or a cool-looking quick-release steering wheel, can each knock a £100 or £200 hole in the old piggy bank. Yet costs are containable by careful shopping.

The purchase of a cheap donor car is one source of parts, the price of the vehicle inevitably being a fraction of the value of the sum of its parts.

A browse through the enthusiast motoring press – *Autosport, Cars and Car Conversions* and *Motoring News* in particular – or through such motor club magazines as the *750 Bulletin*, can be rewarded by bargains among the classified advertisements. Motor racing enthusiasts are natural hoarders, but from time to time they clear out their lofts and lock-ups to make way for more junk.

Then there are such Aladdin's caves as Jester Racing at Chertsey, who break racing cars for their still serviceable specialist parts. Here high-quality, and often little-used, components from the professional formulae can be bought for a fraction of their cost new.

Of course, as will shortly be revealed, not all 750 cc running gear is specialist tackle. Some road car parts are perfectly adequate for racing application, in which case a visit to your local previously owned, damaged vehicle reallocation specialist, or scrap man as he is sometimes known, could produce the very item you are looking for.

So what's needed?

## TRANSMISSION

Formula rules state that the gearbox must not contain more than four forward gears, with an operable reverse gear capable of being engaged by the driver while normally seated. Ratios are free.

In theory there are lots of gearboxes that would suit, but in reality there is nothing to be gained by using anything other than the standard Reliant unit, with modified internals. This box has an alloy casing and is therefore light. It is also strong, readily available and naturally fits straight into the back of the Reliant engine. BMC gearboxes have occasionally been used in the past, sourced from the Austin A35 or MG Midget, but that was generally because a hard-up constructor just happened to have one lying in a corner of his garage, rather than a quest for any material advantage.

Close-ratio gears – to keep the engine turning at its most powerful revolutions during gear changes – and straight cut for strength, are available from such specialist manufacturers as Edmonton Tool & Engineering Company in London, and JoMo Racing in the Midlands, and three alternative sets of ratios can be supplied for the Reliant box. A typical ratio set would be 2.58:1, 1.56:1, 1.19:1, and a 1:1 direct top gear.

By taking some metal off the top, the Reliant gear-lever can be drastically shortened to provide a short positive shift. A nice round alloy gear-knob can complete the job, but that's a matter of personal preference.

Worth remembering is the fact that reverse is to be found alongside first in the forward left position on 750 gearboxes, and in the excitement of sitting on a start line awaiting the green light, confusion can occur. Some years ago Iain Sclanders went from pole position to last place at the start of a race at Lydden Hill when he selected reverse rather than first in his DNC3. Interestingly (or perhaps not), Sclanders' car was fondly known as Smokey Joe to one and all, because one day at Snetterton the DNC sprang an oil leak which ignited on contact with the hot exhaust, but nobody, including the hapless driver, noticed the difference for some laps.

On later 850 gearboxes reverse is in the back left position alongside second, with fairly strong spring protection, but a metal guard may be considered, particularly if a remote change is proposed, as with a mid-engined car. On the latest Reliant box reverse is back right, next to fourth. This offers endless possibilities to the heavy-handed hard charger.

The choice of rear axle is free but it must be solid. With the motor industry's current devotion to front-wheel-drive, it is necessary to look towards some fairly elderly benefactors when seeking a propshaft-driven live back axle. Obvious candidates are Ford and BMC, with the Cortina and Escort, the Austin A30 and A35, Morris 1000, Austin Healey Sprite and MG Midget. However the BMC axles and differentials have two notable advantages over the Ford items: they weigh less, and there are a greater number of cw & p (crown wheel and pinion) ratios available.

As a result of the BMC axle finding its way into everything from commercial pick-up trucks and vans to small sports cars, seven diff ratios were fit-ted over the years: 3.7:1, 3.9:1, 4.2:1, 4.5:1, 4.9:1, 5.1:1 and 5.3:1. Ever since the Austin-powered days, all these ratios have been tried, but today many drivers manage with just two alternatives. The 4.2 is suit-able for most British circuits, with the lower-geared 4.5 pop-ular for tighter tracks such as Lydden, Pembrey, and possibly the Silverstone National course with its tortuous Luffield com-plex of bends. Perversely, because revs equal power, par-ticularly when applied to a restricted engine, some brave souls fit a 4.5 or even a 4.9 diff for a circuit such as Snetterton, the aim being to extend their engines fully, almost to the point of going ballistic, when given some beans along Revett Straight. But when you consider that more than 8,000 rpm can be seen on a tachometer by running a 4.2 at the Norfolk track, any more revs with a lower cw & p can only bring on an early engine rebuild or a broom and shovel for the scat-tered internals of your pains-takingly assembled power unit.

Prior to installing the axle in a 'Clubmans'-style car, it is stan-dard practice to cut 3 in (75 mm) off the left-hand side. By offsetting the diff in this way (see Fig. 31), the propshaft run-ning from the offset engine and gearbox is allowed to operate in a reasonably direct manner. Such an arrangement also pro-vides extra room for fat drivers' bums to be installed within the right side of the chassis.

A Morris 1000 axle facilitates this arrangement rather well, for by shortening the left side by 3 in an A30, A35 or Midget drive shaft can be used on that end, being 3 in shorter than the Morris 1000 shaft.

Finally, there is no need to use expensive silicone trans-mission oils. EP80 grade, good-quality road oils from A.P., Castrol or Girling are fine.

## WHEELS AND TYRES

In a formula where grip is always going to exceed power, it is important not to fit wheels and tyres that are too wide. To do so will result in speed being lost through corners due to tyre scrub, ponderous handling, and aerodynamic drag down straights.

A 13 in diameter wheel of 6–8 in rim width is recom-mended, and indeed the cur-rent mandatory 'control' tyre renders such a choice essential. Alloy wheels are also recom-mended as they are strong, reduce unsprung weight and aid brake cooling, unlike their steel equivalents. Although pricey new, alloys can be had for half price or less second-hand, but avoid wheels that may have been used for rally-ing. Ten miles on a flat tyre against the clock through Kielder Forest does little for the sealing properties of alloy rims. There are many makes to choose from, but Revolutions seem to strike an impressive blend of looks, quality and price.

During the early years of 750 racing, Austin Seven-based spe-cials raced on skinny wheels covered by any rubber drivers could lay their hands on includ-ing worn remoulds. They were treaded, and ran in all track conditions, rain or shine. Later, fairly unsophisticated treaded racing tyres were adopted, the classic Dunlop D3 'Green Spot', often handed down by Formu-la Fordsters, being a fashion-able choice.

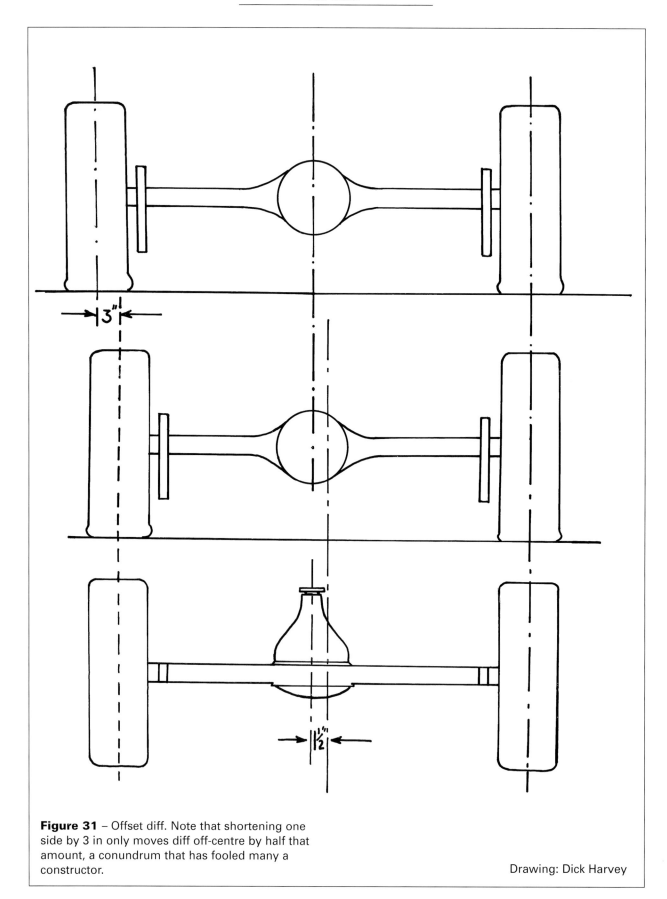

**Figure 31** – Offset diff. Note that shortening one side by 3 in only moves diff off-centre by half that amount, a conundrum that has fooled many a constructor.

Drawing: Dick Harvey

By the later seventies the professional formulae had discovered that a tyre without tread put more rubber onto the track, and combined with softer compounds could provide traction, cornering power and braking far in excess of what had previously been thought possible. These slicks became available on the second-hand market by the early eighties, and were scooped up with alacrity by 750 men eager to replace their 'wooden' D3s.

Not surprisingly, slicks extended the capabilities of these amazing little cars a stage further, but there was a down side. The ever cost-conscious 750MC allowed only a single set of tyres per meeting, and impressive though sticky untreaded rubber is on a dry track surface, its complete lack of any means of water dispersal renders it driver-involving, to say the least, in the wet. The answer was to cut three grooves in the tyre contact surface, longitudinally, and throughout its circumference. Although in practical terms this was little more than a gesture towards water displacement, it enabled drivers to feel a little less uneasy about venturing out onto a rain-soaked circuit.

Goodyear G50 Formula 3 covers were a common choice, the compound being just about right for a 750 car, having been designed for a form of racing which, like 750F, was characterized by a surfeit of grip over power. Furthermore, many F3 teams, running on tight budgets in an increasingly expensive form of motor racing, were pleased to get a few bob for their discarded rubber, much of which had plenty of life left in it, in order to keep their ambitious young South American

stars competitive on new tyres.

This transitional rubberwear period, which lasted several seasons, was characterized by a growing interest among competitors in meteorological predictions during the week prior to a race. Of course, theoretically a driver could have committed himself to a set of wet tyres should the forecast have been for rain, but in reality most racers could only afford one set of tyres anyway, so went with the grooved slick. These had considerable limitations if it was really wet: Dick Harvey recalls one wet Snetterton meeting when, forced to feather the throttle down Revett Straight to avoid the Darvi aquaplaning, he was overtaken by the DC+ of Mike Street and the DNC of John Richardson both travelling backwards. Ironically, it was an incident at the same circuit not long afterwards that was to bring about the end of this era of 750F tyre choice.

In addition to poor wet weather performance, the grooved slick provided a cornering sensation known irreverently within 750 paddocks as the 'three bite shuffle'. Upon turning into a corner, each of the three grooves would load up in sequence, adopting a stable attitude only when all three were fully loaded. This phenomenon also led to uneven wear, as loadings were not necessarily equal upon each section of the tyre.

The incident which led to the introduction of a control slick and free choice of wets, as allowed today, occurred during a sudden cloudburst at Snetterton, when most of an otherwise healthy 750 field hit standing water at Richies and flew so far off the track that they practi-

cally qualified for air miles.

Since 1988 a Yokohama slick has been the formula's mandatory tyre, although a free choice of wet weather covers is allowed. The Yokohama, a 160/515 x 13 (Code No. 811), originates from Formula Ford 2000, and is also currently used in Formula 4 and Sports 2000. Compared to a grooved slick, an ungrooved Yoko simply turns into a corner immediately and without drama. Being light, a 750 car can race for several seasons on the same set of tyres, which are more likely to lose performance through old age than wear. When, after the stresses and heat of a race distance, the tyres no longer pick up stones in the paddock, it is safe to say that they are knackered (technical term used in the rubber industry).

New Yokohamas cost around £75 each. Expect to pay half of that or less for used ones. They come from the factory with 3–4 mm of usable rubber, and will fit rim widths of 6–8 in. Recommended pressures vary according to the temperature of the day, the aim being to allow the tyres to reach working temperature quickly but not to overheat, although this is rarely a problem with the power and weight of a 750 car. Anyone who has ever driven on the road with a very soft tyre knows that lower-pressured tyres warm up quickly, so on a cold day, 14 psi may be sufficient. 16 psi is about average, rising to as much as 20 psi for a hot race.

Always use the same gauge as readings can vary enormously, and swapping instruments with fellow drivers can confuse matters. However it is worth knowing that your local Weights and Measures office will check your gauge against their accurately calibrated master meter without charge.

Although the choice of wet covers is free, most 750 drivers currently opt for the fully treaded Bridgestone 170/510 x 13. Originating from the Formula Vauxhall series, this is a soft compound tyre with moulded grooves. Costing around £100 new, these can be picked up for as little as £20 used. Higher pressures should be used in these compared to slicks, in order to 'dome' the tread surface to optimize the drainage of water; 20–22 psi is about right. Avon and Yokohama wets are also available in a similar size.

Used slicks can of course be hand-cut to a wet-tyre pattern to save cost, however the rules of the formula insist upon at least four circumferential grooves of a minimum 7 mm width, cut to the full depth of the surface rubber. This is relatively easy on a tyre that is fairly new, but less so when the rubber is older and harder, particularly if the odd stone has been deeply embedded.

Tyres should be stored in a cool dark place, although in reality they tend to get left on the car. This is alright provided the tyres are away from heat and light. A rubber eraser left in the sun on a window sill for an hour or so will effectively demonstrate how sunlight can reduce soft rubber to a brick.

## BRAKES AND STEERING

Despite a lightweight 750 car not requiring a great deal of stopping power, effective brakes are a valuable weapon in the racing driver's arsenal. With a similar amount of power beneath each competitor's right foot, the benefits of being able to outbrake an adversary are considerable. Good brakes give a driver confidence, and this is a quality that cannot be over-estimated.

As Triumph Herald, Spitfire, Vitesse and Vauxhall Chevette, Victor and Viva uprights, or components modelled on them, are popular among 750 car constructors, brake discs from the same sources make sense.

Some go their own way. Jim Dallimore for example converted his Hague (fitted with modified Mini uprights and drum brakes) to discs by using a four-pot Metro set-up, but it was heavy.

Skimming the disc to reface its braking surfaces not only improves braking performance, it also allows quicker warming up and cooling, but don't overdo it. Then for the serious late brakers, cooling may be further enhanced by cross-drilling the disc.

Caliper choice tends to accord with choice of disc, two-pot Triumph Herald and Spitfire, or Vauxhall Victor and Viva being widely favoured. Avoid single-pot swinging calipers. Jon Harvey uses ex-F3 Ralt calipers on his Darvi 92J, but choice of pads is limited and they tend to be too hard, fierce retardation resulting.

Although discs all round are not strictly necessary to stop a car of the 750 racer's speed and weight, the replacement of the original drums from the live back axle has a number of points in its favour. Discs save weight, are easier to maintain, do not have the balancing difficulties inherent with drums, are self-adjusting, and are not afflicted by a drum's tendency to fill with oil from hard-pressed axle seals during energetic cornering.

For many years it was common practice to replace the standard single leading-shoe drum arrangement at the rear with the twin leading-shoe set-up from the front of a Morris Minor 1000, in order to balance braking with the discs fitted to the front of the racer. However, until the mid-1970s most 750 cars were still racing on drums all round.

When choosing discs and calipers it should be appreciated that more braking is required at the front than the rear. Two to three times as much, in fact. Accordingly, larger calipers are needed at the front of the car than at the rear.

A good starting point would be to employ $1^3/4$–2 in dia pistons in front calipers acting upon 10–11 in dia discs, and $1^3/8$–$1^1/2$ in dia pistons in rear calipers acting upon 8–$8^1/2$ in dia discs. A $5/8$ in master cylinder would be appropriate for both front and back, and under normal circumstances the balance bar could be set about centre.

On his Darvi Mk 6, Dick Harvey used Mini Cooper aluminium calipers in conjunction with 11 in front and 9 in rear discs – a happy combination, one might think. But the car proved impossible to balance in terms of braking with the rears tending to lock up, and no adjustment to the balance bar or changes in master cylinder sizes had any effect. The problem was eventually solved by fitting a Mini compensation valve into the rear brake line.

In the days when twin leading-shoes were used on rear drums, it was very often necessary to use a $3/4$ in master cylinder at the back because of the larger fluid requirement. This had the added advantage of lowering line pressure to the rear brakes.

Standard pads are fine for racing. They are available, cheap, and reach working temperature quickly, but normally never heat up enough to fade.

Modern racing cars are required to have two separate hydraulic braking systems which, in the event of one failing, allow braking to be maintained on at least two wheels. The most straightforward way to achieve this is to use two single master cylinders in parallel, each with its own fluid reservoir, one operating the front brakes and the other the rear through separate pipe systems, with the refinement of an adjustable balance bar capable of splitting braking effort between front and rear as required (see Fig. 32). The bar must be set properly so that if one end of the car loses its stopping power, the bar locks up and actuates the other end.

Finding a suitable single master cylinder in a scrap-yard is no longer the work of a moment. Modern road cars, whilst required to have dual braking systems, use a single non-adjustable master cylinder to serve both circuits. They are frequently piped to connect one front wheel and one rear diagonally, and have a double reservoir subdivided internally, so for the racing man are practically useless.

Early Anglias and Heralds were equipped with the type of single master cylinder we are after, although specialist suppliers such as AP Racing can also provide them – at a price. Master cylinders should be solidly mounted on a bulkhead directly ahead of the brake pedal, as the braking force exerted upon a circuit is directly proportional to the distance between pedal and master cylinder rod in the region of 5:1. Fluid pressure is in fact halved for any given pedal movement by having two master cylinders, but this should be no problem in a car weighing 357 kg (7 cwt) or less. Servos are definitely out, adding weight, reducing pedal feel, and encouraging wheel lock-up.

Brake hoses with stainless steel braided outers and PTFE inners, as supplied by such companies as Goodridge, eliminate spongy pedal feel under demanding conditions and resist abrasion and corrosion. They can also work out cheaper than buying conventional piping as you can buy the exact length you need. Regular DOT4 fluid from AP, Castrol or Girling is quite adequate for 750 racing use.

A Formula Ford or similar single-seater pedal box can be bought for a tenner or so from a specialist breaker. Discs and calipers are about the same per pair. Although possibly a bigger job to fit, superb little alloy four-pot calipers and large-diameter thin discs are in every motor cycle breaker's yard, and are well worth checking out.

For racing, a high-ratio steering rack is essential. It will add to the car's agility, convey accurate information in respect of the behaviour of the front wheels to the driver, and allow him to keep his hands in a set position on the steering-wheel rim without recourse to shuffling, no matter how tight the bend being negotiated. Herald racks are popular, giving $1^{7}/8$ in of rack travel per steering-wheel turn (for comparison purposes, a Mini gives $1^{1}/2$ in, while a quick rack for an Escort gives $2^{1}/4$ in). However, a central pinion single-seater rack ($2^{1}/2$ in per wheel turn), either undamaged second-hand or even new, is ideal. A safety bonus with the use of a centrally controlled rack, as found on a single-seater, is the necessity to use an angled linkage in the steering-column of a 750 car due to its offset driving position. In a frontal collision such linkage will collapse, whereas a more direct mechanism can be, disconcertingly, punched straight back towards the driver.

As for the choice of steering-wheel, this is likely to boil down to personal preference and cost, although *Bondage Quarterly* was surely correct when it remarked that there is nothing quite like the looks and tactile experience offered by leather or suede, allegedly. They certainly provide excellent grip under all conditions and, in terms of accident protection, represent a giant step forward over the bakalite and wood-rimmed wheels of yore. Momo wheels look like the dog's bollocks but cost about the same as a small flat in Belgravia, so consideration should perhaps be given to an Alpha or Mountney which do the same job for much less cash. A 10 in diameter wheel is about the right size, and serious thought should be expended upon the incorporation of a quick-release mechanism. Seven-Fifty car cockpits are pretty tight, and it may be necessary to vacate one quickly, even if only to reach the paddock bar in a hurry following a race.

# INSTRUMENTS

Simplicity is the key. There is

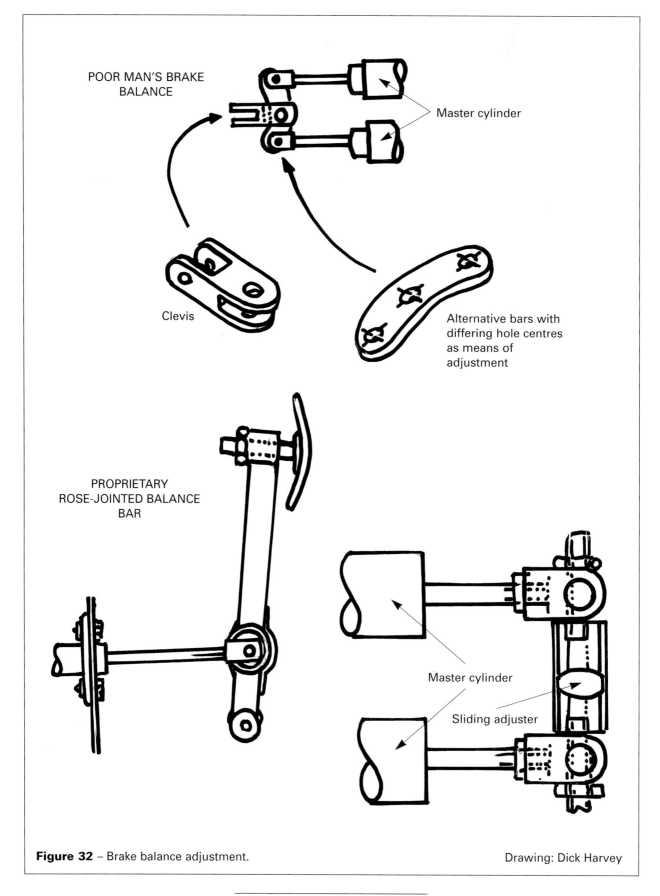

POOR MAN'S BRAKE
BALANCE

Master cylinder

Clevis

Alternative bars with
differing hole centres
as means of
adjustment

PROPRIETARY
ROSE-JOINTED BALANCE
BAR

Master cylinder

Sliding adjuster

**Figure 32** – Brake balance adjustment.

Drawing: Dick Harvey

enough going on during a motor race to hold a driver's attention without the distraction of an instrument panel from the Starship *Enterprise*.

Essentials are a rev counter, oil pressure and temperature gauges, and a water temperature gauge. There are several makes to choose from. Elliot, Stewart Warner and VDO are good value for tachometers, Lucas, Raceparts, Stewart Warner and VDO for pressure and temperature gauges.

As for normal readings, you need: an idling speed of 1,500 rpm, and a safe 8–8,500 rpm through the gears with the odd burst up to 9,000 on the tachometer; an oil pressure of 40–60 psi; oil temperature of 80–100°; and water temperature of 80° with a maximum of 100°. Some drivers put a red line or mark on their instrument glasses to denote maximum safe or normal readings. Then in the heat of battle all instruments can be checked at a glance. Alternatively they may be angled so that needles point upright when all is well, to the left when reading low, to the right when reading high. The oil pressure gauge should be supplemented by a large orange warning light activated by a switch sensitive to any drop below 25 psi. A wing-mounted indicator repeater from a small road car is ideal, and will grab the attention of any pilote, no matter how engrossed in a dice, if lit.

Incidentally, excessive oil temperature is a sure warning that all is not well within the engine's bottom end, and shouldn't be ignored. Alterations in regular oil pressure readings, even of a few psi, are also a strong hint of forthcoming trouble and indicate the

need to look inside in good time.

Switches may be restricted to the activation of ignition, fuel pump, and the obligatory red warning lamp that has to be displayed on the rear of a car during wet races. The latter should contain the only circuit with an in-line fuse in case of a nudge from behind. Toggle switches are best, and you are required to mark the 'off' position for the ignition clearly so that marshals can kill the electrics in an emergency. It is also mandatory to mount a clearly marked master cut-out switch externally; if an Autolec, this incorporates a red plastic removable key which is useful for security. This cuts out all feed from the battery and must be positioned on the lower main hoop of the roll-over bar, or at the lower part of the windscreen mounting if fitted, on the driver's side.

A push-button starter switch is required to bring the engine to life once the master and ignition switches have been turned on. As the Dellorto carburettor has a habit of flooding when first coaxed into action, this can be avoided by switching on the fuel pump only when the motor has consumed the petrol which has been lying in the float chamber. This procedure caught Dick Harvey out some seasons ago at Lydden Hill. Having qualified next to Richard Stephens's Gallard on pole, the Darvi's motor spluttered and died as the pack drove around the circuit to the start line on the parade lap. By the time Dick realized that he had not switched his pump on, he had rolled to a halt and was thus instructed to start the race from the back of the grid. But like all good stories, it had a

happy ending, as a suitably irritated Harvey stormed through the field to snatch the lead on the final lap from a startled Stephens.

The only other switch to note is the handle which triggers any onboard fire extinguisher, should it be fitted. Such a system is not mandatory, and the carrying of a hand-held extinguisher securely fixed within easy reach of the strapped-in driver will suffice, but if a plumbed-in extinguisher is in place within the cockpit, an externally mounted grip must be clearly marked.

## MIRRORS AND SEATING

There is an important relationship between mirrors and seating as they, together with pedals, dictate a driver's most effective operating position. To be able to sit comfortably and securely, with the pedals falling naturally beneath your feet – close enough together for heel and toe gear-changes but not close enough for two to be caught at once in error – and to be able to glance into either mirror without losing sight of what is directly ahead, is the aim. Of course it does no harm, when starting racing as a novice, to impress the Clerk of the Course with your awareness by making a few well-timed gapes into the mirrors when passing race control.

Wind-cheating racing mirrors are available from such specialist suppliers as Demon Tweeks and Merlin Motorsport, and should be easily adjustable for fine-tuning at the track.

Purpose-made competition seats, although readily available, don't always lend themselves to the narrow confines of a 750 car's cockpit. A home-made seat can be moulded to the exact shape of the driver within the space available, and is cheap. This is done by filling a substantial plastic dustbin liner with two-pack polyurethane foam which, when mixed, generates heat and expands to form a tough foam structure. By sitting on the bin liner as it is being filled, the driver's shape is mirrored in the profile created, though you should remember to support the liner above the cockpit floor by a couple of lateral wooden blocks to allow downwards expansion.

As the reaction between the liquids is quite violent, the driver should wear a couple of additional bin liners over his lower and upper body to protect himself. He will look a complete prat, but even the most kinky won't appreciate hot polyurethane over the nether regions should an expanding bag burst. This is actually a three-man job: one sitting, one pouring, and one holding open the neck of the bin liner being filled. The foam seat can be used as it is, covered in tank tape, or a GRP mould taken from it and a permanent seat made. The secret is to proceed carefully step by step, with the liquids being added gradually. They are available from racing specialists such as Merlin, or from your local glassfibre stockist.

Finally, seat belts. To avoid 'submarining' out of a four-point harness, a six-point harness should be fitted, to include two shoulder straps, an abdominal strap, and two crutch straps, with six separate chassis fixings and a single central release mechanism. They are not cheap, but they could save your life, and will most certainly hold you in place during hard acceleration, braking and cornering. Luke, Sabelt and Willans are probably the best-known makes.

One last thing. A 10 cm square head restraint positioned approximately 5 cm behind a normally seated driver's helmet is mandatory. This must be capable of restraining a helmeted head without the possibility of the head moving past the restraint or being trapped between it and the roll bar, and be able to contain a 17 kg mass decelerating at 5 g. How is the finished article tested? Answers on a postcard.

# Chapter 9

# THE END IS NIGH

**C**oming out of Luffield for the last time, you take a perfect line, floor the throttle early, snatch top, and sprint towards the chequered flag. Pursuers, former champions all, having stuck doggedly to the shapely tail of your fleet creation for ten hectic laps, suddenly fall back, stunned by this final burst of speed. The flag drops and an admiring crowd is acknowledged with a cheery wave. A famous victory is yours . . .

An urgent knock at the garage door and a stern 'Dinner's getting cold' shatters the illusion of a perfect summer's day at Silverstone, and awareness of winter rain beating down onto a felt roof returns. Reluctantly you climb out of the bare chassis balanced on stands and return to the warmth of the house.

With chassis and bodywork finished and painted, engine built and running gear assembled, a place on the grid is in sight. But for the completed car to function in the most effective manner possible, it must be set up correctly.

The key to setting up a car is to approach the task carefully and methodically, and the aim is to achieve balance throughout the chassis, with everything pointing or leaning in precisely the right direction.

To achieve such balance, everything must relate accurately to everything else, and to ensure this a central point of reference is required against which critical dimensions may be checked. This datum point must be as far as practicable from the components to be positioned, and located at a point that is unlikely to be affected should the car be involved in a minor shunt.

The middle of the centre bulkhead (the one immediately ahead of the driver on a 'Clubmans'-style car, or immediately behind on a mid-engined design) is a good datum point. However, to safeguard its integrity during minor indiscretions, it is wise not to mount suspension pick-up points directly onto the bulkhead itself, so that forces are not transmitted into its structure should a wheel make contact with something solid, like a marshal's post!

Once a datum point has been established, the assembly of components may begin, but keep a record of critical measurements so that, should repairs later become necessary (heaven forbid!), these figures may be used to restore the car's set-up.

## REAR AXLE

The live rear axle must be installed centrally and parallel to the chassis cross members. This is done by firstly laying the four radius arms on a workbench, then equalizing their lengths by screwing the rose-joints in or out of the extremities of the arms. The axle is next hung at each end from the chassis by either its dampers or slave-links, the latter being made of rigid lengths of metal drilled to correspond with the damper length at normal ride height. Such rigid links should be retained, for they are a useful measure of chassis integrity following a bump. If the links no longer fit, something has moved.

With the axle suspended, the radius arms may be fitted. In a perfect world they should mate perfectly with the eyes on axle and chassis, but in reality there is always one that fails to keep the appointment. This means that some adjustment to the rose-joints must be made, but try to keep the arms as equal in length as possible.

Having pre-marked the centre of the chassis and the centre of the axle, ignoring the fact that the diff is likely to be offset by 3 in, the two should be lined up and lateral linkage assembled, be it Panhard rod, Watt's linkage, Mumford, or whatever. Then finally, by careful measurement between points on the axle and the datum point, the axle's lateral and longitudinal correctness can be verified, making sure it is in the middle and square. On some cars this can present extreme physical difficulties due to components getting in the way of tape measurements. However the insertion of lengths of stick or string, where a tape will not fit, can often do the trick.

Another ploy for checking squareness is to run a piece of string around the car sitting on its wheels. Where front track differs from rear, say by 2 in, an inch-square block of wood can be placed outside each wheel at the car's narrower end to compensate. If the car is not true it should be readily apparent as the string runs across the wheel faces.

## FRONT HUBS

When assembling the front suspension, the bottom wishbone is a good place to start. As with the rear radius arms, place the lower wishbones on the bench, adjust for equal length each side, bolt into position, then examine for uniformity by measuring the distance between the datum point and the outer extremity of each wishbone

where it joins the hub upright. The reading should be the same on each side of the car.

Next equalize the upper wishbone lengths, then, using slave-links as dampers, bolt the arms into place. It is now possible to carry out castor and camber adjustments by altering the rose-jointed ends of the upper wishbone, although it will sometimes be necessary to shim (using washers) top (and sometimes bottom) wishbones fore and aft to avoid major differences in rod-end lengths. On some cars it may be easier to do it all on the lower arms. Whichever is chosen, it is simpler to adjust one or the other rather than both, and this approach also ensures that at least one pair of wishbones remains absolutely equal. Of course ideally, when a wishbone on one side of the car is adjusted, that on the opposite side should be changed in the same way to maintain equality of length, but tiny irregularities in upright shapes, chassis pick-up points, wishbone sizes and, dare one suggest it, chassis squareness come into play, with the result that wishbone balance is often less than straightforward once disturbed.

Paddocks are full of cars which have not benefited from such attention to detail, and their crab-like progress once out on the track is a direct result.

With the upright in place, and checked for verticality with a spirit level, the castor may be set. Castor is the amount by which the hub upright is allowed to lean backwards or forwards from the vertical and, by association, the amount the upper locating arm – in this case the wishbone – is allowed to sit ahead or behind the

lower link. Positive castor, which is where the upright leans backwards from the vertical, results in heavier steering and greater self-centring according to angle. Anything between 2° and 11° has been tried on the Darvis, and Dick Harvey currently uses a setting of 4° positive on his 91-D. However, he considers the importance of having both sides of the car set up equally to far exceed the importance of the settings themselves, having felt little difference between them.

Whilst some self-centring is desirable for straight-line stability, too much can prove an embarrassment. Take the negotiation of Shaws at Mallory Park, a walking pace right-hand hairpin with very fast approach. Here a 750 pilote is required to brake hard, change down, apply lots of steering lock, perhaps snatch an even lower gear, and employ a little opposite lock as power is directed to the tarmac as soon as possible for a speedy exit. With all this going on, the last thing you need is fierce self-centring, particularly when only one hand is guiding the wheel during a gear-change, and a quick trip into the cheap seats could easily be the unpleasant result.

Sticky racing slicks have a natural aversion to pointing in anything other than a straight line, so they possess natural self-centring. Accordingly it has been the subject of considerable debate amongst petrolheads as to whether any castor is required at all on a slick-shod 750 car.

Large adjustments in castor are generally made by spacing top wishbones fore or aft at the inboard pick-ups. Fine adjustments are then made by winding the inner rod-ends in or out as required. Winding the front one out and the rear one in will increase castor but will affect camber too, which will need correcting. This can be done crudely by rotating the rose-joint half a turn at a time in the bush at the end of the wish-bone. For fine adjustment, other than using spacers or adjusting the lower wishbone, a left-hand-right-hand thread bush floating in the top wish-bone end-tube is necessary.

Camber (the amount by which the wheel leans inwards or outwards) cannot really be determined until the car is tried on a track, so the best starting point is to set it vertical. If the suspension geometry is work-ing effectively, it should give negative camber on bump to compensate for roll, and so keep the outer wheel upright through a corner and the maxi-mum rubber in contact with the road. It is therefore a case of driving the car for a few laps, then observing whether the entire contact surface of the tyre is reaching working tem-perature. In the absence of a pyrometer, the back of one's hand is very useful, being remarkably sensitive to temper-ature variations. If the inside of the tyre is warmer than the out-side, there is too much negative camber; vice versa and there is too much positive. Not only will such imbalance adversely affect the car's handling, it will also lead to uneven tyre wear.

As with castor, it is an advan-tage, in terms of simplicity, to adjust camber at the top wish-bone rose-joint. Darting about between upper and lower arms introduces too many variables, and there is a real danger of losing the balance so carefully gained on the bench by equal-izing wishbone lengths. On some cars it may be easier to set castor and camber on the lower wishbones, but the principle remains the same.

The steering rack should be positioned parallel to the ground, at right angles to the car's centre line, and centrally. The rack should also lie level with the top wishbones if pos-sible (less easy with outboard than inboard suspension), this being an effective operating position which eliminates the evils of 'bump-steer'. Try to avoid the fundamental mistake of fitting a forward-mounting rack to rearward-facing steering arms, or vice versa. The embar-rassment of turning the steer-ing-wheel in one direction only to have the car turn in the other is almost too great to contem-plate. The clue is that rearward-facing arms require the pinion on top of the rack, and for-ward-facing ones underneath.

Tracking should be set with a little toe-in, say 1/16 in, to coun-teract the front wheels' ten-dency to toe-out naturally once on the move. Toe-out enhances a car's ability to turn into a corner with alacrity, but scrubs off speed along the straights. Formula 1 cars are set up with toe-out as they can afford to invest 20 of their 650 bhp in search of better turn-in. A 750 racing car cannot.

So with nothing more expen-sive than a tape measure, spirit level, a couple of spanners, considerable patience, and a little swearing, much of the car can be set up on trestles or sim-ilar set level and flat, virtually single-handed. The use of solid slave-links made, say, from old rose-jointed suspension arms ensures a constant ride height is simulated without having to rely upon a pal's weight being brought to bear inside the cockpit, where he will inevitably become extremely bored and restless.

## SPRINGS

The choice of springs, dampers and roll-bars is a fairly scien-tific one, but fortunately there are plenty of tried and tested selections on current 750 cars that may be followed according to your car's configuration. However, should you wish to go your own way, or at the very least make a well-informed decision, there is no better place to start than Allan Staniforth's *Race And Rally Car Source Book* (G.T. Foulis).

Coil-spring rates are a func-tion of wire diameter, number of coils and coil diameter. Accordingly, should your sus-pension design require a spring of a certain length that subse-quently proves too soft, it is possible to uprate that length of spring by increasing the wire diameter, reducing the number of coils, or both.

Springs are available off the shelf at any number of motor sporting factors, but a useful man to know is 750 racer Dan White, whose company, Sus-pension Supplies Sheffield, manufactures springs for many of the big names in suspension including Leda and Spax. Well-versed in the needs of the 750 man, Dan may be able to make the exact spring you are look-ing for, or even pick it off the shelf.

And what exactly are you looking for? On a typical out-board-suspended car, 150–200 lb springs at the front and 80–120 lb at the rear. However, in respect of front springing, much depends upon the angle at which the spring is required to

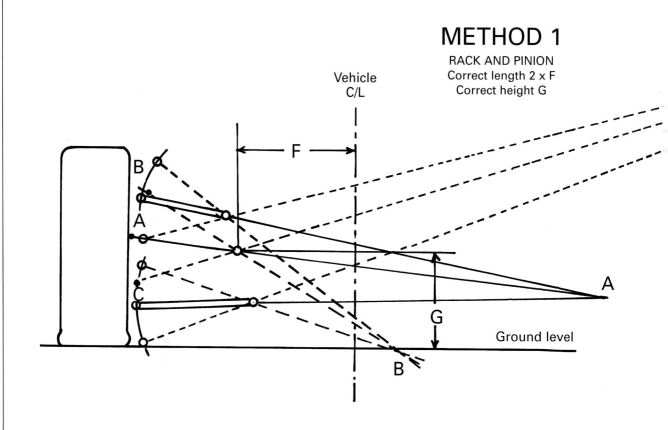

METHOD 1
RACK AND PINION
Correct length 2 x F
Correct height G

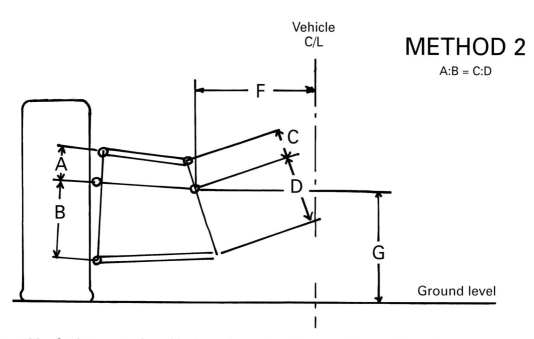

METHOD 2
A:B = C:D

**Figure 33** – Setting up steering with alternative rack positions and their relationship to bump steer.

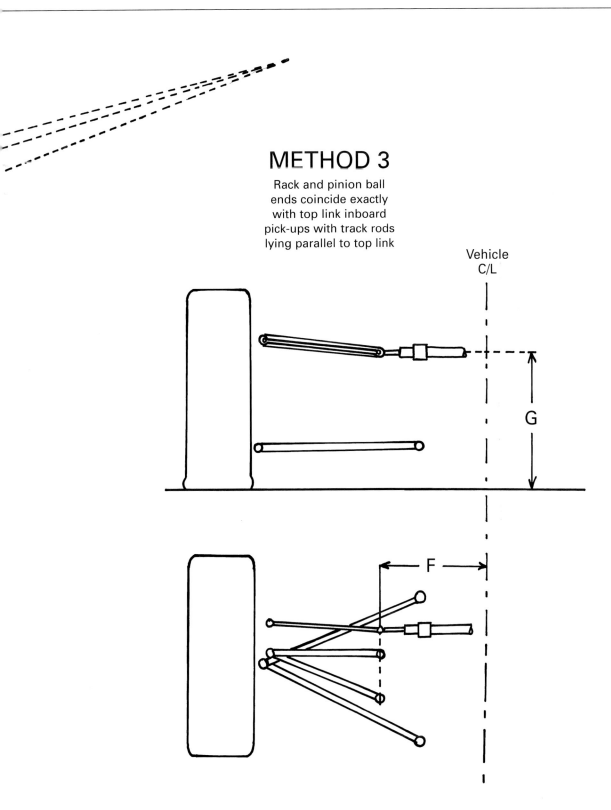

# METHOD 3

Rack and pinion ball
ends coincide exactly
with top link inboard
pick-ups with track rods
lying parallel to top link

Vehicle
C/L

G

F

Drawing: Dick Harvey with permission from Allan Staniforth

work. The greater the angle from vertical, the more the spring's rate is reduced. For instance, the Bob Couchman Darvi, which uses parts and suspension geometry from the ex-Chris Gough Jo Mo, employs 350 lb front springs.

Naturally, a front-engined 'Clubmans' configuration car will have different spring needs to a mid-engined 'Sports Racer'. The low-line outboard-suspended and front-engined Marrow runs 150 lb front springs and 110 lb rear, while the similarly suspended but mid-engined Darvi 877 uses 230 lb front springs and 160 lb rears – an interesting comparison but not one of great meaning unless all the variables involved (e.g. leverages, wheel rates, frequencies, etc.) are known. In a one-make formula, say Renault Clios, a rate of spring found to work well on one car will do so on any other, as all the variables are the same. But in 750 racing, where the constructor driver is king, it is impossible to recommend an ideal spring, given the suspension variations likely to occur, and advice has to be confined to likely rate ranges.

Once selected, the spring should be 'scragged' prior to fitting. Brand-new springs which have never been compressed will fatigue a little when initially squashed, therefore they are put into a vice or spring compressor, wound up solid, and left overnight. After 24 hours or so, the initial sagging will have taken place and the springs can be released. Should they at that stage wish to remain compressed, it is time to have meaningful discussions with your spring supplier.

Before fitting the spring over the damper unit, carefully lubri-

cate the spring platform and top collar which retain the coil. This makes adjustment of the platform much easier when the spring-damper unit is attached to the car. And as the platform is easier to lower than raise, due to the force of the spring acting upon it, better to wind it up the damper a good way prior to assembly and the adjustment of ride height.

With coil-spring on the car, and damping fully soft, the first step towards setting the desired ride height is to sit in the car and jump up and down. Pretend it's your first victory. Then roll the car backwards and forwards a few times and allow the suspension to settle.

Only now can the ride height be measured. This may be done with a tape measure, but a better way is to build a triangular wooden block with heights from ground level marked along the rising edge. This can then be wedged under each corner and measurements taken. Typically, $2\frac{1}{2}$ in front and $2\frac{3}{4}$ in rear are aimed for, and by adjusting the spring platforms each corner may be set in turn. However, it should be realized that raising a front corner will lower the diagonally opposite rear, so care must be taken to keep platform heights as equal as possible at each end of the car and across each axle.

A constructor at the posh end of the paddock would now seek out some sophisticated corner weight equipment. Experienced Darvi constructors Harvey and Harris doubt its value when applied to asymmetrical two-seaters, and having spent many a puzzled hour toying with corner weight gauges, are convinced that a 750 car can be set up equally

well in the manner described above.

Now, with some damping wound on, the car may be tried on a circuit. There the recommended procedure is to do a few laps, return to the paddock, then find a level piece of ground and, without leaving the car, get someone to recheck the ride height with the calibrated block and readjust as necessary.

# DAMPERS

Bilstein, Koni, Leda and Spax are the leading manufacturers of reasonably priced dampers available in this country. All are available gas-filled and adjustable, apart from Bilstein which are non-adjustable, but they tend to be valved for a wide range of applications unless expensively manufactured to order. Most 750 practitioners opt for the Spax, which is a fair compromise between price, quality and flexibility of range, but it must be fairly obvious that what is designed to work on a two-ton Jaguar may not be ideal for a 750 car, despite working well enough on the face of it.

For the perfectionist there is AVO. Operating out of the former Spax factory in Jersey, Rod Avon can engineer a gas-filled damper, adjustable for rebound, to suit a specific car. Bespoke AVO products have been successfully used for several years by the multi-championship winning Darvi stable and by ex-champion Bob Simpson. Competitively priced, they are well worth considering, and have just set up a UK depot in Northamptonshire.

Settings are a matter of experimentation. Start soft, then stiffen to the point where the car feels well balanced under cornering forces, and free from excessive lift and dive under acceleration and braking. The secret of getting the best out of any racing car is smoothness, and this is particularly true with a 750, with its modest power. Sliding around is scrubbing off speed and time wasted, so handling that is ultimately neutral is the aim. Some degree of understeer into a corner is essential, otherwise if all available grip has been used up during entry, the application of power on exit can only result in time-sapping oversteer. What is required is a stable and neutral attitude when full throttle is applied on leaving a corner.

Beware of running the rear of the car too hard. Twenty-five per cent of the vehicle's weight is at the back, jumping up and down in the form of the axle. Fail to damp that movement effectively and the tail will take over the car, and in no time at all you will be picking the contents of a gravel trap out of the bodywork.

## ROLL BARS

To use its proper title, the anti-roll bar is the constructor driver's tool for fine-tuning his car's handling. Sensitivity to small roll-bar adjustments is indicative of a car that is working well in all other respects; no reaction to large roll-bar changes is a sign of there being something fundamentally wrong with the car's set-up elsewhere. It will be worth pure gold to spend time and effort finding out just how to calculate roll bars and their effects on car handling.

Once made of solid steel, roll bars now tend to be tubular. There are two reasons for this.

First, tubular steel offers a greater strength-to-weight ratio than a solid bar, while secondly, as a result of lighter weight, there is less of a penalty for using larger diameters of bar for greater stiffness.

The bar should be mounted in solid nylon or alloy block bearings across the chassis. On a car with outboard front suspension, the bar arms are rose-jointed to the outer ends of the wishbones – usually lower, and as close to the wheel as possible. An inboard-suspended car's front roll bar usually has blades rose-jointed to the rocking arms via linking arms. At the back of the car the roll-bar blades or arms are rose-jointed to the rear radius-arm mounts, or a nearby point on the axle casing.

The calculation of roll-bar stiffness has been left to the learned tomes listed in Appendix B, however a typical front roll bar would be 14 or 16 g, 3/4 in dia CD tubular steel and a rear, 18 g, 3/4 in dia CD tubular steel. Note that if of equal length, typically 3 ft on an outboard-suspended car, the rear bar will be less stiff than the front due to the lighter gauge. Stiffness is a function of length, diameter and gauge.

If it is accepted that a car has, say, 3 in of wheel travel, a front roll bar, wishbone-operated, will be required to resist the twisting action of the blade moving 3 in. On an inboard-suspended car, that 3 in of travel will translate into a top rocker-arm movement of perhaps less than 1 in, with a much shorter bar to act against it. Though the shorter bar is stiffer, a heavier gauge may still be required on an inboard roll bar to provide comparable stiffness to a lighter gauge out-

board arrangement.

The uprating of front springs can also have a significant impact on roll-resistance. Dick and Jon Harvey experienced this phenomenon on their inboard-suspended Darvis when, in order to counteract bottoming-out under braking, they uprated their front springs. This solved their bottoming problem but upset the car's previously good balance due to the stiffer springs' direct influence upon the car's overall roll-resistance, and this puzzled the brothers at first as nothing else had been changed. The solution was to soften the front roll bar, which, combined with the uprated springs, restored the original roll-resistance.

To adjust a roll bar of certain diameter and length without altering its mountings, the suspension pick-up points on the blades may be rotated, or the length of lever arms varied, in order to exert more or less leverage, or the gauge of steel can be changed.

## WINGS

At 750 racing speeds, aerodynamics aids only really make themselves felt in third and fourth gear corners. Therefore the effectiveness of your wings and optimum settings can only be established on the track. Begin with zero angle-of-attack and increase that angle one end of the car at a time with roll bars set fully soft. Front wings do not contribute a great deal to drag as they are of smaller area than rears, and probably display greater aerodynamic efficiency, so you can afford to put more angle on the front than rear for maximum downforce. At the rear, the airstream is disturbed by the bodywork

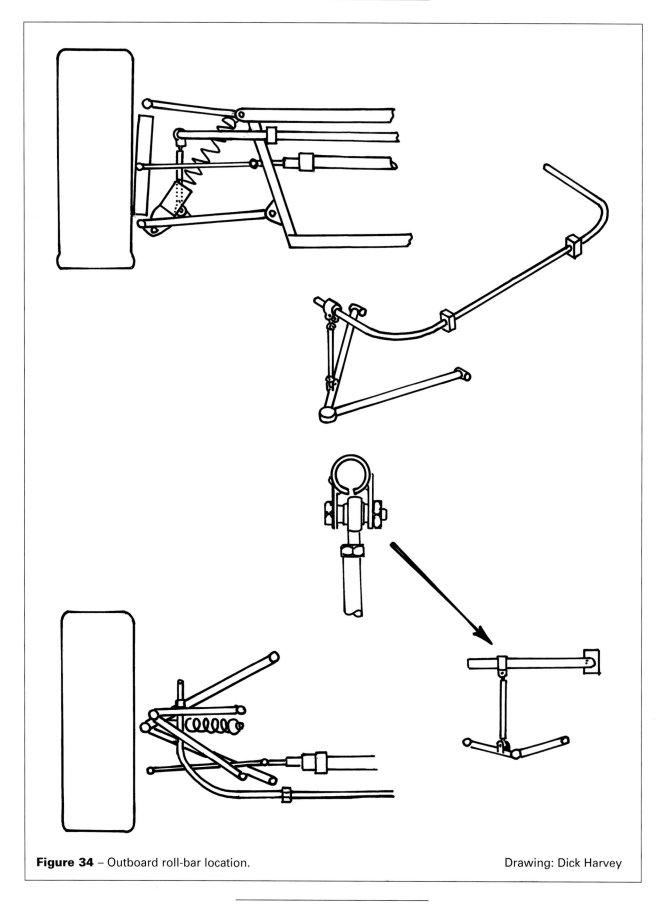

**Figure 34** – Outboard roll-bar location.

Drawing: Dick Harvey

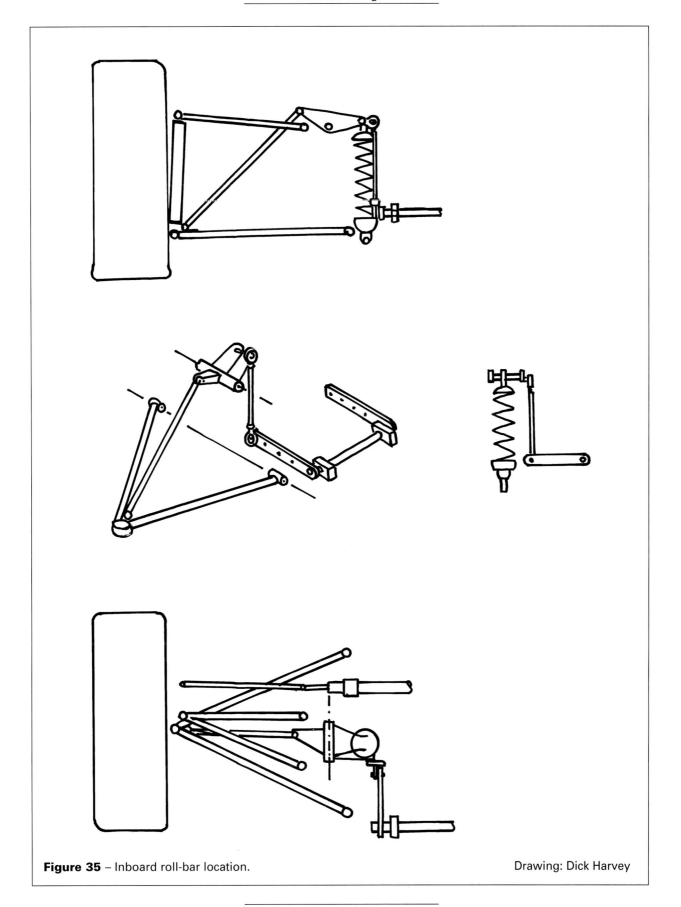

**Figure 35** – Inboard roll-bar location.

Drawing: Dick Harvey

and therefore does not hit the back wing either at right angles or parallel to the ground. Accordingly, what may appear to be an angle-of-attack of barn door proportions is merely a response to air hitting it at perhaps 30° from the ground.

## FIRST DRIVE

Any old piece of smooth tarmac well away from the public road is fine for what the F1 boys would term a 'systems check'. That is a gentle run to ensure everything on the car is working in the manner intended, and sundry fluids flowing around for the first time are not flowing onto you or the road. However, to run the car in properly, and to learn something about it, a track test is essential.

Estoril, Jerez and Paul Ricard are likely to come a little over budget, therefore a Wednesday at Mallory Park, one of the 750MC test days at Goodwood, a sunny Thursday at Three Sisters near Wigan, Lancashire, or any other reasonably priced

British circuit deal advertised in the motor sporting press is worth considering.

The only drawback may be that some tests may be unmarshalled. In such a case it is wise for drivers and their helpers to get together to arrange look-outs, and position a road car with keys in the ignition at the track entrance. Some years ago, during an unmarshalled session at Goodwood, those watching from the paddock heard the distant sound of a Formula Ford falter, a squeal of tyres, and an ominous thud. Leaping into a waiting car, they sped around the track to the scene of the shunt to find the hapless driver upside-down in a ditch. She was quite unhurt, but the value of rapid assistance was not lost on her.

Once arrived and unloaded, warm up the engine to working temperature, then take the car out onto the track for five laps, using full but not sustained revs. Pay close attention to oil pressure and oil and water temperatures as the pistons, bores and bearings bed in. If all is

well, do another ten laps using the brakes for slowing rather than the gears. Give the engine plenty of revs but feather it a little down the straights.

The car is now ready to be given some umpty, so off you go for some serious lappery. These engines are built to rev. Tootling around at 6,000 rpm for 50 laps will just result in a carbon build-up at the top of the bores, so that when revs are eventually increased, the rod stretches a few thou more and the rings go bang.

The only problem with open testing is that you could find yourself on the same track as a Formula 3000 car or the like, in which case you will spend so much time watching the mirrors that you will learn nothing about your car. This is the reason why some 750 drivers use the first couple of races with a new car as test sessions, for then at least they are amongst machinery of similar performance against which they can make direct comparisons.

# Chapter 10

# A STRANGER IN PARADISE

That feeling arrives on Monday morning a week before the race. A potent cocktail of anticipation, anxiety and excitement. It begins in the brain, drops to the stomach, and becomes lodged in the bowels. The moment you get out of bed it's there, a portent of something very special about to happen in your life.

The car is almost ready. Designed by you and built with the help of pals too numerous to mention, it has taken longer than expected, much longer. And you are reminded of that irritatingly true and much-quoted adage, 'Any job will occupy the time available'.

There are still numerous small things to do to the car, and you eye the list pinned to the garage wall apprehensively, but the main tasks are completed, the racer runs, and only details and fine-tuning remain to occupy the diminishing number of evenings left.

The season is already two races old, and you have missed both, but that's no problem as the weather was foul. But by setting a realistic target, Round 3, a superhuman effort has finally seen the car's prepara-

tion accelerate to within sight of the starting grid. Twelve of the 750 Championship races remain, and with points from your best eight results allowed to count, there is plenty of time to make an impact.

Personal preparation is ahead of that of the car, although you remain in shock from the bills. There was the mandatory purchase of the RACMSA Novice Racing Driver Start Pack (£35), containing your *Motor Sport Year Book*, racing licence application form, and video which you watched attentively. Flag signals were committed to memory, you marvelled at one of the all-time great F3 jump-starts, were not fazed by the monumental accidents shown to warn the nutters, and were amused by the irony of former touring car combatant Mike Smith imploring the racing newcomer to drive carefully.

Passed fit to race by a bemused, and at least forty-five quid richer, GP, you attended a Novice Racing Driver Course (£135) at an RACMSA-approved school. There, in the classroom, the basics of car control were explained, the video watched

again and discussed, then out on the circuit your driving was assessed. First the instructor demonstrated the correct lines in one of the school's hot hatches, impressing with his smoothness, then you took the wheel and were evaluated, not for speed, but for general competence on the track.

Back in the classroom came the written exam and old childhood fears, thought long forgotten, returned. There were 25 multiple-choice questions to be answered and a 55 per cent pass mark required, with six questions relating specifically to safety all having to be answered correctly. To your relief, you passed, as did the rest of the class, despite one pupil being under the misapprehension that 'heel and toe' down changes involved braking with the left toe and accelerating with the right heel. (He was a rally driver, and claimed to have been doing it that way for years.) Your driving was also deemed to surpass the minimum requirement (65 per cent pass mark) and your shortcomings were analysed, vindicating those winter evenings spent in front of the fire reading

Alain Prost's *Competition Driving* and Jackie Stewart's *Principles Of Performance Driving* when you should have been labouring in the garage. There were a few more words of advice about helmets and protective clothing, then you were allowed to part with a further £35 for a National 'B' race licence from the RACMSA.

With a wallet already £250 lighter, you then visited a speed shop for some serious spending. Heeding sound advice from guys with limps, who looked as though they knew what they were talking about, you bought a good-quality full-face helmet (up to £300+) and a decent, multi-layer Nomex fire-proof race suit (£200+). Although not obligatory, you also wisely added to your kit bag a pair of Nomex gloves (£25+), boots (£60+), underwear and socks (£60+) and balaclava (£10+).

Now, approximately £900 worse off (second-hand items could have drastically reduced the race kit expenditure and, ignoring the old joke about a £60 helmet for a £60 head, perfectly adequate RAC-approved skid-lids start at this price), you were almost ready to race in the knowledge that you were well protected, your outfit would last many seasons, and you looked the business.

All that now remained was racing membership of the 750 Motor Club (£45 including joining fee), registration for the 750 Championship (free), and a race entry (£90).

Some days prior to the race meeting an entry list, final instructions and entry passes arrive. A nine-race programme reflects all the racing car types accommodated by the 750 Motor Club: Formula 4 (1600

and 2000 cc single-seaters), Formula Vee (1300 cc single-seaters), 750 Formula, Formula 1300 (1300, 1600 and 2000 cc sports racers), 750 Trophy (pre-war and period sports and single-seaters), Roadgoing Sportscars, Hot Hatches, Kit Cars (roadgoing front-engined) and Super Sports (front- and mid-engined slick-shod kit cars).

You note the 750 race as being Event Seven, with signing-on at 8.30 a.m., novice drivers' meeting 9.30, scrutineering 10.30, practice at midday, and racing starting at 2.00 p.m. Some of the 25 names on the 750 race entry list you recognize, including your own; most you do not. You hope there will be other first-timers competing so that you are not doomed to circulate alone at the tail of the field.

As the week progresses, the car's preparation nears completion. So does yours. Visits to that little gym, recently joined, are stepped up. Well, it's next door to a good pub, isn't it? Every evening, following the news, you await some mention of Saturday's weather, but the Meteorological Office stubbornly refuses to commit itself on the subject of weekend precipitation, and you brood about a nasty-looking area of low pressure lurking above the Irish Sea.

At the office, a less than totally committed workforce starts to turn its attentions to the weekend. When enquiries are made about your plans, colleagues are suitably impressed by the answer. On a scale of one to ten, where taking the cat to the vet's scores three, visiting the mother-in-law gets four, and going to the garden centre rates five, driving in a motor

race is good for at least eleven.

Friday evening comes at last. As you leave the office you wonder what tales there will be to tell when you return on Monday. At home the tow car is loaded. Spares, tools and trolley jack; oil, water and petrol; and four wheels shod with treaded 'wets' go in the back. The trailer is hooked up and racing car loaded and secured. Finally, before darkness falls, the white number backgrounds on nose and sides receive your black race numbers, and a black novice cross on yellow square is fixed to the tail.

That evening you try to relax, and are almost able to ignore that big black cloud hovering over the circuit on the weather map, but not quite. You go to bed early with a warm *Autosport*, set the alarm for an ungodly hour, and much to your surprise fall asleep.

As tyres crunch on broken concrete passing through the circuit gate, it's just getting light. Outlines of the bridge across the track, a grandstand, and advertising hoardings can be made out against a grey early morning sky, whilst wide-mouthed speakers up poles wave slowly in the breeze like giant daffodils. These are powerful images for the black belt motor racing enthusiast beyond help, and a lump finds its way into your throat.

As you rumble across the old bridge, you can just see the track below. Within hours you will be down there racing, and that feeling which has come and gone since Monday returns with a vengeance.

After entering the paddock and parking in the area allocated for 750s, you shiver as the warm interior of the car, super-heated by several hours of motorway travel, is exchanged for the coolness of the morning. The racer is unloaded and you join the queue for signing-on at the circuit office. The time is 8.25 a.m.

Those awaiting the opening formalities of going motor racing are an eclectic bunch, far removed from the famous racing drivers seen on television. They range from teenagers to pensioners, are of all shapes and sizes, and there are several ladies. There is much lively chat, predominantly about who has just bought what, new modifications to old nails, and previous daring deeds. Everybody knows each other, or that's the way it seems to the newcomer, and everyone appears to look and sound very confident. But in time the difference between truth and bull-shit will become apparent, and the saying 'The older I get, the quicker I was' will hold real meaning.

Good-humoured barracking

greets the officials when the office opens a couple of minutes late, and in no time you are signing the competitors' sheet next to your race and competition licence number, picking up a scrutineer card and programme, and handing over your licence for signing, hopefully, at the end of the race. To gain such a signature, of which ten are required to upgrade to a National 'A' licence, you must in the opinion of the Clerk of the Course not only complete the race distance but also 'drive in a responsible manner'. Sometimes even this is not enough, and you are reminded of the story of a conscientious fellow who painstakingly restored a Lotus for several years prior to entering it in his first motor race. Qualifying on the back of the grid, he completed the race a distant last and lapped. Then, much relieved that his pride and joy was still in one piece, he went to collect his signed

licence. However, there was a message at the office: despite finishing the race and driving in a perfectly safe manner, assiduously observing all flag signals, his licence could not be signed as, in the opinion of the Clerk of the Course, at no time had racing speeds been reached. A real message from hell, and the motor racing equivalent of being told one is bad in bed!

You now make your way to Race Control, a rather grand name for a Portakabin perched above the pits. The time is 9.25 a.m.

Within the hallowed confines of his lair, the Clerk of the Course (God's representative on earth chosen to attend motor sporting occasions) explains to those present, none of whom have raced at the circuit before, the horrors await-

*Race day: Dick Harvey and Peter Herbert discuss the finer points of queuing in the rain for scrutineering. (Allan Staniforth)*

ing them at various points around the track. He reminds you all that motor racing is not a contact sport. Then, with a

*Scrutineering: the Darvi 91-D gets the full attention of Dallas Smith as its owner looks on anxiously. (Allan Staniforth)*

look normally reserved by magistrates for those who molest small furry animals, he tells how he will descend like a free-falling fridge on anyone daring to overtake under a yellow flag.

With the assistance of an unpaid helper – well, he is get-

ting to see cars racing for free, after all – you push the racer towards the scrutineering bay and join another queue. Yes, it's just like Russia. At this point your uncle arrives. He is not actually a blood relative, rather an experienced competitor who, with the encouragement of the organizing club, has agreed to take you under his wing. Uncle admires your car, runs a trained eye over the features likely to receive particular attention from the scrutineers, introduces some fellow 750 guys standing close by in the queue, and advises you to get out onto the circuit at the back of the bunch for practice so that a couple of steady laps can be had before the mirrors are filled by the quick men storming past.

Eventually it's your car's turn to be wheeled in front of the men in white coats. The time is 10.45 a.m.

You release the Dzus fasteners with a screwdriver and remove the engine cover, and a small grey-haired man with a Chief Scrutineer armband and a look that says he has seen it all before pounces on this newcomer to the paddock. Road wheels are tugged to find play, the steering-wheel is jerked to detect lost motion, throttle return springs are tested, brake fluid reservoirs and catch tank examined, pipes fondled for leaks, seat belts tugged, master switch tweaked, rear light checked, and many more things inspected before, to your intense relief, the car is passed fit to race. There is a quick look inside your new helmet for the RACMSA-approved sticker, and at your race suit for required British Standard or FIA approval label, then the scrutineering card is exchanged for a

*Post-scrutineering: with 'passed' ticket firmly in hand, Dick Harvey engages in a frank exchange of views with scrutineer Dallas Smith, while Mick Harris cringes out of sight. Not that there was much to worry about, as the Darvis of Mick Harris, Dick and Jon Harvey were nominated the three best-prepared 750s of 1994 by Mr Smith. (Allan Staniforth)*

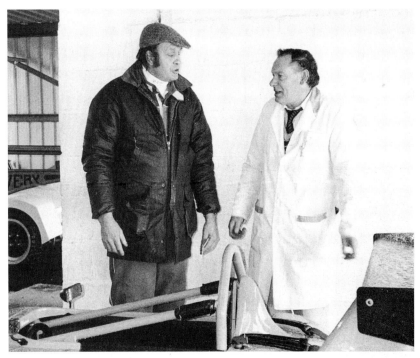

stamped and signed scrutineer's pass ticket which is proudly fastened prominently within the cockpit.

As the racer is pushed back to its spot in the paddock, the sun reluctantly breaks through a curtain of grey cloud, and while your helper checks fuel, oil and water levels, you set the tyre pressures. Your car is the

*Preparing to disengage the brain: strapped into the restricted confines of the 91-D, Dick Harvey readies himself for practice. (Allan Staniforth)*

centre of considerable attention amongst the 750 racing fraternity. This is as genuine as it is inevitable. You have not just turned up with the latest Formula Ford from Van Diemen, Seven from Caterham, or Escort

RS Cosworth from Ford, all of which, exciting though they may be, are available off the shelf. This is your car, there is nothing else quite like it, and 750 racers know and respect that. They have been there.

*Assembly: the Harvey attention is fully focused upon the task ahead, while Mick Harris's Darvi 877 and Phil Hoare's DNC Mk 5 (17) can be seen beyond. (Peter Herbert)*

In the privacy of the changing room you step into your racing gear. The bare walls, timber bench and cold floor remind you of school, when, on cold winter days, you were sent out onto a bone-hard pitch to play football. Now no-one is making you do anything, and you want to go motor racing. The time is 11.30 a.m.

Soon you will be called to the assembly area next to the pits to await practice. Your helper has warmed up the car, the sun is becoming quite warm, and inside your driving suit you calmly concentrate upon the job in hand.

Once in the assembly area, your calmness evaporates. You have been to the toilet half a dozen times, but the harness buckle resting on your bladder fools it into thinking you must go again. You pull on your balaclava and helmet, and panic when the chin strap becomes twisted through the buckle.

You take a deep breath and try again. It goes straight through and tightens. You pull on your gloves and check the mirrors for the hundredth time. You feel yourself sweating beneath your balaclava. Its partly the heat of sitting in the sun wearing so much clothing, and partly fear. Why are you putting yourself through this? You could be selecting bedding plants at a garden centre right now.

Quite suddenly you are off.

A marshal waves, an engine bursts into life, then another, then another. Your gloved finger flicks down the ignition switch and pokes the starter button. The engine coughs then dies. You panic and try again, this time with the fuel pump switched on, and the little Reliant is up and running.

Into the pit road, then onto the track, you move steadily up through the gears and check the instruments. As your uncle advised, you are at the back of the field, and whilst everyone warms up their brakes and tyres you are able to keep pace. Despite a half-day's testing at another circuit, you are impressed by the width of this one, and you check out the marshals' posts as the first lap is completed.

*Tension takes drivers different ways: Nigel Cowley cracks a gag above the noise of angry exhausts as he awaits admittance to the track. Chris Gough's CGR1 (8) and Richard Stephens's Gallard J11 (24) can be seen behind. (Peter Herbert)*

On the second lap every-body steps up the pace, and as you pass the pits you wave to your helper that all is well. By lap three (you lose count after lap one) you are getting a feel for the course. The car is going well, better than you dared hope, and you try to set a time. The result is some untidy driving. Braking is left too late and a wheel locked, an application of full throttle too early causes a lurid tail slide compounded by over-correction, and too much speed on a poor line results in a wide exit from a corner and a trip onto the grass.

By lap five your driving is back under control. You slow down, mentally regroup, then attack again. At this point the front runners fighting for pole position rocket past. They come on you so quickly that no sooner have you seen flashes of colour in the mirrors than they are gone. You are unable to comprehend how they can go so quickly. Steadily, lap by lap, others come by, and you try to keep them in sight for as long as possible before you are overtaken by another and the

process begins again.

You start to enjoy yourself, there is no longer any fear. Then suddenly out comes the chequered flag and it's all over, and you enter the pit lane after one final lap and park back in the paddock.

Climbing out of the car and nonchalantly tossing helmet, balaclava and gloves onto the seat, you feel great and wonder what all the fuss was about. You check the car over, refuel, and chat with fellow competi-tors about a shared experience. Then all of a sudden you feel hungry and thirsty, and repair to the circuit restaurant. The time is 12.45 p.m.

On a board inside the circuit office, times are displayed. As if waiting for exam results, a bunch of drivers has already gathered by the door. Hoping for a miracle but expecting rather less, you anxiously scan the 750 race list. You are not slowest, there are two other drivers behind. One is another novice, the other spent most of practice in a sand trap. Having completed the necessary three laps before his excursion, he will be allowed to race.

*Practice makes perfect: Dick Harvey joins the marshals in the cheap seats after a locking back brake causes him to spin. (Dick Harvey collection)*

During the lunch break, as the hard-worked marshals and officials at last have a chance to don nose-bags, you take a stroll around the paddock and absorb the atmosphere.

A British Racing Green Austin Seven Ulster, surroun-ded by a jolly bunch of bearded coves, is having a holed radia-tor repaired. A yellow West-field, tail jacked high in the air, is receiving a replacement drive shaft on loan from a spectator's Escort parked nearby. Mean-while, an attractive blond novice in a Peugeot 205GTi is the centre of considerable attention as she finds herself surrounded by several new uncles.

In the rear window of another hot hatch appear the prophetic words 'There will now be a short intermission in this marriage for THE RACING SEASON', whilst a driver walks past with the words 'NO FEAR, NONE AT ALL, NOT EVEN A

*High jinx at lunchtime: Nigel Mansell, enjoying a guest drive in Richard Stephens's Gallard, scans his 'comfort zone'. (Peter Herbert collection)*

LITTLE BIT' written across the back of his sweatshirt. As the race approaches you wish you could share these sentiments.

A heady mix of sizzling hot dogs and Castrol R pervades the air, and you buy a pair of ear plugs from a goody stall, only to learn later that they cost half the price from Boots'.

You watch the first couple of races half-heartedly from the grandstand and worry about the gathering grey clouds. In the paddock other drivers cast anxious glances skyward, but nobody makes any sudden moves towards wets. Then it's time to line up in grid order in the assembly area. The time is 3.30 p.m.

Sitting in the car awaiting the

*Awaiting the green light: Mick Harris sits in his Darvi 877 on the front row of the grid. (Peter Herbert)*

call to the grid, a fresh fear consumes you. The fear of the unknown has been replaced by the fear of getting hurt. Was it not Mark Twain who said, 'Sport is like war without the shooting?'

The previous race ends and it's time to go. The field of 750 racers drives around the circuit and takes position on the grid. The sky remains threatening and butterflies perform a rain dance in your stomach. You switch off the engine to avoid overheating and wait.

At three minutes to go, a siren sounds and a board is held high. You tighten your seat belts, stomach muscles needing no such assistance. At two minutes the siren wails again and up goes the board. You glance towards the pits and grandstand and realize all eyes are on you. At one minute the siren goes off once more followed by the raising of the board. You start the engine. There is a 30-second warning, a waving of a flag, and you are

away on the green flag parade lap.

As you enter the back straight the sun comes out and you feel better. Fear turns to excitement. Back on the grid, beneath the watchful eye of an observer, you ease the front tyres up to the line delineating position 23. Then, with clutch pushed home and gear-lever firmly in first, you peer across the sea of colourful wings and helmets towards the starter's light tower.

After what seems an age, the red light comes on, and all around you exhaust notes harden. You build up the revs in the knowledge that in between four and ten seconds' time a green light will start the ten-lap race, and an amazing calmness descends over you.

Green replaces red. You drop the clutch, get too much wheelspin, ease the accelerator, and you're away. Despite good intentions to drive a circumspect first lap, a gap opens between the two slow-starting

cars ahead and on reflex you go through it – by which time you are approaching the first corner with foot hard down as those ahead are braking hard, and smoke rises from the front tyres as they lock in your attempts to avoid an embarrassing collision.

Through the first corner and the ones that follow you hold your position, as the cars you have passed fill your mirrors. On the back straight confidence returns, and when the car in front misses a gear you move up into 20th place.

Already the field is spreading out, and each time the pits are passed, your pit board announces how many laps to go. The last car you passed is fighting back, and through corners its driver's superior experience is bringing the nose right under your rear wing. But your newly built and fresher engine

*The green light: Chris Gough's CGR1 leads Mick Harris's Darvi 877. (Steve Jones)*

*Close stuff: Phil Myatt (Marrow), Phil Shepherd (Darvi), Andy Jones (Marrow) and Alan Avery (Avalan) engage in a mid-race dice. (John Gaisford)*

has the legs down the straights and you are able to open up a small gap, only for it to close once more whenever the track turns.

By lap six you are getting tired, missing apexes and occasionally gears. But with second wind, and a determination to stay ahead that you didn't know you had, you go deeper into corners, get onto the power earlier, and smooth your lines.

On lap nine the leaders come past and you give them space.

*The chequered flag: an elated Mick Harris crosses the line first, narrowly ahead of Chris Gough's CGR1. (Dick Harvey collection)*

Post-race debriefing: Mick Harris explains how he did it. Left to right: Lisa and Bob Simpson, Mick Harris, Jon and Dick Harvey. (Dick Harvey collection)

Almost too much, in fact. Your adversary gets alongside in the confusion, but by holding your line through the following bend you edge ahead again. Then it's the chequered flag and the race is finished. By being lapped you only did nine laps to the winner's ten, but what do you care?

Afterwards, in the paddock, as you remove a Nomex balaclava soaked from your exertions, you reflect on 15 of the most exciting minutes of your life. This must be paradise, and when your race-long adversary comes over to shake you by the hand, you are no longer a stranger.

In the races and seasons ahead you will become quicker and more determined as a driver, and will develop your car out of all recognition compared to how it is today. But for the moment you have finished your first race in a car of your own design and construction. You have become a 750 Racer.

# SPORTING & TECHNICAL REGULATIONS 1996

## – 750 FORMULA CHAMPIONSHIP

# 750 FORMULA CHAMPIONSHIP

# SPORTING & TECHNICAL REGULATIONS 1996

1.  SPORTING REGULATIONS - GENERAL

1.1  TITLE & JURISDICTION: The 750 FORMULA CHAMPIONSHIP is organised and administered by the 750 Motor Club Ltd in accordance with the General Championship Prescriptions of the RAC Motor Sports Association [RACMSA] and these Championship Regulations.

RACMSA Championship Permit No:
Race Status: NATIONAL B.
RACMSA Championship Grade: Dii.

1.2  OFFICIALS:

1.2.1.  Co-Ordinator: R.G.Knight, West View, New Street, Stradbroke, Suffolk. IP21 5JG. (01379 384268)

1.2.2.  Eligibility Scrutineer: D.Lovie, Greenside, Appleshaw, Andover, Hants. SP11 9BS.

1.2.3.  Championship Stewards:
F. Blann, 9 Saxon Close, Portchester, HANTS.
B. Smith, 12 Speart Lane, Heston, MIDDX.
V.Ayres, 26 Heywood Avenue, Maidenhead, BERKS.

1.3.  COMPETITOR ELIGIBILITY: Only individuals who are fully paid up valid membership card holding members of the 750 Motor Club Ltd will be permitted to declare themselves as entrants; trade and association entries will not be permitted. Advertising permits and Entrants Licences are not permitted. Competitors may only carry decals as detailed in 5.17.1 of these regulations.

1.3.2.  Drivers and Entrant/Drivers must be fully paid up valid membership card holding members of the 750 Motor Club Ltd, be registered for the Championship and hold a valid RACMSA National B Race Licence or be in possession of a valid Licence & medical, issued by the ASN of a member country of the European Union, Monaco, Norway, San Marino or Switzerland.

1.3.3.  All necessary documentation must be presented for checking at all rounds when signing-on.

1.4.  REGISTRATION:

1.4.1.  All drivers must register for the championship by returning the Registration Form with any Registration Fee to the Co-Ordinator prior to the Final Closing date for the first round being entered.

1.4.2.  There is no Registration Fee.

1.4.3.  Registrations will be accepted from 1st January 1996 until the closing date for the last round of the championship.

1.4.4.  Registration numbers will be the permanent Competition number for the Championship.

1.5.  CHAMPIONSHIP ROUNDS: The 750 FORMULA Championship will be contested over a minimum of 12 Rounds, details of which, once confirmed, are available from the Co-Ordinator.

1.6.  SCORING:

1.6.1.  Points will be awarded to Registered Competitors listed as classified finishers in the Final Results as follows:-

1st-15; 2nd-14; 3rd-13; 4th-12; 5th-11; 6th-10; 7th-9; 8th-8; 9th-7; 10th-6; 11th-5; 12th-4; 13th-3;
All other finishers - 2; all starters who non-finish - 1.

1.6.2.  The totals from the best 8 qualifying rounds will determine the final championship points positions.

1.6.3.  Ties shall be resolved by, when more than one competitor have equal totals, adding their next highest or subsequent highest scores until a conclusive result is found. If that fails to find a winner, the highest number of best results shall be taken into account.

1.7.  AWARDS:

1.7.1.  All awards are to be provided by the Organising Club unless agreed otherwise.

1.7.2.  Per Round: Trophies to 1st, 2nd and 3rd.

1.7.3.  Championship: As per the list published in the 750 Motor Club Limited's Year Book for the respective year.

1.7.4.  Bonuses:

Per Round: Not applicable.

Championship: Any monies which are available from sponsorship after the payment of expenses will be distributed as starting money at the end of the season on the basis of the total number of race starts by competitors who have started in at least 5 events during the season.

1.7.5.  Presentations: Garlands and Trophies are to be provided for presentation after race results are declared final. Prize money and Bonuses shall be posted to the Entrants within one month of the results being declared final after each season.

1.7.6.  Entertainment Tax Liability: Not applicable.

1.7.7.  Title to all Trophies: In the event of any Provisional Results or Championship Tables being revised after any provisional presentations and such revisions affecting the distribution of any awards the Competitors concerned must return such awards to the 750 Motor Club Competitions Secretary in good condition within 7 days.

2.  SPORTING REGULATIONS - JUDICIAL PROCEDURES

2.1.  ROUNDS: In accordance with Section O of the 1996 RACMSA Yearbook and any additional regulations of the 750 Motor Club Ltd.

2.2.  CHAMPIONSHIP: In accordance with Section O of the 1996 RACMSA Yearbook and any additional regulations of the 750 Motor Club Ltd.

3.  SPORTING REGULATIONS - CHAMPIONSHIP RACE MEETINGS & RACE PROCEDURES.

3.1.  ENTRIES:

3.1.1.  The Organisers are responsible for mailing Supplementary Regulations/Entry Forms to all Registered Competitors in sufficient time for entries to be made prior to the published selection-of-entry dates for each round.

3.1.2.  Competitors are responsible for sending in correct and complete entries with the correct entry fees prior to the closing dates which shall be as per the entry form for each round.

3.1.3.  All correct entries are to be acknowledged, advising the Competitors of acceptance or otherwise, within 5 days of receipt by the Organising Club.

3.1.4.  Incorrect or incomplete entries (including driver to be nominated entries) are to be held in abeyance until they are complete and correct and the date of receipt for acceptance of entry purposes shall be the date on which the Secretary of the Meeting receives the missing or corrected information or fee.

3.1.5. Any withdrawal of entry or driver/car changes made after acceptance of any entry must be notified to the Secretary of the Meeting in writing. If driver/vehicle changes are made after the publication of Entry Lists with Final Instructions, the Competitor concerned will be accepted in accordance with B12.1.12.

3.1.6. The maximum entry fee for each round shall be:
Private Entry: As per the Supplementary Regulations.
Trade Entry: Not applicable.

3.1.7. Entry fee refunds will be as per the policies of the Clubs organising each round - as published in their Supplementary Regulations for each round.

3.1.8. Each Race Meeting Organiser may accept up to 20% more entries than specified on the Track Licence for each Circuit and all accepted competitors may practice; selection for the race is in order of the fastest laps in the correct practice session.

3.1.9. In the event of any rounds being oversubscribed the Organising Club may, in liaison with the 750 Motor Club Limited, at their discretion run qualification races.

3.1.10. Irrespective of the date of receipt of entries (provided they are received prior to closing date and are correct) preference will be given to the entrants in the then current championship positions. The remaining entry allocations will be made up from those entrants who have not yet achieved a current championship score, in order of receipt of their entries. Reserves are to be nominated on the Final List of Entries published with the Final Instructions or Amendment Sheet Bulletins. All reserves will practice and replace withdrawn or retired entries in Reserve Number order. If Reserves are given grid places prior to issue of the first grid sheets for any round, the times set in practice shall determine their grid positions. If reserves are given places after the publication of the grid sheet and prior to cars being collected in the official 'Assembly Area' they will be placed at the rear of the grid and be started without any time delay. Otherwise, they will be held in the Pitlane and be released to start the race after the last car to start the GREEN FLAG LAP or last car to take the start has passed the startline or pitlane exit, whichever is the later. Such approval to start MUST be obtained from the Clerk of the Course.

3.1.11. Reserves who practice in the correct session and set a time will take precedence, in reserve number order, over any accepted entry whose practice times are disallowed, or who does not set a time during the official practice for the championship race.

3.2. BRIEFINGS: Organisers must notify competitors of the times and locations for all briefings in the Final Instructions or Official Race Day Bulletins for the meetings. Competitors must attend all briefings.

3.3. PRACTICE: The minimum period of practice to be provided is to be as specified in the RACMSA Regulations J.4.4.1. in respect of circuit lengths. Should any practice session be disrupted, the Clerk of the Course shall not be obliged to resume the session or re-run sessions to achieve the championship criteria and the decision of the Clerk of the Course shall be final.

3.4. QUALIFICATION: Each driver must complete a minimum of 3 laps practice in the car to be raced and in the correct session in order to qualify for selection and order of precedence as set out in the RACMSA regulations and the Clerk of the Course and/or Stewards of the Meeting shall have the right to exclude any driver whose practice times or driving are considered to be unsatisfactory - as per RACMSA Regulation J 4.4.3.

3.5. RACES: The standard minimum scheduled race distance shall be 10 laps whenever practicable but should any race distance be reduced at the discretion of the Clerk of the Course or Stewards of the Meeting, it shall still count as a full points-scoring round.

3.6. STARTS:

3.6.1. All race start countdowns are to have a maximum elapsed period of 5 minutes from the time all cars are released to form up on the grid to the start of the Green Flag lap(s) in the formation specified on the track licence for each circuit.

3.6.2. The countdown procedures/audible warnings sequence shall be:-
3 minutes to start of green flag lap - Close Pitlane Exit
2 minutes to start of green flag lap - Clear grid warning/grid closed.

1 minute to start of green flag lap - start engines/clear grid.
30 seconds - visible and audible warning for start of green flag lap.

3.6.3. The use of tyre heating/heat retention devices, tyre treatments and compounds is prohibited.

3.6.4. Any car removed from the grid after the 3 minute stage or driven into the pits on the green flag lap shall be held in the pitlane and may start the race after the last car to take the start from the grid has passed the startline or pit exit lane whichever is the later.

3.6.5. Any drivers unable to start the green flag lap or start are required to indicate their situation as per RACMSA regulation J 13.10.2. and any drivers unable to maintain grid positions on the green flag lap to the extent that ALL other cars are ahead of them, may complete the green flag lap but MUST remain at the rear of the last row of the grid but ahead of any cars to be started with a time delay.

3.6.6. Excessive weaving to warm-up tyres - using more than 50% of the track width - and falling back in order to accelerate and practice starts, is prohibited.

3.6.7. A five second board will be used to indicate that the grid is complete. The red lights will be switched on 5 seconds after the board is withdrawn. In the event of any RED/GREEN starting lights failure the starter will revert to the use of the Union flag.

3.7. RACE STOPS:

3.7.1. Should the need arise to stop any race or practice, RED LIGHTS will be switched on at the Startline and RED FLAGS will be waved at the Startline and all Marshals signalling points around the circuit. This is a signal for all drivers to cease circulating at racing speeds, to slow to a safe and reasonable pace and to return to the starting grid area which will automatically become a Parc Ferme area. Cars may not enter the pits unless directed to do so. Work on cars already in the pits must cease when a race is stopped.

3.7.2. If the race leader at the time of the Red Flag being displayed has not completed 3 laps the race will be null and void and will be re-started with drivers in their original grid positions. Retired competitors may be replaced by reserves who shall be started from the back of the grid. Gaps on the grid created by retirements must not be closed up prior to the start of the race. The Clerk of the Course is to be responsible for determining the length (in laps) of any re-started race.

3.7.3. If the race leader has completed more than 3 laps but less than half the originally scheduled number, the race may be run in two parts with an aggregate result produced. Drivers must have started the first part and been classified in the results of the first part to qualify for the second part. The grid for the second part shall be the classification order of the first part as per RACMSA Regulation J.5.4.4.

3.7.4. If the leader has completed more than half of the race distance or duration it shall not be re-started and the results will be declared in accordance with RACMSA Regulation J.5.4.4.

3.8. RE-SCRUTINY: All vehicles reported involved in contact incidents during races or practice must be re-presented to the Scrutineers before continuing in the races or practice.

3.9. PITS AND PITLANE SAFETY:

3.9.1. Pits: Entrants must ensure that the RACMSA, Circuit Management and Organising Club Safety Regulations are complied with at all times.

3.9.2. Pitlane: The outer lane or lanes are to be kept unobstructed to allow safe passage of cars at all times. The onus shall be on all drivers to take all due care and drive at minimum speeds in pit lanes.

3.9.3. Refuelling may only be carried out in accordance with the RACMSA Regulation J. 14, Circuit Management regulations and the SRs or Final Instructions issued for each Circuit/Meeting.

3.10. RACE FINISHES: After taking the chequered flag drivers are required to: - Progressively and safely slow down, remain behind any competitors ahead of them, return to the circuit exit road as instructed, comply with any directions given by Marshals or Officials and to keep their helmets on and harnesses done up while on the circuit or in the pitlane.

3.11. RESULTS: All Practice timesheets, grid sheets and Race Results are to be deemed PROVISIONAL until all vehicles are released by Scrutineers after post-practice/race scrutineering and/or after completion of any judicial or technical procedures.

4. CHAMPIONSHIP RACE PENALTIES:

4.1. INFRINGEMENT OF TECHNICAL REGULATIONS:

4.1.1. Arising from post-practice scrutineering or judicial action:

Minimum Penalty - The provisions of RACMSA Regulation O.3.3.

4.1.2. Arising from post-race scrutineering or judicial action:

Minimum Penalty - The provision of RACMSA Regulation O.3.5.(b).

For infringements deemed to be of a more serious nature the Clerk of the Course and/or Stewards of the Meeting may invoke the provisions of RACMSA Regulation O 3.5. (a) and/or (c).

4.1.3. Additional specific Championship penalties:

a) The 750 Motor Club Limited reserves the right at all times to reject any car which it considers represents an attempt to defeat the spirit of the regulations, even though it complies with the letter of them.

b) In order to maintain standards of conduct, the 750 Motor Club Limited will monitor all Officials/Observors reports of adverse behaviour at race meetings. If any individual is included on two such reports during one racing season he will receive written warning from the 750 Motor Club Limited that his driving/behaviour is to be specifically observed at future race meetings. Any adverse reports during this period of observation could result in official RACMSA action and will result in a 750 Motor Club Limited Championship Stewards' enquiry, with possible loss of Championship points and refusal of further race entries.

4.2. Infringement of non-technical RACMSA Regulations and the Sporting Regulations issued for the Championship:

As per RACMSA Judicial Procedure Regulations.

5. TECHNICAL REGULATIONS

5.1. INTRODUCTION: The following Technical Regulations are set out in accordance with the RACMSA specified format and it should be clearly understood that if the following texts do not clearly specify that you can do it, you should work on the principle that you cannot.

5.2. GENERAL DESCRIPTION: The 750 FORMULA CHAMPIONSHIP is for Competitors participating in two-seater, front or rear engined, open or closed sports-racing cars.

5.3. SAFETY REQUIREMENTS: The following Articles of RACMSA Appendix Q Safety Criteria Regulations will apply:- 1.5.4a or 1.5.1; 2.1.3; 3.1.1; 3.5; 5; 6; 7.1.4; 8; 9; 10; 11; 12; 13.

5.4. GENERAL TECHNICAL REQUIREMENTS & EXCEPTIONS:

5.5. CHASSIS: The chassis must have as the main longitudinals, two 50mm x 50mm x 1.5mm (2in x 2in x 16swg) square steel tubes into which the suspension loads shall be fed directly or indirectly. At the rear of the driver/passenger space, the centre lines of the two main longitudinals must be at least 76.2cm (30in) apart consistent with 5.6.1.1.v. With any suspension they must extend to within 15cm (6in) of the vertical planes through front and rear wheel centres. No lightening holes are permitted in these longitudinals, but a 6mm hole must be drilled in each longitudinal to enable the thickness to be checked. These holes must be positioned such that they are readily accessible and should be taped over to prevent the ingress of water.

5.6. BODYWORK:

5.6.1. Modifications Permitted:

1. General:

COCKPIT:

i) There must be only one cockpit opening to serve both driver and passenger space. The opening must be large enough to accept, with it's longest side transversely at the rear of the opening, a horizontal quadrilateral frame with hinged joints, one side 81.3cm (32in) long, two opposite sides 45.7cm (18in) and the fourth side 63.5cm (25in).

ii) In checking the cockpit opening any obstruction caused by the bracing members for a roll over bar may be ignored.

iii) Closed cars must provide similar unobstructed area at drivers/passenger shoulder level.

iv) The centre line of the driver's seat must be at least 17.8cm (7in) from the centre line of the car.

PASSENGER SPACE:

i) The passenger space, exclusive of the seat structure if fitted, measured at floor level must be at least 27.9cm (11in) wide at the rear of the cockpit and at least 70cm (28in) in length to the front of the footwell. The footwell must be at least 15cm (6in) wide, and 25.4cm (10in) high. These dimensions must be maintained over this area.

ii) If an integral seat structure is incorporated in this space it must be no higher than 17.8cm (7in) above the 70cm (28in) floor line and at least 12.7cm (5in) below any structure over any part of the passenger space.

iii) The driver/passenger space must be clear of and not divided by any chassis members other than those forming the propshaft tunnel in front engined cars, or roll over bar braces. It is permitted to locate the fire extinguisher in the passenger space.

iv) Any cover over the passenger space and/or forming an extension to the windscreen alongside the driver must be constructed only of supple and flexible fabric and must be easily removable.

v) It must be possible to drop into the driver/passenger space through the driver/passenger space opening at right angles to the longitudinal centre line of the car an inverted 'U' shaped member with legs 76.2cm (30in) apart (measured over the outside of the legs) held vertically so that the difference in height of the legs does not exceed 76mm (3in) when one of the legs is on the lowest floor level.

2. Interior: As defined above.

3. Exterior: AEROFOILS

i) Aerofoil devices ahead of the front wheels are permitted, but must be below the top of the front wheel rims and not exceed in width the centre line of the front tyres. They must form a continuous part of the bodywork.

ii) A rear aerofoil is permitted. Chord must not exceed 30cm (11.8in). Maximum width to be full body width or outermost track whichever is the greater.

iii) Any rear aerofoil or bodywork must not overhang the rear of the vehicle by more than 70cm (27.5in) measured from the centre line of the rear wheels. The height of any bodywork or aerofoil must not exceed 90cm (35.4in) with the driver aboard, measured from the ground, excluding safety roll over bars, or bodywork of closed cars between the centre line of the front and rear wheels.

iv) Any forward facing horizontal splitter attached to the lowest edge of the front bodywork may not exceed the maximum overall width of the wheels or bodywork whichever is the greater.

4. Silhouette: Not applicable.

5. Ground Clearance: In accordance with RACMSA regulation E.13.19.10.

5.6.2. Modifications Prohibited

1. General: Any in contravention of 5.6.1.

2. Interior: Any in contravention of 5.6.1.

3. Exterior: There shall be nothing to obstruct wholly the drivers sight from the normally seated position of another

car to the front or either side.

4. Silhouette: Any in contravention of 5.6.1.

5. Ground Clearance: Any in contravention of 5.6.1.

5.7.    ENGINE

5.7.1.    Modifications Permitted: The engine must be a Reliant OHV of up to 857cc capacity.

i) A standard Reliant cylinder block/crankcase must be used with bores not exceeding 62.5mm + wear allowance of 0.2mm dia., measured at the maximum point of piston ring travel.

ii) A standard Reliant crankshaft with stroke of 69.1mm must be used.

iii) Connecting rods are free, but must be of ferrous metal.

iv) A standard Reliant Cylinder head must be used, subject to the following:-

a) Ports and combustion chambers may be modified by the removal of material.

b) The ports must remain in their original place in the side of the head.

c) There must be no more than two valves per cylinder and these must remain in parallel to each other and in the manufacturer's original position.

v) The camshaft is free, but must remain in the manufacturer's original position, retain chain drive and be the sole means of operating the push rods and valves.

5.7.2.    Modifications Prohibited: The addition of material in any form other than for the replacement of valve seats or guides is prohibited. Down draught heads are prohibited.

5.7.3.    Location: Front or rear.

5.7.4.    Oil/Water cooling: Free within overall periphery of bodywork.

5.7.5.    Induction Systems: Carburation shall be by only one carburettor choke. Forced induction, fuel injection and external slide throttles are prohibited. The 750 Motor Club reserve the right to modify the regulations in respect of the carburation; this will be done by publishing a notice which will be circulated to all registered competitors and by publication in the Bulletin. Such a change to become effective not less than 21 days after the despatch of the notice to registered competitors.

5.7.6.    Exhaust systems: Exhaust systems are free, provided they comply with RACMSA regulation E.13.16..

5.7.7.    Ignition systems: Only ignition systems using one trigger, inside the distributor or external, to initiate the low tension current will be permitted. Any system that requires more than one sensor or input to provide another signal/voltage for any electronic/microprocessor control system will not be permitted.

5.7.8.    Fuel delivery systems: Free.

5.8.    SUSPENSIONS: Suspension systems are free, subject to RACMSA regulations.

5.8.1.    Permitted modifications: Free subject to RACMSA regulations.

5.8.2.    Prohibited modifications: Any in contravention of RACMSA regulations.

5.8.3.    Wheelbase/track: Free.

5.9.    TRANSMISSIONS

5.9.1.    Permitted modifications: Free subject to 5.9.2.

5.9.2.    Prohibited modifications: Automatic transmissions, torque biasing, locked or limited slip differentials. Non-standard magnesium alloy bell housing, gearbox casing and tailshaft. A bevel-driven, live rear axle from a series production car must be the sole means of driving the rear wheels. The use of any electronic traction control system is prohibited.

5.9.3.    Transmissions & Drive ratios: Axle and gearbox ratios are free. Gearbox must not contain more than four forward gears and must contain an operable reverse gear capable of being engaged by the driver whilst normally seated.

5.10.    ELECTRICS

5.10.1.    Exterior Lighting: Not applicable.

5.10.2.    Rear Fog Light: To RACMSA regulation Q5.

5.10.3.    Batteries: An electrically powered starter motor, and battery, are mandatory and must be operable by the driver whilst normally seated and must be capable of repetitive starts.

5.10.4.    Generators: A charging system is not required.

5.11.    BRAKES

5.11.1.    Permitted Modifications: Free.

5.11.2.    Prohibited Modifications: Not applicable.

5.12.    WHEELS / STEERING

5.12.1.    Permitted Options: Free.

5.12.2.    Prohibited Options: Any in contravention of RACMSA regulations.

5.12.3.    Construction & Materials: Free.

5.12.4.    Dimensions: Free.

5.13.    TYRES

5.13.1.    Specifications: Wet tyres are free but as a minimum the tread pattern must have at least four circumferential grooves of at least 7mm width cut to the full depth of the tread.

5.13.2.    Nominated Manufacturers:
Slick tyres must be YOKOHAMA. Size - 160/515-13. Code No :811. Size and code numbers must be clearly visible.

5.14.    VEHICLE WEIGHT: No restrictions.

5.15.    FUEL TANK / FUEL

5.15.1.    Types: Free.

5.15.2.    Locations: Free.

5.15.3.    Fuel: Only pump fuel as defined is section P of the current RACMSA Blue Book may be used. The use of power boosting or octane boosting additives by competitors in any fuel is prohibited.

5.16.    SILENCING

5.16.1.    Specification: To current RACMSA regulations.

5.17.    NUMBERS & CHAMPIONSHIP DECALS

5.17.1.    Positions: Racing numbers must be affixed in accordance with RACMSA regulations. Only 750 Motor Club and Championship Sponsors decals as issued for the current year may be affixed to the vehicle; failure to display these on both sides of the car will render the driver ineligible for Championship points. Decals from previous years must be removed.

5.17.2.    Suppliers: Club and sponsors stickers may be collected at the first race meeting in which the vehicle is entered.

6.    APPENDICES:

6.1.    Race Organising Clubs & Contacts

6.2.    Commercial Undertakings:
Trade Support Vehicle Decals & Overall Patches
Promotional Activities

6.3.    Qualification Races: Not applicable.

**MOTOR CLUB**

*COMPETITIONS SECRETARY*
**ROBIN KNIGHT**
WEST VIEW, NEW STREET
STRADBROKE. SUFFOLK IP21 5JG
TELEPHONE: 0379 384268
FAX: 0379 384055

## Important Notice to all 750 Formula Competitors - 8 February 1995

### Re: Carburettor Restrictor - change of regulations for 1995.

At the Annual Formula Discussions in November, debate was held regarding the carburettor restrictor regulations. The 750 Formula Committee at its next meeting proposed, and recommended by majority, that the regulations should be changed as follows:-

1.  That the rules regarding carburation should be altered, the only restriction being that only one carburettor choke may be used.

2.  That valve sizes should be restricted to standard production size.

These two matters were raised at the Racing Technical Committee meeting on 17th January 1995. That committee endorsed point 1 above, with the rider that the regulation should remain unchanged for 2 years. In respect of point 2 above, the RTC could not endorse that change, since regulations have already been approved by the RACMSA for 1995 and, unlike the restrictor regulation, there is no machinery for change at such short notice.

The recommendations were put forward at the Board meeting on 7th February as follows:-

1.  5.7.5 Induction Systems - to be changed with immediate effect (and to remain in force throughout the 1995 and 1996 seasons without further change) to read:-

    'Carburation shall be by only one carburettor choke. Forced induction, fuel injection and external slide throttles are prohibited. The 750 Motor Club reserve the right to modify the regulations in respect of the carburettor restrictor; this will be done by publishing a notice which will be circulated to all registered competitors and by publication in the Bulletin. Such a change to become effective not less than 21 days after the despatch of the notice to registered competitors'.

2.  That consideration be given during 1995 to the restriction of valve sizes to those of the standard engine.

<u>Those recommendations were endorsed by the Board of Directors and accordingly the required 21 day notice is being given to all competitors by way of this letter and a notice in the Bulletin.</u>

750 Formula Official:

I regret to advise you that Chris Gough has resigned his position as Formula Official. His efforts and hard work over the years are to be applauded and will be missed. The remaining committee members will be asked to recommend a replacement, which will have to be approved by the Board of Directors.

Robin Knight. (Competitions Secretary).
cc      Board Directors.
        Racing Technical Committee.

*GENERAL SECRETARY*
MIKE PECK COURTHOUSE St. WINIFREDS RD. BIGGIN HILL KENT. TN16 3HR. TEL: 0959 575812  FAX : 0959 540094

Registered Office: (552948 London) 100 Baker Street, London W1M 1LA. VAT Registration Number: 195 3216 55

# 750 Formula Championship

## 1996 CHAMPIONSHIP REGISTRATION FORM

I am a racing member of the 750 Motor Club and intend to compete in championship rounds in 1996. Please register me as a competitor and send me entry forms for all 750 Motor Club promoted events.

NAME : ............................................................................................................... AGE : ........

ADDRESS : ...................................................................................... POST CODE : ............................

Tel (Daytime) . ................................................... Evenings : ...................................................

750 Motor Club Membership No :.......................... Expiry Date : ...................................................

Preferred Competition No (if any) : ...................................................................................................

Have you raced under RACMSA regulations before?    YES ❑    NO ❑

If yes, are you prepared to assist a Novice

Driver at, and leading up to, their first race?    YES ❑    NO ❑

Make/Model/Name of Car :...............................................................................................................

Year of Construction : ...................................................................................................................

Did you design/build the car? ...........................................................................................................

Any known history of car? ...............................................................................................................

..............................................................................................................................................

Class B:    Competitors who, during the previous 5 years, have not been placed in the top 6 places in the 750 Formula Championship or have not finished in the top 3 positions in any 750 Formula Championship race, may register to score points in Class B as well as the overall championship.

Do you wish to register for Class B?    YES ❑    NO ❑

DECLARATION: I have read and understand the Technical & Sporting Regulations for the Championship and agree to be bound by them.

Signed : ................................................... Date : ...................................................

---

Please complete and return this form to:-
Robin Knight, 750 MC Comp Sec, West View, New Street, Stradbroke, Suffolk. IP21 5JG

---

# *Appendix B*

# FURTHER READING

*Advanced Race Car Suspension Design* by Steve Smith (Steve Smith Auto Sports)

*Automobile Suspensions* by Colin Campbell (Chapman and Hall)

*Build To Win* by Keith Noakes (Osprey Publishing Ltd)

*Competition Car Suspension* by Allan Staniforth (Haynes)

*Competition Car Suspension: Design, construction and tuning* by Allan Staniforth (G.T. Foulis)

*Design of Racing Sports Cars* by Colin Campbell (Chapman and Hall)

*Engineer To Win* by Carroll Smith (Aero Publications Inc.)

*Gas Flow in the Internal Combustion Engine* by W.J.D. Annand and G.E. Roe (G.T. Foulis)

*High Speed – Low Cost* by Allan Staniforth (Patrick Stephens Ltd)

*Practical Gas Flow* by John Dalton (Motor Racing Publications Ltd)

*Prepare To Win* by Carroll Smith (Aero Publications Inc.)

*Race and Rally Car Source Book* by Allan Staniforth (Haynes)

*Racing Car Design and Development* by Len Terry and Alan Baker (Robert Bentley Inc.)

*Racecar Engineering and Mechanics* by Paul van Valkenburgh (Dodd, Mead & Co.)

*Racing and Sports Car Chassis Design* by Michael Costin and David Phipps (Batsford)

*Scientific Design of Exhaust and Intake Systems* by Philip H. Smith and John C. Morrison (G.T. Foulis)

*The Design and Tuning of Competition Engines* by Philip H. Smith (G.T. Foulis)

*The New Glassfibre Book* by R.H. Waring (Model and Allied Publications Ltd)

*The Sports Car: Its Design and Performance* by Colin Campbell (Chapman and Hall)

*Theory and Practice of Cylinder Head Modification* by David Vizard (Interauto Book Co. Ltd)

*Tune To Win* by Carroll Smith (Osprey Publishing Ltd)

# *Appendix C*

# USEFUL CONTACTS

**Alloy Wheels International Ltd**
Priory Road
Strood
Rochester
Kent ME2 2BE
Tel: 01634 290700

*Revolution wheels*

**A P Racing**
Wheler Road
Seven Stars Industrial Estate
Coventry
Warwicks CV3 4LB
Tel: 01203 639595

*Brakes*

**Autosport Directory**
*Autosport*
60 Waldegrave Road
Teddington
Middlesex TW11 8LG
Tel: 0181 943 5000

*Motor sport A–Z guide*

**AVO (UK)**
Unit 10B, Leyland Laurence
   Industrial Estate
Irthlingborough Road
Wellingborough
Northants
Tel: 01933 270504

*Shock absorbers*

**Avon Tyres Ltd – Racing Division**
Bath Road
Melksham
Wilts SN12 8AA
Tel: 01225 703101

*Tyres*

**JWE Banks**
St Guthlacs Lodge
Crowland
Peterborough
Lincs PE6 0YP
Tel: 01733 210316

*Koni shock absorbers*

**BMTR**
11 Washington Street
Birmingham B1 1JS
Tel: 0121 643 7656

*Avon tyres*

**Bridgestone-Firestone Ltd**
Birchley Trading Estate
Oldbury
Warley
West Midlands BG9 1DT
Tel: 0121 552 3331

*Tyres*

**Contact Developments**
13 Boult Street
Reading
Berks RG1 4RD
Tel: 01734 598955

*Dellorto carburettors*

**Delta Motor Sport**
Unit 17, Vanalloys Business
   Park
Stake Row
Nr. Henley-on-Thames
Oxon
Tel: 01491 682011

*Setting-up services, etc.*

**Demon Tweeks**
Hugmore Lane
Llan-Y-Pull
Wrexham
Clywd LL13 9YE
Tel: 01978 664466

*Mail order competition parts*

**Dunlop Motorsport, SP Tyres UK Ltd**
Fort Dunlop
Birmingham B24 9QT
Tel: 0121 306 2675

*Tyres*

**Dzus Fastener Europe**
Unit 3, Rockfort Industrial
   Estate
Wallingford
Oxon OX10 9DA
Tel: 01491 837142

*Fasteners*

**Earls Performance
   Products**
Unit 17, Silverstone Circuit
Silverstone
Northants NN12 8TL
Tel: 01327 858221

*Hoses and fittings*

**Edmonton Tool &
   Engineering Co. Ltd**
Second Avenue
Edmonton
London N18 2NW
Tel: 0181 807 4412 and 01707
   875752 (evenings)

*Close-ratio gears and
machining*

**Dick Harvey Racing
   Services**
3 Keens Close
Totteridge
High Wycombe
Bucks HP13 6TP
Tel: 01494 534789

*750 Formula and racing
specialist*

**Haynes Publishing**
Sparkford
Nr Yeovil
Somerset BA22 7JJ
Tel: 01963 440635

*Motor Manuals*

**Jester Racing**
29 Charlton Lane
Shepperton
Middlesex TW17 8QB
Tel: 01932 788779

*Competition parts, new and
used*

**Jo Mo Motor Racing**
Bell Cottage
Rising Lane
Lapworth
Warwicks B94 6JD
Tel: 01564 3314

*Close-ratio gears*

**Kent Performance Cams
   Ltd**
Units 1–4, Military Road
Shorncliffe Industrial Estate
Folkestone
Kent CT20 3SP
Tel: 01303 248666

*Camshafts and timing gear*

**Koni Shock Absorbers**
c/o Camberley Auto Factors
57e Mytchett Road
Mytchett
Surrey
Tel: 01252 516797

*Shock absorbers*

**Leda Suspension**
Unit 33, Hanningfield
   Industrial Estate
Chelmsford
Essex CM3 8AB
Tel: 01245 400668

*Suspension*

**Lifeline Fire and Safety
   Systems Ltd**
1 Portway Close (off
   Torrington Avenue)
Coventry
West Midlands CV4 9UY
Tel: 01203 471207

*Fire extinguishers*

**Mallock Racing**
Unit 3, Salcey Lawn
Salcey Forest
Nr. Hartwell
Northants NW7 2HY
Tel: 01604 863504

*Competition parts*

**Merlin Motorsports**
Castle Combe Circuit
Chippenham
Wilts SN14 7EX
Tel: 01249 782101

*Competition parts*

**Morris Lubricants**
Castle Foregate
Shrewsbury
Shropshire SY1 2EL
Tel: 01743 232200

*Oils*

**Piper Cams**
2 St Johns Court
Ashford Business Park
Ashford
Kent TN2 0SJ
Tel: 01233 500200

*Camshafts*

**RAC Motor Sports
   Association Ltd**
Motor Sports House
Riverside Park
Colnbrook
Slough
Berks SL3 0HG
Tel: 01753 681736

*Motor racing's governing body*

**Raceparts UK Ltd**
Unit 3, Rockfort Industrial
   Estate
Wallingford
Oxon OX10 9DA
Tel: 01491 837142 and 837740

*Competition parts*

**Revolution Competition
   Wheels**
Temple Manor Works
Priory Road
Strood
Rochester
Kent ME2 2BE
Tel: 01634 720227

*Alloy wheels*

**750 Motor Club**
Robin Knight, Competition
  Secretary
West View
New Street
Stradbrooke
Eye
Suffolk IP21 5JG
Tel: 01379 384268

*Race organizers*

**Rod End and Spherical
  Bearings International**
Enterprise House
181 Garth Road
Morden
Surrey SM4 4LL
Tel: 0181 330 4499

*Rose-joints, etc.*

**Spax Ltd**
Telford Road
Bicester
Oxon OX6 0UU
Tel: 01869 244771

*Shock absorbers*

**Suspension Supplies Ltd**
92 Burton Road
Sheffield S3 8DA
Tel: 0114 275 3723

*Springs*

**Terrapin Services**
Rose Cottage
Top Wath Road
Pateley Bridge
Harrogate
N. Yorks HG3 5PG
Tel: 01423 711228

*Suspension design and setting
up*

**Yokohama HPT Ltd**
Unit D6, Horton Park
  Industrial Estate
Hortonwood 7
Telford
Shropshire TF1 4EX
Tel: 01952 677999

*Tyres*

# INDEX